*Soviet Foreign Policy since
the Death of Stalin*

THE WORLD STUDIES SERIES

General Editor: JAMES HENDERSON, M.A., Ph.D.,
Senior Lecturer in Education with special reference to Teaching of History
and International Affairs, Institute of Education, University of London

Editorial Board: MOTHER MARY de SALES, M.A., Principal Lecturer in
History, Coloma College

JOSEPH HUNT, M.A., Senior History Master, City of London School

JAMES JOLL, M.A., Professor of International History, London School of
Economics and Politics, University of London

ESMOND WRIGHT, M.A., M.P.

VOLUMES PUBLISHED

Malaysia and its Neighbours, J. M. Gullick.

The European Common Market and Community, Uwe Kitzinger, Fellow
of Nuffield College, Oxford.

The Politics of John F. Kennedy, Edmund Ions, Department of History,
Columbia University, New York.

Apartheid: A Documentary Study of Modern South Africa, Edgar H.
Brookes.

Israel and the Arab World, C. H. Dodd, Department of Government,
University of Manchester, and M. E. Sales, Centre for Middle
Eastern and Islamic Studies, University of Durham.

The Theory and Practice of Neutrality in the Twentieth Century, Roderick
Ogley, Department of International Relations, University of
Sussex.

The Search for Peace, D. W. Bowett, The President, Queens' College,
Cambridge.

Soviet Foreign Policy since the Death of Stalin

H. Hanak

School of Slavonic and East European Studies, and
University College, London

LONDON AND BOSTON
ROUTLEDGE & KEGAN PAUL

First published 1972
by Routledge & Kegan Paul Ltd
Broadway House, 68–74 Carter Lane,
London EC4V 5EL and
9 Park Street,
Boston, Mass. 02108, U.S.A.

Printed in Great Britain by
C. Tinling & Co. Ltd
London and Prescot

ISBN 0 7100 7215 5

listed 1973

Feb 24 '77

Contents

page

page

page

PART II: THE SOCIALIST COMMONWEALTH

(*a*) Reconciliation with Yugoslavia

(*b*) Poland and Hungary in 1956

(*c*) Relations among socialist states

CONTENTS

ix

PART III: THE SOVIET UNION AND THE
THIRD WORLD

General Editor's Preface

The World Studies Series is designed to make a new and important contribution to the study of modern history. Each volume in the Series will provide students in sixth forms, Colleges of Education and Universities with a range of contemporary material drawn from many sources, not only from official and semi-official records, but also from contemporary historical writing from reliable journals. The material is selected and introduced by a scholar who establishes the context of his subject and suggests possible lines of discussion and inquiry that can accompany a study of the documents.

Through these volumes the student can learn how to read and assess historical documents. He will see how the contemporary historian works and how historical judgments are formed. He will learn to discriminate among a number of sources and to weigh the evidence. He is confronted with recent instances of what Professor Butterfield has called 'the human predicament' revealed by history; evidence concerning the national, racial and ideological factors which at present hinder or advance man's progress towards some form of world society.

In presenting these documents, Mr Hanak has put into the hands of students a key with which they can unlock many of the doors of Soviet foreign policy and so obtain a degree of access to its mainsprings. It is possible to examine the relationship of the USSR to the Capitalist States (Part I), to the Socialist Commonwealth (Part II) and to the Third World (Part III).

'A Soviet communist', writes the author in his conclusion, 'would not differentiate between the aims of communists and the aims of the Soviet Union.' The documentation of recent Russian history, here made available, should enable the scholar to judge for himself whether such non-differentiation is in fact possible.

JAMES HENDERSON

Volume Editor's Preface

The Union of Soviet Socialist Republics is a totalitarian state. It has a parliament, the Supreme Soviet, but only one political Party. The Supreme Soviet meets for a few days once or twice a year. It approves the budget and passes a few laws, always unanimously. It sometimes receives reports from the prime minister or the foreign minister on foreign policy. The Soviet state and Soviet society are guided and governed by the Communist Party of the Soviet Union. The Party, like the state, has a democratic apparatus. In fact the leaders of this Party are not accountable to the membership. The Party by itself or through its subsidiary organs, controls every aspect of the life of society and of the citizen. Nothing is too insignificant for its attention. Soviet foreign policy is conducted by the state organs, that is by the Council of Ministers and by the Foreign Ministry. However, foreign policy is the special concern of the Party. In many aspects of foreign policy, especially in relations with other communist states and other communist parties, the Party is both a guiding and an executive organ. Although the minister of foreign affairs is an important member of the state hierarchy he has rarely been an important member of the Party hierarchy. Only seven men have been ministers (or commissars as they were known before 1946) of foreign affairs since 1917. Of these only three have held important party office: Trotsky (who held the portfolio of foreign affairs for less than a year), Molotov and, at a junior level, Shepilov. With the exception of Trotsky, none of the incumbents of this high state office has ever been arrested, executed or murdered. In the bloody annals of Soviet history it is the only such office whose chief has escaped purging. The foreign minister is an important executive official: he is not a decision maker. Typical is the present incumbent of this office, Andrei Gromyko. He was appointed foreign minister in 1957 after he had served as ambassador in Washington and

London, and had been permanent representative at the Security Council. Foreign policy is made by the Praesidium (or the Politburo as it was known under Stalin and is so called again) or by the real head of the state and Party, the party secretary. Foreign policy is a Party matter.

Nearly all the documents used in this volume come from Soviet publications. Most of them are government or party statements or have appeared as articles in the Soviet press. As the press is totally controlled, articles in it are either inspired by Party-state organs or have their approval. All such statements, whether emanating directly from a Party or state organ or from the press, have a propaganda purpose. They must not, however, for this reason be dismissed. Propaganda is not always untruthful and unless there is evidence to the contrary it may be believed. In any case, such statements can sometimes be checked or compared with other Soviet statements or with statements emanating from abroad. In this context Chinese comments are particularly important. Second, Soviet statements vary very much in the way matters are treated, and in what is treated, what is left out, and in the order of appearance in a certain document.

In this volume I have been concerned to explain Soviet foreign policy in its own words, selecting from a vast amount of material that which seemed significant to me and illustrative of a particular event. Its very language is different from that of western diplomacy.

Acknowledgements

The editor and publishers wish to thank the following for kind permission to print in this volume extracts from the works cited:

The American Association for the Advancement of Slavic Studies at the Ohio State University for translation from *The Current Digest of the Soviet Press*, published weekly by The Association, by permission of *The Digest*.

The New York Times Company for the secret letter of the Communist Party of the Soviet Union, 24 March 1966, Copyright 1966, reprinted by permission

The M. I. T. Press for *Sino-Soviet Relations 1964–1965* edited by W. E. Griffith, Copyright 1967

Oxford University Press, under the auspices of the Royal Institute of International Affairs, for *Comecon* by Michael Kaser

Macmillan & Co. Ltd. for *Thirteen Days: The Cuban Missile Crisis* by R. F. Kennedy

Abbreviations

CDSP Current Digest of the Soviet Press (compiled by the Joint
    Committee on Slavic Studies, New York)
SN   *Soviet News* (distributed by the Press Department of the
    Soviet Embassy, London)

CCCPSU	Central Committee of the Communist Party of the Soviet Union
CCP	Chinese Communist Party
CDSP	*Current Digest of the Soviet Press* (compiled by the Joint Committee on Slavic Studies, New York)
CPCS	Communist Party of Czechoslovakia
CPR (or PRC)	Chinese People's Republic
CPSU	Communist Party of the Soviet Union
CSR	Czechoslovak Socialist Republic
DRV	Democratic Republic of Vietnam
FRG	Federal Republic of Germany
GDR	German Democratic Republic
PPR	Polish People's Republic
PRC (or CPR)	Chinese People's Republic
SN	*Soviet News* (distributed by the Press Department of the Soviet Embassy, London)

Introduction

Expansion has been a characteristic feature of Soviet foreign policy ever since the revolution of 1917. In that year and for some time afterwards Lenin and the other directors of Soviet policy waited for their revolution to act as a signal for communist take-overs in other parts of the world and thus to save the Russian revolution, then in dire peril of extinction. When these revolutions outside Russia either failed to materialize or were suppressed, the Bolsheviks sought to spread the revolution by force of arms. They were stopped at Warsaw and driven back.

The expansionist character of communism was also seen in the attitude that the Bolsheviks took to the non-Russian nationalities of the old Tsarist empire. Many of these had set up independent states. Lenin, as a good Marxist, was hostile to the claims of national self-determination. For tactical reasons he had, however, supported national claims because the Tsarist empire could be weakened in this way. When, however, the Bolsheviks became the heirs of these Tsars they were prepared to grant national independence only to those whom they could not conquer. Thus an independent Poland, Finland, Estonia, Latvia and Lithuania arose on the western borderlands of the old empire. The independence of the last three of these was to be brief. In 1940 they were annexed by the Soviet Union. The eastern areas of Poland were seized in 1939. Bessarabia, another border area of Russia, was taken from Rumania in 1940. Finland alone was successful in resisting the Soviets in the winter war of 1939. Indeed the spirit of expansionism was not derived only from Marxism-Leninism but also from old Russia. Stalin, a Georgian and not a Russian, was the exponent of this policy. Port Arthur, on the Dairen Peninsula in Manchuria, was returned to Russia in 1945. It had been lost to the Japanese in 1905.

Soviet expansion has never been reckless. Caution has also been a typical characteristic. Communists are not in a hurry. Victory is inevitable but the road to victory is beset with dangers, ambushes, losses and suffering. In 1918 at Brest-Litovsk a humiliating peace was signed with the Germans and their allies in order that the revolution be preserved. Lenin described it as a 'breathing-space'. Under Stalin, caution was elevated to the level of state policy. Stalin knew how weak the Soviet Union was. He was prepared to see the communists suppressed in China in 1927 and in Germany in 1933 with hardly a murmur of protest. In the course of time both Chiang Kai-shek and Hitler became allies of the Soviets.

The benevolent neutrality that the Soviet Union practised towards Germany in the first two years of the Second World War resulted in a vast extension of Soviet territory in Europe. But this 'breathing-space' ended with the German invasion of June 1941. In spite of appalling losses—twenty million dead, that is 10 per cent of the population—Soviet Russia survived. In the great battles of Stalingrad and the Kursk Bulge Hitler's armies were so badly mauled that they never recovered. At the end of the war the Red Army controlled most of eastern and half of central Europe. This military advantage was turned to political uses and the whole area came under the control of communist governments loyal to Moscow. Perhaps to Stalin's surprise this expansion scared the western powers, and they quickly sought to purchase safety in unity and in the permanent presence of American troops in Europe. Stalin, cautious as ever, realized that for the time being the days of expansion had come to an end. Instead, he turned to the congenial task of preparing a new purge directed against those who had profited by the liquidations of their predecessors in the late thirties. Then, on 5 March 1953, Stalin died.

Within a matter of months the process of liberating the Soviet Union from the cult of the dead dictator had begun. In the field of foreign policy there was a relaxation of tension in the strained relations between the Soviet Union and her erstwhile partners in the grand alliance against Nazi Germany. The Thaw, as it became known, was not, however, a sudden phenomenon. There were signs already in the last years of Stalin's life that the policy of maximum hostility to the west had outgrown its usefulness. After an initial period of staggering success the borders of Soviet power became stabilized along a frontier in Europe running from the Baltic to the Adriatic seas. Beyond that the Soviets could not move. The strike movements in France and Italy inspired by the communist parties and the communist-led trade unions did not achieve their political aims. The guerrilla war in Greece was liquidated by Stalin's order and in 1948, the year that Czechoslovakia fell under communist control, Finland showed her determination to remain independent in spite of her proximity to the Russian colossus. The Berlin blockade of 1948 and 1949 showed both the determination of the three major western powers to defend this militarily indefensible outpost and their technical competence in keeping the population of West Berlin supplied by air. Most seriously of all the vicious quarrel between Tito and Stalin resulted in an actual contraction of Soviet power. For the time being Yugoslavia was isolated from the communist world but in the brighter world now dawning her example and her ideas were to have a divisive influence on the people's democracies of eastern Europe.

In Asia the dynamics of revolution had not yet been exhausted. In 1949 Mao Tse-tung's armies brought over six hundred million Chinese under communist control—three times the population of the Soviet Union. This fantastic success was, however, a mixed blessing for the Soviet Union. China would never be a satellite of the Soviet Union. Still, in 1953 there were no signs that the everlasting and fraternal friendship of the Soviet and Chinese peoples would turn to bitter enmity.

In Indo-China the armies of the communists, centred around the Democratic Republic of Vietnam in the North, were gradually driving the French out of Vietnam. In other parts of Asia the communists had been checked. Burma, Malaya, the Philippines, Indonesia and India had all been victims of communist agitation and in some cases of communist insurrection. In all of them insurgency had been at least temporarily checked. But the greatest defeat came in Korea. When in June 1950 the armies of the People's Republic of Korea crossed the 38th parallel, dividing North from South Korea, the world became once more the witness to a *Blitzkrieg*. Within a matter of weeks the North Koreans had overrun most of the peninsula with the exception of the extreme south-east corner, the perimeter of Pusan. It was into this small area that the United States put its troops and armaments and under the leadership of General MacArthur not only drove the North Koreans out of the South but proceeded to liberate the North. In December 1950, as they approached the Yalu River which separates Korea from Manchuria, they were met by a greater adversary. Chinese 'volunteers' descended upon them and the rapid advance was followed by an equally rapid retreat. In 1953 the Korean stalemate was ripe for solution.

THE THAW

The reappraisal of Soviet foreign policy, which had already begun under Stalin, was given a new direction and was pursued with considerable energy by the new leaders of the Soviet state, G. M. Malenkov, Stalin's designated successor, L. P. Beria, the police chief, and V. M. Molotov, an old Bolshevik who had been minister of foreign affairs until 1949 and who immediately resumed his old post. Beria did not remain in the leadership for long. In July he was arrested and unmasked as an enemy of the people, an imperialist spy and a would-be restorer of capitalism. Before the end of the year a special court passed on him and some of his associates the inevitable verdict of death. It seemed that the death of Stalin, like the deaths of some of the Tsars, would be followed by a period of troubles. That it did not do so shows much for the strength of the Soviet system and for the iron discipline of the communist party. Still, it is reasonable to believe that these internal dangers imposed great caution on the directors of Soviet foreign policy. Malenkov, too, did not survive for long. In September 1953 Nikita Khrushchev replaced him as first secretary of the Party and in February 1955 N. A. Bulganin replaced him as prime minister. Fate was kinder to Malenkov than to Beria. He was demoted to running the electrical power industry, sent on a tour of Britain and finally in 1957 expelled from the Central Committee of the Party as a member of the 'anti-Party group' and relegated to running an electric power station in East Kazakhstan. Indeed between 1953 and 1957 a similar fate befell a whole series of rivals and friends of Khrushchev: Molotov was expelled from the inner leadership in 1957 and later even from the Party; his successor at the foreign ministry, Shepilov, was equally demoted; Bulganin was stripped of his premiership in 1957; K. Y. Voroshilov, another old Bolshevik, was stripped of his functions and humiliated also in 1957; Marshal Zhukov, the war hero and the man who had helped Khrushchev outwit his rivals when they had deposed him in the Praesidium of the Party in 1957, was to enjoy his prominence for a few months only.

The Soviet leaders were impelled to their policy of relaxation for external reasons too. Not only was the period of late Stalinism causing an isolation of the Soviet Union and positive dangers for it but there was also a realignment of forces in the west. Attempts were being made to establish a west European army. The attempts failed when, in the summer of 1954, the French Parliament refused to ratify the agreement establishing the European Defence Community. But this did not stop the rearmament of Germany. By the Paris Agreements a rearmed Germany joined NATO. The barrage of Soviet propaganda against a German army, against the supposed Nazi tendencies of the Federal Republic and against the expansionist aims of West German capitalism, has always had some success. It is unlikely that it has ever been genuine, though of course the Soviets are never likely to applaud the strengthening of any of their adversaries. But in 1949 the Soviet Union became a nuclear power, in 1953 it exploded its first hydrogen bomb and in 1957 it sent the first satellite into space. The development of nuclear armaments and the means of delivery made the establishment of a German army a much smaller risk for the Soviet Union than it would have been in the years immediately after the war. Indeed in 1957 it allowed the Red Army to reduce its manpower.

The European problem was connected with the change of administration in Washington. The Eisenhower administration, brought to power in the backlash of anti-communism, had as its secretary of state John Foster Dulles, a dedicated and fervent anti-communist. Above all, the administration inherited from the presidential election campaign an extremely bellicose vocabulary. Communism was not only to be 'contained', it was to be 'rolled back' and the peoples of eastern Europe were to be 'liberated' while Chiang Kai-shek was to be 'unleashed' on mainland China. The United States would not hesitate to go to the 'brink' of war. This absurd phraseology meant very little as the events of Hungary in 1956 were to show, and the Chinese cannonade of Matsu and Quemoy in 1958. Of course, the Soviet leaders could not know this and therefore the policy may have had some effect on them. But the policy was useful to the Soviets in another way. Dulles's language probably did not frighten them—after all for forty years they had been using similar language in order to intimidate the west—but it most certainly frightened America's allies in Europe who tried to restrain American policy.

Winston Churchill had been the first to suggest a meeting with the new Soviet leaders in order to see whether a compromise with them was possible. In 1953, with the succession crisis not yet settled in the Soviet Union, the Russians were not keen on it. However, in January 1954 a Big Four foreign ministers' meeting did take place in Berlin. The Soviets suggested that a provisional German government be set up by the West and East German regimes and that this government would hold all-German elections under conditions of 'genuine freedom which would preclude pressure on the voters by big monopolies'. The west was no doubt right in its belief that the Russians would prevent genuinely free elections—the East German uprising of June 1953 and the flood of refugees from East to West Germany was a clear indication as to the result of such elections.

The Berlin Conference was followed by another one at Geneva. This ended unsuccessfully, but the Soviets announced their readiness to meet again to discuss Korea and Indo-China. The Korean armistice had been signed in July 1953 after the South Korean government had been put into the right frame of mind by a Chinese offensive against a sector of the front held by it. In the April conference in Geneva China was represented by its foreign minister Chou En-lai. Early in May the French-held fortress of Dien Bien Phu fell to the Viet-Minh. The new French premier, Mendès-France, undertook to achieve a settlement by 20 July or resign. Within minutes of the time limit this was achieved. The settlement established a communist state in the North, and the states of Laos, Cambodia and South Vietnam in the South. The United States refused to put its signature to the agreement.

The conference was a great success for the Chinese. For the first time they had taken part in a major international conference. The continuance of war would have created the danger of American bases close to China's frontier. The Russians, too, were pleased to extricate themselves from an increasingly dangerous situation. For the west in general, whatever the feeling of the American administration may have been, the ending of the war in Korea and Indo-China was an indication of the great relaxation of international tension. Indeed everyone could be pleased except the unfortunate people of Vietnam, to whom the conference brought only the briefest period of respite before they were plunged into an even more murderous war.

There were other real signs of relaxation. Austria was another of the divided countries of the world. Attempts to settle its problems had been described by Dulles as a labour of Sisyphus—ever rolling a stone to the summit of a mountain only to find that it rolled down just before reaching the top. Suddenly in February, however, Molotov announced that the Soviets were prepared to drop their previous demand that the Austrian and German problems be treated together. In April 1955 the Austrian chancellor, Raab, was invited to Moscow, and on 15 May the Austrian State Treaty was signed in Vienna and the armies of the four occupying powers departed from Austria. No doubt from the Soviet point of view this was the policy of abandoning exposed salients and bases—in the same year the base of Porkkala near Helsinki was returned to Finland and Port Arthur to the Chinese. But Austria had a greater significance. It was perhaps meant as an indication to the West Germans that the Soviet Union was prepared for concessions if West Germany broke or loosened its close links with the western powers which had been much strengthened at the end of 1954 and in the early months of 1955. It should be borne in mind that from the Soviet point of view a ring of neutralized states adjoining the western borders of the satellite empire would be of very great strategic importance.

In July 1955 a conference of the heads of government took

place in Geneva and the discussions between Eisenhower, Eden, Mollet, Bulganin and Khrushchev were cordial. This was followed by a further foreign ministers' conference. Neither of these conferences solved the problems of divided Germany, or collective security in Europe or of disarmament, but they did show the Soviet leaders as reasonable and polite men anxious for the peace of the world. From this point of view, the 'spirit of Geneva' was of value to the Soviets. Indeed the statesmen at these meetings addressed world opinion rather than each other. But between these two Geneva conferences one important result was achieved. In September the German chancellor, Konrad Adenauer, negotiated in Moscow an agreement establishing diplomatic relations between the two countries.

THE NEW DOCTRINE AND THE NEW LEADER

'The Thaw', or 'the spirit of Geneva', required a change in the ideological basis of Marxism-Leninism. Lenin had taught that war between capitalists was inevitable. The capitalist system had within it the contradictions that caused war. Lenin also believed that the capitalist states would try to destroy the Soviet state by war, and the period of intervention from 1918 to 1919 provided the evidence for this theoretical belief. However, in *The Economic Problems of Socialism in the USSR*, Stalin's last major work published in 1952, it was stated that war among capitalist states was more likely than a war between the capitalist states and the Soviet Union.

Under the old dictator a real change of policy was perhaps not possible. Under a new leadership, anxious for a détente with the west, it was. Unlike Stalin they were aware of the destructiveness of nuclear weapons. Stalin had taught that the outcome of a war would not be decided by surprise or by accident but by 'permanently operating factors' such as 'the stability of the rear, the morale of the army, the quantity and quality of divisions, the armament of the army, the organizational ability of the army commanders'. This became a very dangerous doctrine when applied to a world where nuclear weapons would be decisive.

Moreover, the Soviet leaders knew that they were inferior to

8

the Americans in the number and quality of nuclear weapons and in the means of delivering them. Attempts to catch up with the Americans, to achieve nuclear parity, were vigorously pursued but were not to succeed. Attempts to by-pass American superiority by placing rockets on Cuba not only failed, but also put the Soviet Union into the humiliating position of having to retreat in the face of American threats.

Under these circumstances the sensible policy was one of preserving peace with the capitalist world. Peaceful co-existence, a Leninist concept, but one which is particularly connected with the foreign-policy activity of Khrushchev, was a phrase which was repeated, explained, asserted and reasserted in thousands of speeches by Soviet leaders and in even more newspaper and magazine articles. It did not exclude the possibility of war. Clearly the Soviet Union would defend itself in case of attack. Still, there is no reason to suppose that at any time since 1953 the Soviet leaders believed in the likelihood of an armed attack. What was more significant, the doctrine did not exclude the possibility of support for national liberation movements. Yet, even here the Soviets were cautious and, unlike the Americans, their armed forces have rarely been involved in armed combat since 1945. Military supplies and some Soviet military personnel have been sent to Cuba and to North Vietnam. The only area where there has been massive Soviet military aid and the actual involvement of some Soviet military personnel in fighting has been in Egypt.

The policy meant in fact that the Soviet Union could maintain good relations with the west and at the same time undermine its positions. Peaceful co-existence, it has frequently been stated, creates the most favourable conditions for the struggle of oppressed peoples against their oppressors, for the struggle of the workers in the capitalist countries against their exploiters. Capitalism, it was felt, could be destroyed by these means. It could also be weakened by internal contradictions or by another financial economic crisis such as the one which shook the world in 1929. It could be weakened or even destroyed by the revolution of the oppressed and the exploited. Yet when in the late 1960s student rebels posed a threat to capitalism, neither the communist parties nor the Soviet Union showed any enthusiasm for the youthful and unorthodox revolutionaries.

All this meant that considerable pressure would have to be maintained against the west in the hope that its nerve would break. Yet the pressure would have to be applied with caution because the west could not be provoked to military action, so socialism and capitalism would have to co-exist. The world of capitalism would shrink until it would be no larger than a button. Khrushchev, always the master of the colourful metaphor, described the relations thus: 'The world now consists of socialist and capitalist countries. They can be regarded as two communicating vessels. At present, as regards number of states, the capitalist vessel is fuller. But this is a temporary state of affairs. History is developing in a way which will reduce the level in the capitalist vessel while the socialist vessel will get fuller.' Under these circumstances, war was wasteful of men and materials and in any case unnecessary.

Paradoxically, the policy of peaceful co-existence was an aggressive policy. Gone was the caution of Stalinist days. As Khrushchev and his successors have denied themselves the privilege of a frontal attack on the western world, they have sought to undermine it by seeking out its vulnerable spots. This policy has been successful, although it is also risky. It has meant more confrontation, not less, with the western powers.

Khrushchev dominated the internal and external policy of the Soviet Union from 1955 until his sudden overthrow in October 1964. In contrast to Stalin and also in contrast to the Brezhnev-Kosygin leadership he was a leader who liked to keep in the public eye, who was concerned with public relations. This attitude, which evoked a certain grudging admiration from the west and even affection from western public opinion, seems to have made no appeal to Soviet public opinion, and was clearly regarded by the Soviet élite as undignified and unbecoming to the world's chief communist and the chief executive of a great power. Certainly his drunkenness, his vulgarity and his outbursts of fury—real or feigned, like the famous example when he thumped his shoe on the table at the General Assembly of the United Nations—were considered unbecoming.

Unlike Stalin he travelled much both in the socialist and capitalist countries. He had an insatiable curiosity about other countries—a curiosity which had been stifled in Stalinist Russia. He would, no doubt, have agreed with the adage that travel broadens the mind. He was fascinated by the technological advances and innovations that he saw in capitalist countries. He saw no reason why communists should not imitate the technology and technique of western industrialism.

His travels had other reasons than pure self-education. His diplomacy was personal in the sense that he believed that problems could be solved by direct confrontation with the leading statesmen of the world. In the socialist world this led him to summon the Moscow conferences of 1957 and 1960 and to put into motion the preparations for a further conference, the meeting of which was postponed, though not cancelled, by his sudden removal from power. It led him also to such confrontations with the Chinese as at Bucharest in 1960. In the capitalist world it led him to the Geneva conferences of 1954 and 1955, the meeting with Eisenhower in 1957 and with Kennedy in 1961.

His personal appearances in non-socialist states, his proletarian bearing in foreign and hostile surroundings and the quiet charm of his wife were important elements in the propaganda battle that he was waging with the western world. It projected an image of a reasonable man emerging from a reasonable and peaceful society, and was thus an important element in the whole campaign of peaceful co-existence.

His concern with world peace, with peaceful co-existence, cannot be doubted. Khrushchev was a man of the people. He was concerned with the ordinary people, the kind of people from whom he himself originated. He had none of the Tsarist disregard for the masses as existing only for the greater glory of a semi-divine ruler like Stalin. His drive for peace was conditioned by a belief that this was the best policy for the Soviet state, but that it was also in the interests of the Soviet citizen and in the interests of furthering the cause of world communism. The atom bomb, as he remarked, knew no class barriers.

He did not shrink from using force. He had after all presided over the destinies of the Ukraine at the time of Stalin's blood purge. It was on his orders that the Hungarian revolution was crushed by Soviet tanks. But his favoured instrument was the threat of, rather than the use of, force. The weakness of such a policy was that he was not always in the position to carry out his threat when his bluff was called, as in the Berlin and Cuban crises.

The secret speech delivered by Khrushchev at the 20th Congress of the Communist Party of the Soviet Union in February 1956 signified his predominance in the politics of the Soviet Union. His position was, however, never as supreme as that of either Lenin or Stalin, in spite of a minor cult of personality to which he himself became subject in the period after 1959. The purge of the anti-party group in 1957, the troubles in eastern Europe and the greater troubles with China, the failure to cajole the west either over the question of Berlin or over Cuba, the failure of the grandiose plans for agriculture, and the seemingly easy and speedy way in which he was overthrown in October 1964, all point to an internal position that was weak. In his foreign policy Khrushchev had always to think of the internal position and of his critics in the Praesidium of the Party, and of the effect that his policy would have on China —a slumbering tiger whom communism awoke to new and ferocious energy.

There was a further condition of Khrushchev's foreign policy. Khrushchev was not only the head of the government, 'Chairman Khrushchev', and as such responsible for the well-being, safety and progress of the citizens of the Union of Soviet Socialist Republics, he was also, as first secretary of the Communist Party of the Soviet Union, the head and the arch-conspirator of a movement dedicated to the overthrow of all the governments of the world which were not communist. It is safe to assume that by the middle 1950s the average Soviet citizen was interested in his material well-being rather more than in the spread of world communism. There is no reason to suppose that Khrushchev disagreed with him, but his position was intensely difficult. The Communist Party of the Soviet Union rules the USSR because it is the vanguard of the proletariat with the task of propelling society forward into the era of communism, a vague Utopian existence whose very outlines have never been defined. Moreover, the Soviet revolution can never remain in isolation. The most favourable conditions for building communism in the Soviet Union will be achieved when communism is triumphant all over the world. The Soviet leaders cannot disregard this ideological heritage. It is their permit to govern, their legitimacy. They must therefore press forward to spread communism throughout the world, just as they must prevent the shrinking of the frontiers of world communism.

This problem would have been easier if the Soviets themselves could have been the judges of what constituted revolutionary action. They could always verbalize revolution. They now had the Chinese to watch over them and to remind them of their revolutionary duty. Mao Tse-tung and his comrades in arms had come to power in 1949 after a military struggle that had lasted for more than twenty years. They were experienced and hardened revolutionaries. From 1949 they ruled the most numerous nation in the world. They looked up to their ideological brothers in Moscow, who had, incidentally, done little to help them in their victorious march to power. After Stalin's death the Chinese continued to accept the primacy of Moscow, although none of Stalin's successors ever possessed the international prestige of the dead dictator or of Mao Tse-tung. Considerable economic and military help was received from Russia. The Soviet base at Port Arthur was handed over to China. But this was not enough. The Chinese expected the Soviets to lead the camp of socialism, but to lead it in a certain direction, that is towards more revolution, towards more confrontation with the United States, towards more brinkmanship. Neither Khrushchev nor his successors were prepared to do this. They gloried in their leadership of the camp of socialism but they were even more proud of their leadership of one of the two super powers, able with the United States to determine the destinies of the world. After all, their dependence on the United States was conditioned by the fact that the United States was the only power able to destroy the Soviet Union.

THE RECONCILIATION WITH YUGOSLAVIA

The Soviet leaders were not only forced to reappraise their relations with the world outside the frontiers of communism, they also had to fashion out new relations with the other socialist states. Communism was now a world system containing approximately one-third of the population of the world. Within a few months of Stalin's death the Soviet system in eastern Europe was faced with two revolts. In western Czechoslovakia in the industrial town of Plzeň, the workers, the supposed

13

beneficiaries of the regime, revolted and held the town for three days until they were dispersed by regular forces. More important and more dangerous were the events in Eastern Germany. An attempt to increase the productivity of the workers and at the same time freeze their wages resulted in demonstrations in East Berlin and in all the major cities of Eastern Germany. Within a couple of days the communist government of Walter Ulbricht collapsed and if it had not been for the presence of Soviet tanks—three mechanized divisions blockaded Berlin itself—Ulbricht and his paladins would have been thrown on to the garbage heap of history.

To the Soviets this was a clear warning signal. The repression of Stalinism was as hated in the satellites as in the Soviet Union. The machinery of terror was not dismantled, but the powers of the secret police were put under the firm control of the party. Soviet economic exactions from the satellites were reduced by the return to these countries of joint stock companies which had been a means of exaction. The temporary switch of resources from heavy industry to light and to consumer industries and to agriculture in the Soviet Union and in the satellites was meant to appease popular dissatisfaction. It also caused considerable economic disarray in the commercial relations of the satellites, and was hence a contributing factor to the Polish and Hungarian events of 1956.

One of the most important immediate tasks of the Khrushchev–Bulganin leadership was to regulate the relations with Yugoslavia. On 26 May 1955 a Soviet delegation, consisting of Khrushchev, Bulganin, Mikoyan, Shepilov, Gromyko and Kumykin turned up in Belgrade. Khrushchev in his speech at the airport referred to Tito as 'dear comrade' and finished his speech with the peroration: 'Long live the fraternal friendship and close co-operation between the peoples of the Soviet Union and Yugoslavia.' The amazement of the Yugoslav comrades can be imagined. In 1949 the Cominform had charged that the Yugoslav party was 'in the hands of murderers and spies'. Yugoslavia had now become 'a land of intrepid heroes and tireless workers'. The reception which the Soviet delegation received was cool. Yet Khrushchev did succeed in his main task of re-establishing relations with Yugoslavia, which was now recognized once again as a country building socialism. The first part of the Soviet–Yugoslav *rapprochement* was crowned by the arrival in Moscow of Tito in June 1956.

It may be wondered why Khrushchev had gone to the inordinate lengths that he did to woo Tito. There were a number of reasons. During the period 1953 to 1956 eastern Europe was in disarray, and Khrushchev evidently hoped that Titoism would be convincing proof of how one could have a solid one-party state and yet eschew the oppressive political and economic measures which had by now become inseparable from communism. Tito was willing to play this role. He had become a communist in Russia, he had fought in Spain and he and most of his closest confederates had been brought up in the world of international communism. Alliance with the west, membership of the so-called bloc of non-aligned countries, was something which Stalin had forced on Yugoslavia. Though the re-establishment of state and party relations between Moscow and Belgrade did not result in the jettisoning of Tito's previous internal and external policies, Tito never forgot that the Soviet Union was the leader of a socialist bloc of states.

The Soviet *rapprochement* with Yugoslavia gave practical recognition to the principle that each communist party must find its own way to socialism. But this phrase, like so many of the clichés of Soviet ideology, remained deliberately vague. The same may be said of the view which was now given great prominence, that the relations between socialist states were relations of a new type, qualitatively different from relations which existed between socialist and capitalist states. Stalin, too, had accepted that these relations should be based on equality, independence and sovereignty, and fraternal mutual assistance. But as Gomulka, the Polish leader, had remarked in 1956, 'the principles could not fit within the framework of what makes up the cult of personality'. These theories were now revived by Malenkov and by Khrushchev, but the primacy of Moscow was never to be questioned. Indeed the Soviets tended to compare the relations between socialist states with the relations existing between the Russian Socialist Federal Soviet Republic and the other union republics—hardly a comparison to please the increasingly nationalistic regimes of eastern Europe.

The example of Yugoslavia was soon to be noted by other communist regimes. Tito had got away with it, because unlike

Trotsky he had behind him a party apparatus and because he controlled the machinery of the state. His brand of communism was popular. The close economic connections with the west assured the Yugoslav population a standard of living which neighbours such as the Bulgarians or the Rumanians could not aspire to. There is no reason to suppose that the leaders of the satellite countries desired independence from Moscow's control, but events were in some cases forcing them in that direction. Several of the regimes found that an appeal to anti-Soviet sentiment could make a great difference to their popularity. Industrial modernization required a turn to the technologically advanced west. Finally the direct contacts between the leaders of the satellites and those of the Soviet Union were no longer as close as they had been when these gentlemen had returned to their countries in the baggage train of the Red Army. In 1956 the Poles had been the first to put into high party office men of whom Moscow disapproved—an action unthinkable a year or two earlier.

The two speeches, one 'open' and the other 'secret', delivered by Khrushchev at the 20th Congress of the Communist Party in February 1956 were perhaps the most important reason for what the Italian communist leader, Palmiro Togliatti, was to call 'polycentrism'. The Czechoslovak writer Ladislav Mňačko in a book published in 1963 wrote of the shock given to those 'blindly believing' members of communist parties by Khrushchev's revelations of what is euphemistically called the 'cult of personality'. In other words, the imprisonment, torture and slaughter, on Stalin's orders, of millions of men and women, many of them party members.

The reverberations throughout the communist world were tremendous. On some it was direct. The first secretary of the Polish Communist Party, Boleslav Bierut, died of a heart attack while still in Moscow. The result of it all was a weakening of Soviet control. As Stalin had not been infallible there was no reason to suppose that any of the little Stalins in the satellites were also infallible. Even the wisdom of communist parties was questioned. It is of course true that the condemnations of Stalin drew a clear distinction between Stalin and the Party. While the head was sick, the Party itself remained healthy. Few, however, were to be fooled by this philosophical distinction.

From the point of view of foreign policy and especially of relations with non-communist states, the 'open' speech was more significant. The principles of peaceful co-existence, different roads to socialism and the abandonment of the doctrine of the inevitability of war were all given prominence. Equally significant was the renunciation of violence and revolution in the seizure of power by a communist party. The October 1917 model was the one which had been prescribed for all parties. It was now admitted that communist parties could eschew violence and that they could even come to power by parliamentary means. Admittedly the example chosen, the *coup d'état* in Czechoslovakia in February 1948, was hardly one to encourage the western democracies, but it did clear the road for a more flexible attitude to communist agitation, especially in the non-committed world of Africa, Asia and Latin America. This made world communism more and not less revolutionary.

THE POLISH AND HUNGARIAN EVENTS

The effects of the 20th Party Congress were soon felt all over eastern Europe. Men imprisoned in the late forties and early fifties began to reappear, for example Wladyslaw Gomulka. Others were demoted, for example the Bulgarian premier Vulko Chervenkov and the Hungarian Stalinist Matyas Rakosi. Suddenly the situation reached crisis point. At the end of June 1956 workers in the Polish industrial city of Poznan revolted, under the eyes of western businessmen attending the international trade fair there. The Polish government admitted that the riots were not caused purely by provocateurs and imperialist agents but rather by the 'existence of serious disturbances between the party and various sections of the working class'. In the next few months political life was subject to a process of democratization and when it seemed to go too far, a powerful Soviet delegation headed by Khrushchev, Molotov, Kaganovich and Mikoyan descended on Warsaw. The Poles were not to be intimidated. Gomulka became first secretary of the Party and Marshal Rokossovski, the Russian commander-in-chief of the Polish army, was sent home. In the face of this united resistance by a communist leadership the Soviets gave way. Their wisdom was to be rewarded. The very considerable freedom achieved in Poland was gradually whittled away by Gomulka, and he himself became one of the most trusted political friends of Khrushchev. Indeed Gomulka's so called 'national communism' was restricted to domestic affairs. Polish agriculture remained largely uncollectivized and the Catholic church, in spite of pressures against it at various times, and especially during the millennial celebrations of the Polish state in 1966, was left comparatively free to develop and to flourish. On the stage of world communism as on that of world politics, Gomulka was content to follow the Soviet line.

Hungary, like Poland, had for some time been in a state of excitement and unrest centred mainly on a group of intellectuals known as the Petöfi Club. The tendency of the government to waver between repression and concession simply encouraged the critics. A meeting of students developed into a demonstration and riot on 23 October. The demonstrators soon turned their fury to the statue of Stalin, which they demolished. The riot became a revolution when the secret police fired on the demonstrators, killing some of them. The next day Soviet troops appeared in Budapest. Two days later Imre Nagy formed a new government. An armistice was proclaimed and Soviet troops left Hungary. The old political parties were revived. However, during the night of 31 October to 1 November, Russian troops once more moved into Hungary. Nagy declared the country's neutrality and withdrew his country from the Warsaw Pact. On 4 November the Soviets launched an attack on Budapest. At the same time a new government was established at the headquarters of the Soviet army by Janos Kadar.

The great difference between the Polish and the Hungarian situation was that in the former the Party retained control of affairs while in the latter it lost it. It was shown in Hungary, and again in Czechoslovakia in 1968, that the Soviets would intervene militarily in a situation where the local communist party was losing its leading role in the state and in society.

Nagy's decision to seek a status for Hungary similar to that of Austria would have meant the exclusion of Soviet influence. It would also have threatened the whole satellite empire and so removed the defensive barrier which had been built around the Soviet Union in the years 1944 to 1948. Even ideologically such a back-sliding to capitalism was not permissible. As communism marked a higher stage in man's development a reversal of the trend meant a reversal of the laws of history.

The Soviets drew a number of lessons from the events in Poland and Hungary. Stalinist policy had been unwise—but they had known this for some time. Nationalism could not be outraged in the way it had been in Stalin's days. Some sops to nationalism, to local peculiarities, had to be permitted. The Soviets themselves became the exponents of liberalism in eastern Europe. As they and some of their partners were to tell the Czechoslovaks in the Warsaw letter of 1968, 'we are not the men of yesterday'.

In many ways the Hungarian and Polish events were to strengthen the Soviet position as against the western powers. The Soviets could feel certain that there would be no American intervention in the affairs of 'their' part of Europe and it was in this conviction that they had acted in 1956 and were to act again in 1968. Secondly, the polycentric tendencies so evident in eastern Europe in the twelve years to the invasion of Czechoslovakia provoked similar tendencies in western Europe. De Gaulle was to become the favourite western leader of the Soviets.

THE SOCIALIST COMMONWEALTH

After 1956 the communist world was becoming a more interesting place. Nations submerged under the common yoke of Stalinism were re-asserting themselves. Relations with Yugoslavia never ran smoothly, especially after the Hungarian invasion and again after the Czechoslovak invasion, but no Soviet government ever suggested that Yugoslavia was not a socialist state. The Soviet Union and China were soon to quarrel, at first using Yugoslavia and Albania as proxies. The Soviet leaders proclaimed again and again that the relations between socialist states were based on the absolute sovereignty of each and on the non-interference in each other's affairs. But, in spite of the absence of the kind of organizational links that the Comintern and the Cominform had provided, the Soviet Union still claimed primacy for itself. In the words of

Khrushchev, this primacy was based on the fact that the Soviet Union had been the first to blaze the trail of socialism for mankind, because she was the first to have entered into the period of the extensive building of socialism, and because she was the most powerful country in the international socialist system. In order to give recognition to this role, international party congresses were frequently held. The first in 1957 was a great success. Sino-Soviet differences were already apparent at the next congress in 1960, coming in the aftermath of Khrushchev's direct attack on the Chinese at the Congress of the Rumanian Communist Party in Bucharest earlier in the year.

Yet outwardly unity was preserved, and the fact that eighty-one parties actually turned up was a triumph for the Soviets. The Moscow meeting of 1965, the Budapest meeting of 1968 and the Moscow meeting of 1969 showed the deep splits in the communist world and indeed the shrinking authority of the Communist Party of the Soviet Union.

The congresses, too, underlined the reality of the socialist commonwealth as indeed did the frequent meeting of party functionaries either at party congresses or at specially arranged meetings. In spite of talks of sovereignty and non-interference the communist parties knew their dependence on each other and the dependence of all of them on the Red Army. As it was stated in the programme of the Communist Party announced at the 21st Party Congress: 'The Soviet Union is not pursuing the task of communist construction alone but in fraternal community with the other socialist countries.'

Yet ideology and international jamborees combined with the presence of the Red Army in the German Democratic Republic in Poland, in Hungary, in Bulgaria, in Rumania until 1958 and in Czechoslovakia from 1968 did not remain the only links of empire or means of control. The treaty setting up the Warsaw Treaty Organization was signed on 14 May 1955. Its members were the Soviet Union and all the communist states of eastern Europe with the exception of Yugoslavia. The German Democratic Republic became a member shortly afterwards. A number of factors were instrumental in the signing of this treaty. The Paris agreements which presaged the re-arming of Western Germany and the entry of West Germany into NATO on 9 May resulted in this counter-move. Its birth had therefore some similarity to that of the Council for Mutual Economic Aid (Comecon) which had been founded as the Soviet bloc's answer to Marshall Aid. The Warsaw Treaty had an important propaganda role. Clearly it has always been a Soviet interest to weaken or undermine the western alliance and to dangle in front of it the prospect of an easing of tension. Thus Article 11 stated that while the Treaty remained in force for twenty years it would be dissolved if a system of collective security were established in Europe. There were, however, other reasons for it, too. The Treaty provided a legal basis for the maintenance of Soviet troops in Hungary and Rumania after the Austrian State Treaty had robbed it of its legal rationale. Indeed the Treaty came into force one day before the signing of the Austrian State Treaty.

For the first five years of its existence the organization was quiescent. The highest organ of the pact, the Political Consultative Committee, held only three meetings between 1955 and 1961 and until 1960 no joint manoeuvres were held. The intervention of Soviet forces in Hungary in 1956 was carried out by Soviet troops alone, but acting under the terms of the Warsaw Treaty. It was Kadar's counter-government, created in the camp of the Red Army, which invoked the Treaty.

In 1959 and in 1960 the Soviet Union adopted a new role for its forces. Khrushchev pursued with great tenacity his policy of improving relations with the United States and clearly came to the conclusion that war with the United States was unlikely. The needs and demands of the domestic Soviet sector and the decreasing utility and burdensome costs of large standing conventional forces provided for a sharp reduction of Soviet conventional capabilities and for a significant upgrading of the role of the strategic forces. It was the Soviet aim that the military forces of the east-European allies were now to fill the gap created by the reduction in Soviet conventional forces. Pursuing this course, these forces were now modernized and given some of the more sophisticated weaponry of modern warfare. It seems paradoxical that the USSR decided to give a more active role to these forces at a time when the east Europeans were becoming more difficult to control and when they were all asserting their independence. The Soviets, however, regarded the pact as a means to both military and political unity, just as they saw Comecon as a means to economic and political unity.

It was not until 1968 that the Warsaw Pact was operationally active. The invasion of Czechoslovakia was carried out after joint consultation among Warsaw Pact countries and was undertaken jointly by them. One country, however, did not participate in either the consultation or the invasion. The Rumanians had been pursuing an independent policy for some years. It was inevitable that they should be sympathetic to the Czechs even though they could have had little sympathy for the internal liberalization in Czechoslovakia. The Albanians had by this time severed their links with both the Warsaw Treaty and Comecon.

The Council for Mutual Economic Aid (Comecon) was founded in January 1949 as a reaction to the European Recovery Programme. It, too, remained fairly quiescent until 1956. It did not get its constitution or charter until 1960. There were a number of reasons for the activization of Comecon in the 1960s. First of all the Soviet Union and some of its partners, such as Czechoslovakia and the German Democratic Republic, were keenly interested in economic integration. The Czechs and the Germans, heavily dependent upon imports of raw materials and requiring a stable market for their manufactured products, favoured integration. In 1962, the trade of these countries with China was reduced to a trickle, for political reasons. The Soviets supported the Czech and German position. To them it made economic and political sense.

Secondly the Soviets began to revise their views of the European Economic Community. It had been roundly condemned in the 17 theses of 1959 of the Moscow Institute of World Economy and International Relations but these views were revised in 1962 in the 32 theses. It was recognized that the EEC had in some ways been successful, and that it was an organization that could be emulated. In August 1962 Khrushchev set forth his views in *Kommunist*. Khrushchev drew from the evolution of the EEC—to which Britain had just signified its readiness to adhere—the lesson that Comecon should itself establish 'a unified planning organ, empowered to compile common plans and to decide organizational matters'. As Gomulka put it: 'everyone peels his own turnip and loses by it.'

The crux of the plan lay in the rational allocation of invest-ment. Most big capital projects would better serve the area as a whole than the limited market of one country, and they could be located near the cheapest or most convenient source of materials. Moreover, the Soviet Union was itself willing to reduce its output of some kinds of manufactures if these could be produced more economically in one of the other countries.

This proposal evoked a shriek of protest from the Rumanians similar to their protest at any strengthening of the Warsaw Pact Organization. In April 1964 the Rumanians declared that the idea of a single planning body had the most serious eco-nomic and political implications: 'it would turn sovereignty into a notion without any content.' Plans to use economic integration as a means of political control were revived again after the invasion of Czechoslovakia.

The Rumanian resistance was possible for two reasons. In 1958 the Soviets withdrew their troops from Rumania. Secondly the Rumanians were able to take advantage of the Sino-Soviet split. They maintained good relations with China and Albania. Soon they established good relations with the west, too. They exchanged ambassadors with Bonn. They were visited by De Gaulle. The Russians regarded all this with much distaste and it seemed possible that the Rumanians, too, would become victims of a Soviet invasion. However, the Rumanian Party secretary, Ceausescu, learned from his pre-decessor, Gheorghiu Dej, one lesson: no internal relaxation was the price that had to be paid for achieving independence.

THE SUEZ WAR

The Hungarian revolution was not the only crisis of the autumn of 1956. The Israeli invasion of the Sinai Peninsula and the subsequent Anglo-French intervention gave the Soviets their first big success in the Middle East. The establishment of the state of Israel in 1948, which immediately received *de jure* recognition from the Soviets, ensured that the Middle East would remain a centre of discord. The two rivals for control of the Arab world, Britain and France, were in rapid retreat. It was natural for the Soviets to seek to penetrate into an area geographically close to their own borders and so breach the wall of military pacts which the United States was building around the communist bloc.

The first steps in this policy were marked by propaganda attacks on Israel. This was followed by a willingness of Soviet bloc countries to take Egypt's cotton yarn and rice at above world prices, and in 1955 by the supply of arms from Czechoslovakia. The nationalization of the Suez Canal in July 1956 resulted in the withdrawal of the promise of American aid to build the Aswan Dam. Although the agreement by which the Russians undertook to help the building was not signed until 1958 they immediately led the Egyptians to believe that such help would be forthcoming.

The Anglo-American intervention in the Suez War was a disaster for the west. It diverted the attention of the world from the Soviet suppression of the Hungarian revolution. It showed the military weakness of France and Britain, indeed the political and military ineptitude of Britain. It allowed the Soviets to gain considerable popularity in the Afro-Asian world by their threat to use nuclear weapons against the aggressors. It afforded them the interesting spectacle of the contradictions of capitalism, that is, a sharp conflict between Washington and her principal European allies. It must, however, be remembered that the Americans warned the Soviets that rocket attacks on Britain would be followed by American reprisals.

The year 1956 made the Soviet Union an African and Asian power factor. It did not particularly matter that for a number of years Nasser in Egypt would keep his own communists in prison. What was more important was the extent to which such a country as Egypt was anti-western, and the extent to which she was dependent on the Soviet Union. This dependence became greater as the repeated defeats of Egypt made her ever more dependent on outside help.

The turmoil of the Middle East did not end after the Suez War. In 1957 Eisenhower attempted to limit Soviet influence by promising aid to any state threatened by communist subversion. In 1958 British troops intervened in Jordan and American marines landed in the Lebanon. But the Middle East became ever more troublesome. In 1957 Syria seemed on the verge of a communist take-over. In 1958 in Iraq, General

Kassim attempted a Nasser-type revolution. The permanent irritant, the existence of Israel, kept the Middle East open to Soviet influence.

THE THIRD WORLD

Lenin had seen the potentialities for world communism among the nations of Asia and Africa, most of whom were subject to the imperial government of Britain and France. He saw that the nationalist movements in the colonial and semi-colonial countries could be used to weaken the world system of capitalism. To the communists, therefore, the national bourgeoisie had a dual nature; it could be progressive if it pursued an anti-imperialist policy which accorded with Soviet interests, but it could be reactionary if it allied itself with imperialist forces, that is if it pursued policies which did not accord with the Soviet viewpoint. After the failure of the Soviet offensive in Asia, and especially in China in 1927, the Soviets warned that the national bourgeoisie, frightened by the revolutionary movement, was betraying it. Even after the end of the Second World War this attitude did not change. Moscow found it impossible to believe in the genuineness of independence for such countries as India or Indonesia.

The shift in attitude did not come until after the death of Stalin. It was myopic to pretend that the correlation of world forces had not been altered by the ever-accelerating speed of decolonization. Moreover, the Bandung Conference of 1955 had demonstrated the intensely anti-western attitude that many Asian and African leaders were prepared to take. Chou En-lai had represented China in Bandung, showing a Chinese awareness of this problem.

This change in policy was fundamental. While formerly it had been axiomatic that a socialist revolution could only take place by the efforts of the working class led by the communist party, it was now admitted that the forces of national revolution could make significant strides towards socialism in countries where a numerous proletariat did not exist. Of course not all the countries of Asia could be classed as being ruled by a progressive national bourgeoisie. The government of South

Vietnam, of South Korea, of Japan and even such former French possessions in Africa as the Ivory Coast or Mauritania, were regarded as reactionary and fascist regimes. At the end of the spectrum were countries like Indonesia under Sukarno, or Ghana under Nkrumah, Mali under Mobido Keita, Guinea, Egypt and Algeria, which were countries ruled by one party, with strong socialist elements and with political sympathies which were favourable towards the communist bloc. Somewhere in between were states like India which pursued a policy of 'positive neutralism' and which were recipients of Soviet aid. Similar to India were states like Ethiopia which perpetuated a semi-feudal society, suppressed the communist party, but resisted the temptations of the west.

Soviet aid to underdeveloped countries had been small in volume but great in propaganda potential. Since 1948 the United States has spent over a hundred billion dollars in foreign aid. The Soviet figure is a mere fourteen billion dollars, of which only four billion dollars has gone out of Europe, and of which only about three-quarters has been spent. This figure does not include military aid, which has been very considerable in the case of Egypt, India and North Vietnam. However, the propaganda value of such prestige projects as the Aswan Dam in Egypt or the Bhilai Steel Mill in India has been important.

There are two major reasons for Soviet aid. The first is to buy political influence, though the extent to which influence can be bought by such means is doubtful. In the case of Indonesia the heavy Soviet involvement did not prevent Sukarno from moving towards the Chinese position. Still, in the case of the United Arab Republic and in the case of India such aid, coupled with political and military support, has paid dividends. At the very least one must say that aid gives the recipient country the possibility of choosing between the east and the west. Mossadegh's nationalization of the Iranian oil company in 1951 might have had a very different result had it happened a few years later.

Such foreign trade ventures also have a purely commercial aspect. It was difficult for the Soviet Union and other communist countries to make inroads in the commercial activity of countries whose ties were with the west. In order to capture these markets credit facilities and the inducement of repayment in soft currencies had to be given. In such a way, the excess goods produced by the communist countries, which were exported to China until this trade was stopped in 1962, could find new outlets. Recently the Russians have admitted that foreign aid should be used to stimulate the flow of raw materials into the Soviet Union.

One of the by-products of the Soviet involvement with the peoples of Asia and Africa was a renewed interest in the United Nations. In the years between 1945 and 1950 the Soviet Union had become convinced that the United Nations was being used to further the aims of American policy. The Soviet reaction to this was a boycott of all the organs of the United Nations with the exception of the International Court of Justice. When the absence of the Soviet delegate from the meetings of the Security Council in June 1950 made it possible to dispatch a United Nations force to Korea, it was seen how erroneous this policy had been. Even the return to the Council did not end in the expected result because by the 'uniting for peace' resolution the United States could by-pass the vote of the Soviet Union in the General Assembly. In the years after 1955 the majority of pro-western states was reduced by a flood of newly independent African and Asian states. These had one thing in common: they were all anti-colonialist and they all wanted to avoid being involved in the east-west conflict. Soviet support for their anti-colonialist position was appreciated, as was the economic and military aid that some of them received. In the Congo crisis the Soviet Union found itself in a position of having to put its propaganda into action. Although it disliked military operations under the aegis of the United Nations it had to support the force sent to the Congo because its task was to expel the Belgians and the mercenaries and to stop the secession of the province of Katanga. But in its refusal to pay for these and the other United Nations peace-keeping forces, the Soviet Union found ready support from France.

The Congo events prompted the Soviet leadership to re-appraise the role of the United Nations. Khrushchev proposed to replace the office of secretary general by a three-man commission, representing the communist, the capitalist and the neutralist powers in order to assure that 'the activity of the UN executive will not be to the detriment of any of these groups of states in the world'. In this move Khrushchev miscalculated and he received no support for the troika plan from his Afro-Asian allies.

EUROPEAN SECURITY

Soviet military strategy and foreign policy have sought in Europe two territorial aims. After the establishment of the satellite empire they have sought to preserve communist rule within it and their own influence—the two are not identical. Secondly they have hoped to establish beyond the perimeter of the satellite states a further perimeter of neutralized states, perhaps on the lines of Finland or Austria. This would mean the destruction of NATO, and the activities of De Gaulle were, of course, extremely welcome to the Russians.

On 2 October 1957 the Polish minister Adam Rapacki proposed in the General Assembly of the United Nations a plan for a nuclear clear zone in Poland and the two German states. It was planned that these countries should not possess nuclear weapons, and the nuclear armaments of other powers, that is NATO and Warsaw Pact powers, should not be disposed on these territories. A few days later Czechoslovakia declared its readiness to accede to the plan. It is certain that the Polish government would not have put forward such an important initiative in foreign policy without Moscow's approval.

Equally clearly the plan could not be accepted by the western powers. It would remove their nuclear armaments to the periphery of Europe, though with the development of Polaris submarines, then beginning, this was perhaps not a vital factor. But the removal of the major deterrent weapon would depress the west politically. In any case to all western-European governments it raised the terrifying possibility of an eventual American withdrawal from Europe.

Especially in Great Britain the Rapacki plan was taken seriously. At the foreign ministers' conference in Berlin in 1954 Eden had himself put forward a plan for a demilitarized zone in eastern Europe and this was repeated by Harold Macmillan at a foreign ministers' conference in October 1955. In each case, of course, the western plan talked about a reunited Germany while Rapacki had based his plan on the existence of two

German states. The plan was also taken up with variations by the leader of the opposition, Hugh Gaitskell, and by the former American diplomat, George Kennan, in the BBC Reith lectures.

The Rapacki plan was given official Soviet blessing in a peace plan adopted by the Supreme Soviet on 21 December 1957 and in a Soviet note of 10 January 1958 in which it was stated that the subject of disengagement should be one of the points on the agenda of a summit conference.

Soviet plans for collective security, as for disarmament, were not allowed to become dormant. The Rapacki plan was followed two years later by the Gomulka plan. Two years later again, after Khrushchev's departure, Poland proposed the convening of a conference to examine the problems of European security. In April 1966 the Soviet foreign minister Gromyko officially restated Moscow's desire for an all-European security conference. This was followed in July by the Bucharest declaration. It stated that the pre-condition for a lasting settlement lay in Bonn's hands: the recognition by her of the permanence of political borders and her renunciation of all territorial claims, that is the recognition of the existence of the German Democratic Republic and of the western frontiers of Poland. Bonn too had to renounce nuclear weapons for ever. Six months later, one of the signatories of the declaration, Rumania, established diplomatic relations with Bonn.

In April 1967 a further conference on European security was held in Karlovy Vary in Czechoslovakia. This time representatives of twenty-four communist parties, ruling and non-ruling, attended, and not representatives of governments. The main purpose of the meeting was to weaken NATO by launching a campaign for its dissolution in the treaty's twentieth anniversary year. Even the invasion of Czechoslovakia did not kill the call for such a conference. Both in March and October 1969 renewed calls were made.

Nevertheless, there were considerable differences between such calls as those made by Rapacki and Gomulka, and the situation after 1967. Formerly the Soviets had been aggressive; now they were on the defensive. The transformation of China from an ally into an enemy made a favourable settlement of the European problem more urgent. But such stabilization was difficult. De Gaulle's policy, culminating in his visits to Poland in September 1967 and to Rumania in May 1968 was a threat to Soviet supremacy in the area. An even greater threat was the policy pursued by the German coalition government of Kiesinger and Brandt and by its successor, the Brandt coalition government. Western Germany was beginning to exercise an ever-greater influence on the affairs of eastern Europe and it was important for the Russians to minimize this influence and also to obtain Bonn's recognition for the *status quo*. This meant above all recognition of the Oder and Neisse rivers as the boundary between Germany and Poland. It also meant the acceptance of the thesis of the two German states. In these aims the Soviets were not unsuccessful.

NUCLEAR STRATEGY

On 26 August 1957 the official Soviet news agency, Tass, announced that an ICBM had been successfully tested and that the Soviet Union was now in a position to send missiles, to any part of the world. In September the first earth satellite Sputnik I, was launched, underlining the seeming Soviet superiority in both space research and rocketry. Khrushchev was at pains to underline this superiority in frequent interviews with foreign correspondents. Moreover, he threatened the west with nuclear destruction. America was assured that a nuclear war would rage with no less fury in the western hemisphere. West Germany was informed that it had no chance of survival and Britain was told that its very existence was threatened. For a number of years it was believed that there was a missile gap and that it was in favour of Russia. The Soviets actually made sure that their claims remained vague. Although they maintained that the world balance of forces was now clearly in favour of socialism, they did not actually claim that the strategic balance had shifted in their favour.

From 1960 onwards the Russians began to play down the claims that they had made. They now stressed more urgently than ever the dangers to all men of nuclear war. Such a war, could, in Khrushchev's colourful words, 'destroy our Noah's Ark, the Earth'. The atom bomb was, unfortunately, not class conscious. It would destroy the workers with the capitalists. Clearly the beginning of the differences between the Soviet and Chinese comrades imposed this caution.

It was not only the pacifists in the west who took Soviet claims at their face value. So did the Chinese. The east wind, Mao said, was now more powerful than the west wind. With a population of over 600 million, rising at the rate of fifteen million per annum, the Chinese could view with equanimity the extermination of millions of people. After all it might not be such a bad thing if 100 million Russians were to disappear in a war. A Soviet general had written that 500 to 600 million people would perish in a nuclear war. Khrushchev himself repeated this claim.

At the same time it must not be supposed that the Chinese were actually encouraging the Russians to unleash a nuclear war. But they did feel that the Soviet technological advantage in nuclear weapons and in the means of delivering them (after all they had the words of the prime minister of the Soviet Union for this), could be used much more emphatically to extract concessions from the west, and especially concessions in the Far East. The Russians, knowing their backwardness compared with the Americans, realized that the supposed missile gap could only be used with great caution. The Chinese were greatly displeased to receive only very cautious Soviet support when in 1958 they tried to wrest control of the off-shore islands of Quemoy and Matsu from Chiang Kai-shek.

FROM BERLIN TO CUBA

Plans for European collective security were one aspect of Soviet policy. There were other means of pressure which could be used. On 10 November 1958 Khrushchev announced that the Soviet Union no longer recognized obligations it had assumed under the Potsdam agreement which related to Berlin. This amounted to a demand that the occupation of West Berlin be ended and that a special status for West Berlin be worked out. Thus began the second Berlin crisis, which continued on and off until 1962. Specifically the Russians demanded that the three western powers in Berlin negotiate an agreement liquidating their occupation within six months. Failure to do so would result in turning control of military traffic along the *Autobahn* over to the German Democratic Republic. The Soviet ultimatum was followed in the summer of 1959 by a foreign ministers' conference in Geneva during which the western powers showed some readiness to make concessions. The Soviets rejected this move and when the negotiations were renewed in the spring of 1960 the west was no longer prepared to make concessions. In any case, with Khrushchev's visit to the United States and his talks with President Eisenhower at Camp David, the situation improved. By this time Khrushchev had of necessity weakened his position by postponing his six months' ultimatum continuously. There was little else that he could do. If the west was not going to give way Khrushchev could only enforce his will by military force, and this he was not prepared to do.

In the midst of it all a further meeting was to take place with Eisenhower in Paris in May 1960. But on May Day a U–2 spy plane was shot down over the Soviet Union. Eisenhower's admission of responsibility for the flight wrecked the conference. Khrushchev could hardly meet in friendship with a man whom he had previously portrayed as a man of peace and reason.

The campaign against Berlin was renewed in 1961 with a new president installed in the White House. The Kennedy administration started off badly in the foreign-policy field by the débâcle in the Bay of Pigs and this failure may have encouraged the Russians. At a meeting with Kennedy in Vienna in June, Khrushchev re-activated the Berlin campaign and on 15 June he announced a new deadline on Berlin. 'A peaceful settlement in Berlin must be attained this year.' The Soviets announced an increase in defence spending. The Americans followed suit and more American troops were sent to Germany. On 13 August the authorities of the German Democratic Republic closed the sector border dividing East from West Berlin and began constructing the Berlin Wall. On 17 October Khrushchev again moved the deadline on his ultimatum beyond the last day of 1961. Ten days later there was a sixteen-hour confrontation between Soviet and American tanks at a Berlin checkpoint. However, by mid-1962 the Berlin crisis petered out.

It is impossible to know exactly the reasons for Khrushchev's actions. Berlin is the most exposed sentinel of the western world but one which the west will not surrender. Kennedy's proud boast to the Berliners, 'ich bin ein Berliner', is the clearest public affirmation of this inflexible determination. Why then did Khrushchev seek to dislodge the west just there?

It has been suggested that Khrushchev was so concerned with the problem of dealing with his Chinese critics that he was determined to win a foreign-policy success which would have the effect of muting their criticism. It seems much more likely that Khrushchev, very concerned with the safety and cohesion of the satellite states, wanted such a success both to strengthen the German Democratic Republic, a country playing an ever more important part in the politics of the Soviet bloc, and to impress all the satellite states with Soviet predominance. The crisis of the autumn of 1956 had shaken the whole Soviet system to its foundations and one of the most important aims of Soviet policy since has been to re-integrate the bloc.

It seems surprising that Khrushchev believed he could succeed. One must, however, take his personal position into consideration. Unlike Stalin, he was prepared to take risks, and the risk in Berlin did not seem too great. He clearly did not believe that war by accident could break out, and in case of real danger it was always possible to defuse the situation. But it is unlikely that he considered his chances so low. He was always a man who acted on the principle that *on s'engage et après on verra*. He had personally met his chief opponents, the major statesmen of the western powers, and there is no reason to suppose that he had a high opinion of them. He did not rate either Eisenhower or Macmillan very highly. Kennedy he no doubt respected, but only after the Cuban missile crisis. By that time his days in power were numbered. It was possible that by a show of strength he could force the west to make concessions on Berlin or Germany.

Khrushchev was soon to involve himself in a much more dangerous game than Berlin. In January 1959 Fidel Castro led his group of youthful and bearded warriors into the capital of Cuba, Havana. Soon this revolutionary, the prototype of the student rebels of the sixties, found that his revolution could not succeed without espousing a hysterically anti-American line. In turn this sent him on a search for allies and he turned naturally to the Soviet Union. Three years after he came to power he announced that he had always been a Marxist-Leninist 'and shall be one until my last day on earth', although he admitted that he had only read a small part of Marx's *Das Kapital*. The new Kennedy administration attempted to get rid of Castro by military intervention. Cuban refugees, organized by the CIA, were landed in the Bay of Pigs in April 1961, but were quickly rounded up by government forces.

In 1962 Khrushchev decided to use the island, 'the island of liberty' in Soviet jargon, as a means of achieving a major breakthrough in the nuclear arms race. Intermediate-range ballistic missiles were brought into Cuba.

It seems likely that Khrushchev, realizing the strategic inferiority of the Soviet Union to the United States, as shown, for instance, in his failure to extract any concessions from the west over the problem of Berlin, attempted to reverse this superiority by this stroke. Presumably the missile sites would have been vulnerable to United States air strikes, but it would have substantially improved Soviet capabilities to launch a pre-emptive attack. Both the strategic and the political position of the Soviet Union would have been very rapidly and greatly enhanced. It is possible, also, that Khrushchev hoped to use the missiles as a bargaining counter with the United States for concessions in Europe or the Far East.

Khrushchev miscalculated both the speed with which the United States would discover the preparations, and the violence of its response. For years Soviet propaganda had stressed the essentially war-like nature of the American government. It seems in fact that Khrushchev was so convinced of its peacefulness that he even believed that it would not react with military force against the missiles. On 16 October President Kennedy was informed of the discovery by aerial photography of a missile base on Cuba. On 22 October, after the confirmation of the original information, Kennedy announced a blockade of Cuba. Four days later the Soviets yielded when it became clear that the United States was prepared not only to destroy the missile sites on Cuba or invade Cuba but regarded the Soviet Union as responsible for the crisis and hence could regard the placement of these missiles as a reason to strike at the Soviet Union itself.

Khrushchev, it seems, drew from the Cuban missile crisis the lesson that as it was impossible to overcome the nuclear superiority of the west it was better to come to some agreement on the limitation of armaments. Proposals for some form of disarmament, control of nuclear weapons, atom-free zones in central Europe or the Far East, reduction of conventional armaments, had been going on ever since the war without success. Now there was a minor breakthrough. On 25 July 1963 agreement was reached between the Soviet Union, the United States and Great Britain not to test nuclear weapons in the atmosphere, in outer space or under water. Neither France nor China signed the treaty. In the same summer the 'hot line' between the White House and the Kremlin was established permitting instantaneous communication between the two super-powers. Again this was a small matter, but it did indicate the extent to which the two super-powers were prepared to go to avoid war. To the Chinese critics this was, of course, another example of collusion. In the autumn of the same year the Soviet Union adhered to the resolution, asking all states to refrain from orbiting nuclear devices in outer space.

The fall of Khrushchev in October 1964 did not cause a reappraisal of Soviet policy. He was replaced by I. A. Kosygin as prime minister and by L. Brezhnev as Party secretary. But there were to be no more risky adventures and caution became, as under Stalin, the hallmark of Soviet policy. Unfortunately the unsolved problems of the Middle East and of South East Asia were both an opportunity and a risk. Even in Europe the polycentric tendencies within the bloc, combined with the attractions of the west, forced the Brezhnev-Kosygin leadership to draw tighter the links of empire. Certainly the détente with America continued and agreement was reached in 1968 on the non-proliferation of nuclear weapons. It seemed that the debates in the disarmament committee in Geneva were bearing some fruit. In 1970, too, the prohibitive cost of nuclear weapons and the defence against them resulted in the Strategic Arms Limitation talks in Helsinki.

THE SINO-SOVIET SPLIT

It is safe to assume that the death of Stalin was welcomed by the

Chinese leadership only a little less enthusiastically than by Stalin's heirs in Russia. At least they were not threatened with physical extinction like their Soviet partners. The Chinese had little reason to be grateful to Stalin. The responsibility for the massacre of communists in 1927 to 1928 must to some extent be placed on him. In the years from then until the victory of communism in China in 1949, he seems to have regarded their problems with suspicion, and in 1949 the Soviet ambassador was, according to Mao, the last to take leave of Chiang Kai-shek.

The ogre was dead and the lesser men in the Kremlin could no longer treat Mao in the old way. Moreover China, having under communism thrown off the anarchy of the republic and the lethargy of the later Empire, began to seek its place as a great world power and as the spokesman of the peoples of Asia. From the Soviet point of view China was a socialist state which by its size precluded a satellite status. From this time onwards China was accepted in Soviet declarations as co-leader of the socialist camp though there was never any doubt of the fact that from the point of view of power, of ideology and of historical experience, the Soviet Union was predominant. The Chinese were prepared to accept the Soviet leadership, but the condition of such acceptance was that the Soviet Union should lead in a given ideological direction. Such direction would inevitably bring the Soviet Union into conflict with the United States. In the last resort, whatever the ties of socialist brotherhood may have been, the Soviet Union was dependent on the United States and not on China. She was dependent on the only other power which possessed nuclear weapons and the means of annihilating her.

In fact a détente with the United States could only be achieved at China's expense. The Soviets apparently promised to help the Chinese develop their own nuclear bomb. This promise was withdrawn, and in 1958 the Chinese began their own nuclear programme and successfully exploded their first bomb in October 1964, the day on which Khrushchev was overthrown. To the Chinese the Soviet nuclear umbrella was not sufficient protection, because they knew that the Soviets would not necessarily use it to further China's aims or indeed to protect China in a conflict with the United States. Similar considerations impelled the French to develop their own nuclear force.

It may be presumed that the shared ideology of Marxism-Leninism would have prevented a split between the two powers, and it is possible that it postponed the public polemics. From another point of view, ideology actually exacerbated the conflict. Each specific point of disagreement, peaceful co-existence, policy towards the United States, the role of movements of national liberation, were not seen only from the point of view of the national interest of each country, but had to be fitted into an ideological framework. Therefore each point of disagreement became a disagreement on the whole field of ideology which made the solution of each problem that much harder.

Moreover, in their dispute the two contestants were speaking to a system of socialist states and to a world system of communism. All socialist states acknowledge the necessity for unity and for leadership and have been prepared to accept Moscow as the leader. Theoretically differences between them are hammered out in secret and once a decision is made all communist parties are expected to support it. This is democratic centralism on the plane of inter-state and inter-party relations. Once China challenged Soviet policy she also challenged her leadership.

In spite of the advantages that the Chinese gained by the death of Stalin, Sino-Soviet relations deteriorated. 'To be specific', the Chinese say, the differences 'began with the 20th Congress of the CPSU in 1956'. An Indian communist has reported that the Chinese did not like the way the Russians were handling the Beria case, that their attitude to Stalin was 'obnoxious' and towards Yugoslavia 'cringing'. They regarded the de-Stalinization campaign as something which the Soviets had no right to decide without consulting the world communist movement. Stalin belonged to all communists, not only Russian communists.

Later in 1956 the Chinese intervened, for the first time in history, in the affairs of eastern Europe. Such a move was not welcomed in Moscow, although in supporting Gomulka and condemning Nagy the Chinese certainly aided the Soviets. Early in 1957 Chou En-lai visited a number of east-European capitals.

Yet in 1957 the relations between the two socialist giants seemed better than ever. The Chinese were greatly impressed by the launching of the first satellite and Mao announced that the east wind now prevailed over the west wind. At the meeting of representatives of communist parties in Moscow in November 1957 Mao Tse-tung fully accepted the leadership of the Soviet Union based on this technological breakthrough. China could not be the leader because it 'has not even a quarter of a sputnik, whereas the Soviet Union has two'.

During 1960 the Sino-Soviet and the Soviet-Albanian conflict came out in the open at the 3rd Congress of the Rumanian Communist Party in Bucharest in June 1960. Khrushchev, who attended the Congress, attacked the Chinese, and it was only the Albanian delegate who supported them. The meeting of the eighty-one communist parties in Moscow in the same year continued the polemics begun in Bucharest. In 1960 a purge took place in the Albanian Communist Party which resulted in the arrest and execution of a number of Party members. It seems probable that the Soviets and the Yugoslavs were attempting to overthrow the Hoxha leadership in Albania. For the next three or four years Albania was used by the two sides when they wished to attack each other. Soviet attacks on Albania were understood by everybody to be an attack on China and Chinese attacks on Yugoslavia were understood to be an attack on the Soviet Union. On 20 October 1962 war broke out on the Sino-Indian border, two days before the beginning of the Cuban crisis. The Soviets quite openly supported India, continuing to send them war material. It was to the Chinese 'a complete betrayal of proletarian internationalism'. Indeed, the Soviet support for India in economic and military aid, and in the diplomatic support given to India in her dispute with Pakistan over Kashmir, was undoubtedly one of the main causes of the Sino-Soviet split. The Chinese demanded from their allies fraternal support. After all, they too were communists while India was a watered-down capitalist state. To the Soviets this was the dilemma of great-power status. From the international point of view they saw every reason to support India. To the Chinese involved in border conflicts with India and seeking the leadership of Asia, India was a capitalist adversary. Instead the Chinese came to an agreement with Pakistan. To the Russians this was equally intolerable. When in 1965 war broke out between Pakistan and India the Soviets arranged a cease-fire and invited the prime ministers to meet in Tashkent. With Kosygin acting as a peace-maker a truce was arranged in January 1966. For their part the Chinese supported Moscow over the Cuban crisis, but when Khrushchev withdrew the rockets the Chinese scorn for Soviet cowardice knew no bounds.

From 1960 the Sino-Soviet quarrel was fought in another dimension. To the disagreements over ideology and the disagreements on matters of external policy, there were now also added conflicts over territory. As early as 1962 there were, according to the Soviets, more than 5,000 frontier violations along the immensely extended frontier between the two powers. By 1969 large-scale frontier conflicts took place, especially on the Ussuri River.

The Chinese have pointed to the imperial expansion of the Tsars against China and have demanded two things. In their statements and in some of the propaganda maps that they publish they have made claims against vast areas of the Soviet Far East. They have gone even further. In an interview given to some Japanese journalists in 1963 Mao Tse-tung even accused the Soviets of grabbing German, Polish and Finnish territory in Europe. The Soviets reacted sharply to this attack. Khrushchev, speaking to another group of Japanese journalists six weeks later, pointed out that China was also a multi-national state and equally vulnerable.

It is indeed interesting to note that in December 1963 Khrushchev had addressed a message to heads of states and governments calling for an international agreement on the renunciation of force in settling territorial and frontier disputes. In August 1964 the USSR proposed that a resolution on this theme be included in the agenda of the forthcoming UN General Assembly.

AFTER KHRUSHCHEV

The coincidence of the fall of Khrushchev with the explosion of the first Chinese nuclear bomb made October 1964 a triumphant month for the Chinese. For the new Kosygin-Brezhnev leadership the problem of achieving an understanding with China was of cardinal importance. The removal of 'the greatest revisionist of all time', as the Chinese called Khrushchev, did not put out of the way one obstacle on the road to *rapprochement*. In fact neither the leaders in Peking nor those in Moscow could ever have had much hope that the very fundamental problems dividing them could so easily be spirited away. In November the Chinese presented their demands in an article entitled 'Why Khrushchev Fell', describing him as 'a buffoon on the contemporary political stage'. They demanded an end to de-Stalinization, an end to co-operation with the United States, abrogation of the Partial Test Ban Treaty, expulsion of Yugoslavia from the communist movement on the grounds that the Yugoslav communists were transforming Yugoslavia into a capitalist state, the cessation of all aid to India and an end of Soviet tutelage over the state of eastern Europe. For a time, however, the truce was maintained, that is, until March 1965, when the delegations gathered in Moscow for the consultative meeting of the world communist movement. From then on the situation steadily worsened. The border incidents increased to the point where major skirmishes were fought on the Ussuri River in 1969 and the Soviet embassy in Peking was surrounded by a howling mob of Red Guards.

Yet in some ways the Soviets were getting the better of the conflict. The excesses of the cultural revolution alienated a number of pro-Chinese communist parties and radically reduced the influence of the Chinese in the world communist movement. It certainly weakened the Chinese influence throughout the underdeveloped world. Castro, a very likely candidate for inclusion in a Chinese bloc, was forced to turn to the Russians because they were the only ones who could keep his revolution afloat economically. Further support was lost when in 1965 the Indonesian Communist Party, the largest pro-Chinese party in the world, was wiped out.

The war in Vietnam placed Soviet policy in the position of having to intervene in an area where Khrushchev had feared to tread, but the escalation of the war there made such intervention unavoidable. On the one hand the Soviets had to outbid the Chinese in the aid that they gave to North Vietnam;

on the other hand they wanted to avoid a direct conflict with the Americans.

It was on 30 December 1964 that the Soviets promised North Vietnam aid in case she was directly attacked. The aerial attacks came sooner than expected, on 7 February 1965. In February, too, Kosygin tried to establish the Soviet presence by visiting the capitals of North Vietnam and North Korea. In both capitals he was much welcomed and in various speeches and communiqués it was made clear that neither of the two countries was willing to quarrel with Moscow for the sake of Peking. His reception in Hanoi was particularly cordial and indeed the relations between the two countries have continued to improve. According to a Chinese version Kosygin apparently tried to bring pressure on the North Vietnamese to bring the war to an end. In January 1965 the Chinese wrote that the United States had demanded of the Soviet Union that it should use its influence in Hanoi to stop the aid North Vietnam was giving to the Viet Cong and to prevent attacks on South Vietnamese towns. The Soviet Union passed this message over to Hanoi. Whilst in Peking in February, Kosygin emphasized that the United States should be helped to find a way out of Vietnam. The Chinese turned down this proposal and Kosygin apparently declared himself in agreement with their views. However, on the day that Kosygin returned to Moscow, the Soviet Union sent notes to Vietnam and China suggesting the summoning of a new international conference on Indo-China without first insisting on the withdrawal of American troops. In February, in spite of a negative answer, the Soviets ordered their ambassador in Paris to suggest a conference to De Gaulle. The Soviet Union has not denied this version of events. It has instead pointed to the material aid it has given to Vietnam and this has certainly been considerable. It has also accused the Chinese of preventing the transportation of arms to Vietnam across Chinese territory.

FROM CAIRO TO PRAGUE

In 1967 the Middle East once more reached boiling-point. In 1957 the Israelis withdrew from Sinai in exchange for guarantees of free access to the Gulf of Aquaba and the Straits of Tiran. This right was assured by the presence of the UN peace-keeping force at Sharm el Sheikh which controls access to the Straits. In May the Egyptians gave notice to U Thant, secretary-general of the United Nations, to withdraw the peace-keeping force. In complying, U Thant triggered off the Six-Day War. The Israeli victory was total and to prevent the Israelis dictating peace in Cairo and Damascus, the Russians urged the Arabs to stop fighting. In November the Security Council produced a resolution calling for withdrawal of Israeli troops from occupied territory.

The Soviets hurried to re-arm their defeated allies, providing them with such sophisticated weapons as SAM missiles, and when the Israelis in 1969 and 1970 extended their raids into the Nile valley, Soviet planes piloted by Soviet airmen began the protection of the area. Indeed, the Soviets were facing a problem which had some similarities to that of the Americans in Vietnam. Their aim had been to expel the west. In this they had been successful, and the presence of Soviet ships in the eastern Mediterranean was a very clear sign of this. So was the increasing dependence of Egypt on the Soviet Union. But support for the Arab states also had its dangers. It was expensive in both economic and military aid. It was dangerous because Arab leaders like Nasser would not survive increased Israeli retaliation. The alternative to Nasser was one of a group of extremist guerrilla leaders who could be more amenable to Peking than they were to Moscow. The Soviet Union and the United States became, together, the two peace-makers in the Middle East and the acceptance by Israel, Jordan and the United Arab Republic of the Rogers plan for a cease-fire in August 1970 is a triumph not only for American but also for Soviet policy.

The year 1968 was the year of Czechoslovakia. The speed of de-Stalinization in Czechoslovakia had been slow. Now events moved at break-neck speed. On 5 January the Stalinist leader, Antonín Novotný, was forced to surrender the first secretaryship of the Party to the Slovak Alexander Dubček. In March he resigned also as president. The new leadership was reformist. The abolition of censorship in the press, on radio and in television caused an explosion of criticism and free speech.

The role of the Communist Party was placed under scrutiny. Clubs and organizations standing outside the Party and deriving no support from it made their appearance. Yet the leadership always expressed its loyalty to its alliances, to the Soviet Union and to the Warsaw Pact.

The Soviets and the other Warsaw Pact countries regarded these developments as the first stage of the liquidation of communism in Czechoslovakia. They sought to bring pressure on the Czechoslovaks by open criticism in their own newspapers. Kosygin and a number of Soviet generals visited Czechoslovakia.

The Czechoslovaks were summoned to a conference in Dresden in Eastern Germany, the aim of which was to persuade them to put some limitations on their reform movement. In July they were summoned to Warsaw but refused to come. The participants of the meeting in Warsaw, the Soviet Union, Poland, Hungary, Bulgaria and the German Democratic Republic addressed instead a letter to them. On 17 July the Central Committee of the Soviet Communist Party met to discuss the problem. The military manoeuvres which took place in Poland and Czechoslovakia were an even more direct form of pressure. The June manoeuvres of the Warsaw Pact countries may be regarded as the first intervention, because the Soviet troops showed unwillingness to withdraw. In fact the last Soviet troops did not leave until 2 August. When they finally did withdraw one last attempt at conciliation was made. In the frontier town of Čierna nad Tisou the Politburos of the Czechoslovak and Soviet parties met to hammer out their differences. Success seemed to be assured when a few days later the Czechs met with Brezhnev, Ulbricht, Gomulka, Kadar and Zhivkov in Bratislava to sign a joint communist statement. On 21 August, however, armies of the five Warsaw Pact countries in massive strength rapidly occupied Czechoslovakia.

The occupation of Czechoslovakia created a new situation for the Soviet Union. For the third time the Soviet Union had used military force to impose its rule on a country that it regarded as within its sphere of influence. But unlike the case of Eastern Germany in 1953 or that of Hungary in 1956 the leaders of Czechoslovakia never wavered in their allegiance to socialism. Clearly there were limits to the liberalization that the Soviets were prepared to permit. There were limits also to the doctrine of the separate roads to socialism. This was the first time that the Soviets had used force against a people who claimed to be socialist. Indeed the Soviets reaffirmed in unmistakable terms their right of intervention in socialist countries which were held to have diverged from the path of socialism. The western press termed this the Brezhnev doctrine.

Yugoslavia and Rumania were especially threatened by the new Soviet policy and for a time it seemed that they, too, would be victims of invasion. Harsh words were spoken in Moscow about them.

The Soviet moves were essentially defensive. Attempts were made to strengthen the Warsaw Pact and also Comecon. It was now stated that economic integration could be used by socialist as much as by capitalist states. Clearly economic integration could be used to bolster the unity of the bloc under the Soviet aegis. In Czechoslovakia pressure continued to be applied to the reformers and in April 1969 Dubček was forced out. A new treaty of alliance between the two countries was signed in 1970, strengthening the Soviet grip. Rumania also negotiated a new treaty which marked an improvement in relations.

The invasion of Czechoslovakia has forced on western analysts a re-appraisal of Soviet motives. It is no doubt true that the Soviets are interested in détente with the west, meaning the United States. The invasion has, however, shown that there were certain vital interests that the Soviets were prepared to defend by force. No doubt the Soviets have believed in 'managed change' in eastern Europe, that is that they have discreetly supported reformist elements which had some popular support, like Gomulka and Kadar, rather than discredited Stalinist leaders like Ulbricht and Novotný. But there was always the danger that such reformism could get out of hand, as happened in Hungary in 1956 and in Czechoslovakia in 1968. In each case the Soviets were clearly unwilling to intervene and only did so when every other means of pressure was exhausted. They realized, of course, that such intervention would have the effect of stirring up the spirit of the Cold War and strengthening the cohesion of the NATO countries at a time when the Soviets have attempted to weaken such cohesion.

A very disturbing factor about the invasion was the limit that this action put on the freedom of movement that the socialist states had won. The Czechoslovaks hoped to avoid the wrath of the Soviets by strict adherence to their alliance with them and by fulsome expressions of loyalty. They hoped to avoid the mistakes that Nagy had made. Yet the Soviet tanks moved. So again the catalogue of things which a socialist state in the Soviet sphere of influence is not allowed to do has been lengthened. Indeed, under Brezhnev and Kosygin, unobtrusively but successfully, the Soviets are drawing closer the bonds of empire.

Yet the international crisis over Czechoslovakia was short-lived. The Soviets did not intervene in either Yugoslavia or Rumania as was feared. President Nixon visited Bucharest in 1969 to encourage the Rumanians. Essentially the west recognized that Czechoslovakia was in the Soviet sphere of influence and that an invasion of that country was not an aggressive move against the west. On the contrary the Soviets were acting defensively and so the Czechoslovaks, subject to foreign overlordship, were the innocent victims of the Soviet desire for peace.

PART I

The Soviet Union and the Capitalist States

(a) THE THAW

In this first extract the prominent Soviet writer, Ilya Ehrenburg (1891–1967), a man well known in the west and one who had been closely and prominently connected with the Soviet peace campaign, expresses the dominant mood of the average Soviet citizen. His attacks on German rearmament and on American military preparations would be readily believed by a population which had experienced the fury of the Germans and had been told about the aggressiveness of the Americans. His article also shows the way in which the Soviets differentiate between their opponents in the west: the ruling capitalist classes, yearning for nuclear weapons and an opportunity to use them and the people, seeking peace and understanding.

Ehrenburg was right to prize the year 1954 so highly. The tension which had built up in the previous years was much relaxed. Particularly gratifying from this point of view were the Korean and Indo-Chinese armistices. The Soviet government handed out praise to all the participants of the Geneva negotiations, except the Americans whose obstructiveness it blames. It does not, however, mention the very important fact that the speedy conclusion of the negotiations were brought about by the concessions that the North Vietnamese were prepared, or were forced, to make.

The elections which were to have been held two years later in the whole of Vietnam never took place.

DOCUMENT I. EXTRACT FROM *Pravda* ARTICLE BY ILYA EHRENBURG, 1 JANUARY 1955 (*SN*, 7 JANUARY 1955)

Long, long ago, at a time when people feared evil spirits, they believed that devils and witches held their sabbath late in the night. They were convinced that the evil spirits were particularly outrageous in the hours just before the dawn. This is a fairy tale, but every fairy tale contains an element of truth. The closer the dawn, the more savage and mad grow the forces that love the pitch-black night.

To us the year that has just ended is still our warm, living yesterday. It is hard for us to view it impartially—big events and small worries, sorrows and joys are still too fresh in our memories. But history has taken the year from us.

What will people say in the future as they turn the pages of the annals of our years—years filled with anxieties and hopes— and come to the figure '1954'? . . .

The year 1954 changed a great deal in the world. The peoples will not forget the great victory they won at Geneva. The Indo-Chinese war lasted a long, long time. All the peoples had pro-tested against it. French patriots were persecuted time and time again for their one desire to put an end to the brutal, unjust war that was being waged in France's name but for interests far removed from those of France.

Only a few weeks before agreement was reached in Geneva, America's rulers talked briskly of 'extending' and 'intensifying' the war in Indo-China. They came to the round table un-willingly, under protest, and they tried to walk out and break off the talks. Agreement gave them a pain in their stomachs. They realized that the peoples would remember that a begin-ning had been made and would demand more negotiations. In spite of everything, however, the peoples insisted on what they wanted. The guns fell silent. Supplies of unused napalm re-mained in American warehouses. For a few months, calls to employ atomic weapons stuck in the throats of the wicked charlatans.

Dreaming of fanning another world war, America's rulers concentrated their attention on Europe—a Europe that has not yet rebuilt its ruined cities, that has not yet finished mourning its dead. Using lofty phrases about 'federation', 'community of culture' and 'new forms of a supra-national state' as a screen, the warmongers tried to turn the ancient states of Europe into recruiting centres for the Pentagon. The European Defence

E   47

Community, however, departed this life. America's rulers felt lost, but they did not grow wiser. Instead, they decided to serve up the same sanguinary dish with a different sauce.

What are they interested in? Not, of course, in arguments about imaginary 'federation', nor yet in the preambles or paragraphs of various Bills. Only one thing is important to them—lining up German divisions and moving them into battle. To the generals of the *Wehrmacht*, men notorious for the number of their evil deeds, murderers of millions of women and children, vandals who destroyed Coventry, Rotterdam, Novgorod and Tours, butchers of Oswiecim, Maidanek, Lidice, Oradour, Babiy Yar and other places of execution in Europe, they want to issue not only tanks and guns but thermo-nuclear weapons of which Adolf Hitler did not dare to dream.

And again I ask: What have they achieved? The conscience of the peoples of Europe was shocked. First of all, the French people forced their Parliament to reject the Bill on the rearming of Western Germany. No one can erase the date—24 December. Can there be men so blind as to think that by prevailing on, or frightening twenty-seven deputies they can pass off as the will of the nation a vote which the guardians of the law regard as open to dispute and which the ordinary people regard as indisputably unscrupulous? Do they not realize that the French people will never permit the implementation of treaties which threaten them with death? Indignation is rising in all the countries of western Europe.

Can anyone with a minimum of honesty declare that the British people ratified the Paris agreements, when a minority of MPs supported ratification, or declare that while many MPs abstained from voting when the question of Britain's existence was posed, the British people abstained and will continue to abstain?

Even in Western Germany itself the Social Democrats, who received more votes than any other party at the last elections, openly declare that the German people will not permit a deal which means, first, the division of the country and then a frightful internecine war. The question of restoring the sinister *Wehrmacht* cannot be decided in parliamentary refreshment rooms. Those who dare to issue atomic weapons to a Kesselring or to any other war criminal will have to answer to their peoples sooner or later.

At the beginning of the 'Cold War', which has already brought mankind many disasters, its instigators loved to brandish the atom bomb. They thought they would be able to frighten with their incantations the refractory citizens of the countries that were not to their liking. It is well known that they did not succeed, but in America herself there was a sharp increase in the demand for tincture of valerian and other drugs that doctors prescribe for very excitable people. One would think that today, when the warmongers know full well that the countries they threatened with the atomic weapon have been forced to acquire the same weapon in order to parry the blow, it is stupid to use threats and intimidation.

But in 1954 the warmongers increased their talk of preparing for an atomic attack. Not long ago Bullitt, the former American diplomat, without stopping to think twice about it, suggested 'destroying the industrial centres of the Soviet Union'. One might not pay attention to that, seeing that Bullitt never did have much sense of responsibility. But one cannot ignore the decisions taken by the NATO Council on preparations for an atomic war.

The Belgian minister Spaak revealed the essence of these decisions with sufficient frankness when he said: 'The military demanded permission to prepare for an atomic war. They got it.'

The instigators of war try to fool naive people by assuring them that as soon as the Americans and British accumulate a sufficient supply of atom bombs and hydrogen bombs they can begin talks with the Soviet Union. Aneurin Bevan, the British MP, has said in this connection that everyone now realizes that Britain will be destroyed in the very first stages of an atomic or hydrogen war, that no one denies this and yet it is planned to rely on those weapons in negotiations. Bevan declares that this is the same as saying to the Russians: 'If you don't give in, we'll commit suicide.'

Bevan's words can be understood by all ordinary people. Playing with thermo-nuclear bombs has gone too far. No one believes any longer in the peace-loving tales of the warmongers, who propose restricting atomic war sometime, somewhere and somehow. The common people demand the immediate prohibition of this weapon that is an insult to the conscience of

49

the peoples. The horrors of Hiroshima are not forgotten. Everyone knows what happened after tests of the American H-bomb on Eniwetok atoll—the radio-active poisons, the agonizing death of innocent Japanese fishermen.

The common people say:

> We are tired of fine promises, of talks of which we understand nothing, of the chicanery and red tape of diplomatic offices. We want to save the world from bombs, from radioactive poisons, from destruction. If you do not want to think about the fate of nations, at least think of the fate of your own children. If you are not capable of feeling anxiety for the fate of mankind and its civilization, think of yourself. If you start an atomic war you will not be able to escape either to the Pole or into the stratosphere, or on to the peaks of the Cordilleras. The lethal atoms will seek you out everywhere, and if you do escape alive, others who have escaped will try and condemn you. There is no joking, gentlemen, with things like H-bombs!
>
> The greatest discovery of our age, the fruit of the labour of noble minds, must be used to make life easier, not to simplify death. No matter how strong your bomb is, the people are stronger. It is they who give birth to great scientists, they who mine uranium, they who work in the plants. It is they, the common people of the world, and not you who will decide the question.

The year 1954 brought the peoples a great victory—the Geneva agreement. This victory for peace frightened and enraged the warmongers. They are hitting out rashly. But the peoples will pin down the madmen's arms. The matter now rests with the peoples. They can see to it that the year 1955 is a turning-point, the beginning of a new era—the era of peace.

The Soviet people are engaged in a great and glorious effort. We hate war. Let every man, no matter where he lives, know that if he wants peace, and firmly stands for peace he has many strong and true friends—the entire Soviet people. We shall never take the threats of the warmongers for the voice of the peoples.

Every people wants to live in its own way, and each cherishes its own traditions, its customs, its land. But all peoples hate war, and we know that the conscience of the peoples will never permit the second advent of the bloodthirsty *Wehrmacht*. We know that the conscience of the peoples will succeed in doing away with the atomic weapon. We know that the conscience of the peoples will uphold peace. And from the bottom of our hearts we wish the peoples, near and far, large and small, a peaceful and happy year.

DOCUMENT 2. STATEMENT OF THE SOVIET GOVERNMENT ON THE GENEVA CONFERENCE IN *Pravda* 23 JULY 1954

The Geneva Conference of foreign ministers, convened in accordance with the decision of the Berlin Conference for the purpose of considering the questions of Korea and Indo-China, ended on 21 July.

As a result of almost three months' work, agreements have been signed which put an end to the hostilities in Vietnam, Laos and Cambodia. These agreements are designed to solve important problems connected with the restoration and strengthening of peace in Vietnam, Laos and Cambodia, on the basis—as stated in the final declaration adopted by those taking part in the Geneva Conference—of respect for the independence and sovereignty, unity and territorial integrity of the three states of Indo-China.

The cease-fire in Indo-China opens up before the peoples of Vietnam, Laos and Cambodia the opportunity of economic and cultural advance under peaceful conditions, an opportunity which, at the same time, creates the basis for the development of friendly co-operation between them and France.

The decisions of the Geneva Conference prohibiting the establishment of military bases of foreign states on the territories of Vietnam, Laos and Cambodia, and the obligations undertaken by these latter states to refrain from joining military alliances, and from permitting themselves to be used for the resumption of hostilities, or for the pursuance of an aggressive policy, will be of great significance.

The decision of the Geneva Conference on the organization of free elections in Vietnam in July 1956, creates the conditions for the national unification of Vietnam, in harmony with the national interests and aspirations of all the Vietnamese people.

Adopted as a result of the persistent efforts of the democratic states, this decision is a defeat for the aggressive forces which were working for the dismemberment of Vietnam, in order to convert Vietnam into one of the bases of a projected new aggressive bloc in South-East Asia.

The agreement on general elections to be held in Cambodia and Laos in 1955 by secret ballot and with respect for fundamental freedoms—as stated in the final declaration—is also of major importance.

It cannot but be noted that the adoption of such important decisions was facilitated by the favourable position taken up by the French government, dictated by willingness to co-operate, in line with the national interests of France, and taking due account of the interests of the peoples of Indo-China.

Despite the existence of certain reservations in the agreements signed at Geneva, it is impossible to overestimate the full importance of these agreements, if only for these reasons, and also because the Geneva Conference has succeeded in overcoming a number of difficulties which had arisen over the position adopted by the representatives of the United States, who tried to hamper the successful conclusion of this conference. The United States did not wish to co-operate with France, Britain, the USSR, the People's Republic of China and the other states in the joint efforts which have secured the restoration of peace in Indo-China. The Geneva agreements are an important victory for the forces of peace and a serious defeat for the forces of war. At the same time, the Geneva agreements signify international recognition of the national liberation struggle of the peoples of Indo-China and of the great heroism they have displayed in this struggle.

The fact that the Geneva Conference ended with agreements between the countries concerned was fresh proof of the fruitful results which may be obtained from international negotiations, given good will among the parties concerned, proof that the possibility exists for the similar settlement of important and as yet unsolved international problems.

The Soviet government welcomes the success achieved at Geneva in the settlement of the most important problem—the restoration of peace in Indo-China. The settlement of this problem is equally in line with the interests of the peoples who are defending their freedom and national independence and with the interests of all peace-loving nations.

Along with the most important task of a final peace settlement in Indo-China, the urgent task of a final peace settlement in Korea is also on the agenda.

The Soviet government, like the governments of the People's Republic of China and of the Korean People's Democratic Republic which had already earlier taken the noble initiative in securing a cease-fire in Korea, have themselves done everything they could at the Geneva Conference to secure a successful settlement of the Korean problem. It is a matter of record, however, that the Geneva Conference has failed to produce favourable results on that question owing to obstacles raised by some delegations and chiefly by the delegation of the United States. The Soviet government considers it an urgent necessity that the earliest settlement of the Korean problem should be secured, in the interests of the national unification of Korea and the maintenance of peace in Asia and throughout the world.

The results of the Geneva Conference confirm the conviction of the Soviet government that there are no international differences at the present time that could not be settled through negotiations and agreements designed to strengthen international security, to weaken international tension and to secure the peaceful co-existence of states, irrespective of their social systems.

The Geneva Conference and its results have brought out the important role of the great Chinese people and their state—the CPR—in the settling of international disputes. The role played by the CPR at the Geneva Conference was fresh evidence of its influence and international authority as a great power. At the same time, the Geneva Conference demonstrated anew that the efforts of the aggressive circles of some countries, and of the United States in the first place, to keep the CPR from taking part in the settlement of very important international problems, are entirely against the interests of peace.

The Soviet government believes that, by helping to reduce international tension, the agreements reached at Geneva for a cease-fire and for the restoration of peace in Indo-China create favourable conditions for the settlement of other important outstanding international problems relating to Asia and also to Europe, and in the first place such problems as the ending of the arms drive and the banning of atomic weapons, of organizing collective security in Europe and settling the German problem on a peaceful and democratic basis.

The Soviet government declares that, consistently following its peace-loving policy, it will continue with all vigour and determination its efforts to achieve the successful solution of these problems, a result which would undoubtedly be a very important move towards reducing international tension and strengthening peace and international co-operation.

*

In February 1955 Soviet foreign minister Molotov made a survey of foreign affairs in the Soviet Parliament, the Supreme Soviet. The speech came at the end of the session in which Bulganin replaced Malenkov as premier. One remark made by Molotov caused considerable interest in the west. He said that the Soviet Union was prepared to sign a treaty with Austria by which that country would be neutralized and the occupation troops withdrawn. Previously the Soviets had insisted that the signing of a treaty with Austria would have to wait on the conclusion of a German settlement. On 15 May the Austrian State Treaty was signed in Vienna and the occupation forces withdrawn in spite of the fact that Germany joined both NATO and the West European Union.

Hardly a month later the Soviet government invited Adenauer to Moscow in order that relations between the two powers be normalized. Although the invitation did not come as a surprise to Bonn—unofficial feelers had been put out previously—it did seem to underline the correctness of Adenauer's position. In 1954 the Federal Republic had ratified the European Defence Community. In May 1955 it had ratified the Paris agreements of October 1954 by which the ending of the occupation of Western Germany was confirmed and by which Germany joined the major European alliance systems. The western powers moreover recognized the Bonn government as the government of the whole of Germany, that is also of Eastern Germany. Moscow thundered at Bonn and in a note of 9 December 1954 pointed out the hopelessness of further negotiations in Germany if Bonn ratified the Paris agreements. In spite of ratification, the invitation to Adenauer dangled in front of the Germans the carrot of reunification.

Adenauer arrived in Moscow on 9 September. Agreement was rapidly reached to exchange ambassadors and also for a repatriation to Germany of German prisoners still in the Soviet Union. In a press conference that Adenauer gave before his departure, he said that he had written to Bulganin, saying that the agreement did not affect the final settlement of the German frontiers nor did it affect the legal claim of Bonn to represent all Germany. In other words Bonn refused to recognize the frontier running along the Oder and Neisse Rivers as the frontier separating Germany from Poland and the German Democratic Republic as a second German state.

Yet from the Soviet point of view the resumption of relations was a success too. From that date to this Moscow and East Berlin have pursued the thesis of the two German states. This meant that plans for reunification—in spite of Moscow's claims to the contrary—were no longer seriously studied. This view was underlined by an agreement signed in Moscow on 29 September 1955 between the German Democratic Republic and the USSR. The agreement recognized the full sovereignty of GDR and the office of Soviet High Commissioner was abolished. On 6 October of the same year, Suslov, chief ideologist of the CPSU, announced in East Berlin that 'the government of the German Democratic Republic is the true representative of the German people'.

DOCUMENT 3. SOVIET-AUSTRIAN COMMUNIQUÉ OF THE AUSTRIAN GOVERNMENT DELEGATION TO MOSCOW, 12–15 APRIL 1955 (*SN*, 18 APRIL 1955)

Negotiations, conducted in a friendly spirit, took place in Moscow from 12 to 15 April 1955, between the Austrian government delegation headed by Dr Julius Raab, federal chancellor of Austria, and Dr Adolf Schärf, vice-chancellor, on the one side, and the Soviet government delegation headed by V. M. Molotov, vice-chairman of the Council of Ministers of the USSR and minister of foreign affairs of the USSR, and

A. I. Mikoyan, vice-chairman of the Council of Ministers of the USSR on the other.

As a result of these negotiations, the two sides have established that both the government of the Soviet Union and the government of the Austrian Republic consider it desirable to secure the earliest conclusion of a state treaty on the restoration of an independent and democratic Austria, which should be of service to the national interests of the Austrian people and to the strengthening of peace in Europe.

The Austrian delegation has given an assurance that, in accordance with the spirit of the declaration made at the conference in Berlin in 1954, the Austrian Republic does not intend to join any military alliances or to lend its territory for military bases. Austria will pursue, with regard to all states, a policy of independence which should secure the observance of this declaration.

The Soviet side has agreed that the occupation troops of the four powers should be withdrawn from Austria after the State Treaty with Austria comes into force, and not later than on 31 December 1955.

Taking into consideration the statement of the governments of the United States of America, France and Britain published on 5 April 1955, concerning their desire for the earliest conclusion of the Austrian State Treaty, the delegations of the Soviet Union and Austria have expressed the hope that there are favourable possibilities at the present time for settling the Austrian question through a corresponding agreement between the four powers and Austria.

Furthermore, the Soviet government has agreed, in the spirit of its statement made at the conference in Berlin in 1954, to accept an equivalent of the 150 million dollars provided for in Article 35 of the State Treaty entirely in Austrian goods deliveries.

The Soviet government has declared its readiness to hand over to Austria (apart from the German property in the Soviet occupation zone in Austria on the transfer of which agreement was reached earlier) immediately after the State Treaty comes into force and for appropriate compensation, the property of the Danube Shipping Company (DDSG), including the wharves at Korneuburg, and all the ships and port facilities.

It has also agreed to cede to Austria her rights, under Article 35 of the State Treaty, to the oil fields and oil refineries, including the joint stock company for the sale of petroleum products (ÖROP), in exchange for deliveries of crude oil in amounts agreed on by the parties.

It has also been agreed to open negotiations at the earliest date for the purpose of bringing about normal commercial relations between Austria and the Soviet Union.

The Soviet delegation has informed the Austrian delegation that the Praesidium of the Supreme Soviet of the USSR has agreed to give favourable consideration to the request of the Austrian federal president, Dr Koerner, for the repatriation of the Austrians who are serving sentences in accordance with the ruling of Soviet judicial authorities. After the Soviet occupation troops have been withdrawn from Austria not a single prisoner of war or detained civilian with Austrian citizenship will remain on the territory of the Soviet Union.

DOCUMENT 4. NOTE TO THE GOVERNMENT OF THE FEDERAL RE-PUBLIC OF GERMANY OF 7 JUNE 1955, INVITING ADENAUER TO MOSCOW FOR TALKS (*SN*, 8 JUNE 1955)

The government of the USSR has the honour to state the following to the government of the Federal Republic of Germany:

The Soviet government believes that the interests of peace and European security, as well as the national interests of the Soviet and German peoples, call for the normalization of relations between the Soviet Union and the Federal Republic of Germany.

The experience of history indicates that the preservation and strengthening of peace in Europe depends to a decisive degree on the existence of normal, good relations between the Soviet and German peoples. Moreover, the absence of such relations between the two peoples can only cause disquiet in Europe and increase overall international tension. Such a state of affairs is advantageous to no one except the aggressive forces, interested in retaining tension in international relations. However, any-one who wants peace to be preserved and strengthened cannot fail to wish for relations between the Soviet Union and the Federal Republic of Germany to be made normal.

The peoples of the Soviet Union and Germany are interested more than anyone else in making relations between the USSR and the Federal Republic of Germany normal. It should be recalled that in the years when friendly relations and co-operation existed between our peoples, it was of great benefit to both countries. And, conversely, hostile relations and wars between our peoples, which have taken place in the past, brought them untold misery, privation and suffering.

It was the Soviet and German peoples that suffered most of all in the last two world wars. The peoples of the Soviet Union and Germany in these wars had millions of casualties, several times higher than the casualties of all the other belligerent nations combined. Cities reduced to ruins, villages burned down, great riches of the two peoples destroyed—such were the results of the wars between our countries.

The Soviet government cannot fail to draw the attention of the government of the Federal Republic of Germany to the fact that at present certain aggressive circles in some countries are harbouring plans intended to set the Soviet Union and Western Germany against each other and to prevent an improvement in the relations between our countries. The implementation of the plans of these aggressive circles would lead to another war, which this time would be bound to turn the territory of Germany into a field of battle and destruction. Such a war on German territory, involving the use of modern means of mass destruction, would be even more cruel and devastating in its consequences than any past war.

Developments must not be allowed to follow this course. The impending danger can be averted, if normal relations based on mutual confidence and peaceful co-operation are established between our countries.

As far as the Soviet Union is concerned, she has never, in spite of all the suffering inflicted on her during the recent war, let herself be guided by feelings of revenge against the German people. Evidence of this is the Soviet Union's position, which meets the basic national interests of the German people with regard to the solution of the German problem in the post-war period, and also the good relations that have developed and are making progress between the Soviet Union and the German Democratic Republic, on the firm basis of equality and non-interference in internal affairs.

The Soviet government proceeds from the premise that the establishment and development of normal relations between the Soviet Union and the Federal Republic of Germany will contribute to settling outstanding issues concerning the whole of Germany and must thereby help to solve the principal national problem of the German people—the re-establishment of the unity of a democratic German state.

All this goes to show that making relations between our countries normal is entirely in accordance not only with the national interests of Germany and the Soviet Union, but also with the interests of strengthening the peace and security of all European nations.

The Soviet government also attaches great importance to the establishment of more stable relations between the Soviet Union and the Federal Republic of Germany in the field of trade. It would be appropriate to recall here that the Soviet Union and Germany carried on extensive and mutually advantageous trade in the past, with the commodity turnover amounting at times to one-fifth of the total foreign trade of both countries.

The Soviet Union has extensive trade relations with the German Democratic Republic. Trade between the USSR and the Federal Republic of Germany is of a limited and unstable nature. However, the prerequisites also exist for the development of extensive trade and for the establishment of mutually advantageous economic relations between the Soviet Union and the Federal Republic of Germany, provided there are normal relations between them. The Soviet Union, with its highly developed industry and expanding agriculture, considers it possible to enlarge substantially its volume of trade with West German firms, and this cannot fail to be of great importance, particularly in the conditions of increasing economic instability existing in some countries.

Cultural interchange can play an important part in making relations between our countries normal. Scientific, cultural and technical ties between the peoples of the USSR and Germany are known to be of long standing. These ties have enriched the intellectual life of both peoples, and have had a favourable effect on European cultural development as a whole. Naturally, these traditions can and must serve to promote scientific, cultural and technical co-operation between the two countries.

The Soviet government believes that the abolition of what was known as the Occupation Statute of Western Germany, which restricted her relations with other countries, and also the decree of the Supreme Soviet of the USSR ending the state of war between the USSR and Germany and establishing relations of peace between them, provide the necessary conditions at the present time for establishing normal and direct relations between the Soviet Union and the Federal Republic of Germany.

In view of this, the Soviet government proposes to the government of the Federal Republic of Germany that there be established direct diplomatic and trade relations, and also cultural relations between the two countries.

The government of the Soviet Union, considering it desirable for personal contact to be established between the statesmen of the two nations, would welcome a visit to Moscow, in the near future, of Herr K. Adenauer, chancellor of the Federal Republic of Germany, and any other representatives whom the government of the Federal Republic of Germany might wish to send to Moscow, in order to consider the question of establishing diplomatic and trade relations between the Soviet Union and the Federal Republic of Germany and to examine the relevant issues.

*

The return to Finland of the naval base at Porkkala, west of Helsinki, which the Finns had been forced to lease to the Russians in 1945, may be interpreted as a withdrawal from exposed salients—in the same year the Soviets withdrew from Port Arthur and Austria. It marked also a change in Soviet strategic planning. In the period from the summer of 1955 to the summer of 1956 the Soviet armed forces were reduced by 1,840,000 men. Instead the Soviets were building and testing the sophisticated weaponry of modern warfare.

Pervukhin was at this time a member of the Praesidium of the Party and first deputy prime minister. In 1957 he joined the 'anti-party group' and was demoted.

DOCUMENT 5. EXTRACT FROM A SPEECH OF M. G. PERVUKHIN AT THE SIGNING IN HELSINKI ON 26 JANUARY 1956 OF THE AGREEMENT TO TRANSFER THE NAVAL BASE OF PORKKALA TO FINLAND (*SN*, 1 FEBRUARY 1956)

The Soviet Union's renunciation ahead of time of the right to lease the territory of Porkkala is the result of growing mutual confidence and the establishment of friendly relations between our countries achieved by the joint efforts of the Soviet government and the government of Finland. . . .

The Treaty of Friendship, Co-operation and Mutual Assistance, signed on 6 April 1948, has been of great importance for the development of good relations between our countries. This treaty laid a sound foundation for friendly and good-neighbourly relations between the USSR and Finland, while its prolongation for another twenty years in September 1955 has opened up to both countries broad prospects for the strengthening of these relations.

The Soviet government's decision on the renunciation by the USSR of its right to use the territory of the peninsula of Porkkala and on the withdrawal of the Soviet armed forces from its territory is an important measure aimed at further easing international tension. This decision confirms in a striking way the consistent character of the peace-loving foreign policy of the USSR. It is common knowledge that the Soviet Union now has no military bases on the territories of other states. The Soviet government considers that the existence of the military bases of certain states on the territories of other states cannot fail to hinder the establishment of really firm and peaceful co-operation between nations, based on mutual confidence.

The friendly relations which have been established between the Soviet Union and the Finnish Republic not only correspond to the national interests of our peoples, but are also an important contribution to the maintenance of peace in Europe.

It can be said with confidence that, given the sincere desire of the Soviet and Finnish peoples for close co-operation, no one will succeed in preventing the further strengthening of good relations between our countries.

(*b*) PEACEFUL CO-EXISTENCE

Peaceful co-existence has been a principle of Soviet foreign policy ever since the days of Lenin. Under Khrushchev it was, however, given very much more emphasis than previously. It was a policy suited to a power which, whatever its boastings, was aware of its inferiority to the United States in the military field. It allowed the Soviet Union to live in peace with the capitalist states and yet keep the purity of its doctrine by insisting that this principle was the only means possible with which to undermine the capitalist world and so bring about the final and complete victory of communism. It did not exclude the possibility of war. Indeed support for wars of national liberation ranked high on the list of Soviet priorities. But it did mean that war with capitalism was no longer inevitable.

The 21st 'extraordinary' Party Congress was ostensibly summoned for the purpose of considering the draft of the new seven-year plan, the goal of which was to surpass the United States in the standard of living—a very important element of the doctrine of peaceful co-existence.

DOCUMENT 6. EXTRACT FROM KHRUSHCHEV'S REPORT TO THE 21ST CONGRESS OF THE COMMUNIST PARTY OF THE SOVIET UNION, 27 JANUARY 1959 (*Current Soviet Policies III. The Documentary Record of the Extraordinary 21st Communist Party Congress*, EDITED BY LEO GRULIOW AND THE STAFF OF THE *Current Digest of the Soviet Press*, COLUMBIA UNIVERSITY PRESS, 1960, P. 58)

What new factors will be introduced into the international situation with the fulfilment of the economic plans of the Soviet Union, of all the socialist countries of Europe and Asia? As a result of this there will be created real possibilities for eliminating war as a means of settling international disputes.

Indeed, when the USSR becomes the world's leading industrial power, when the Chinese People's Republic becomes a mighty industrial power and all the socialist countries together will be producing more than half of the world's industrial output, the international situation will change radically. The successes of the countries of the socialist camp will unquestionably exert a tremendous effect on strengthening the forces of peace throughout the world. One need have no doubt that by that time the countries working for the strengthening of peace will be joined by new countries that have freed themselves from colonial oppression. The idea that war is inadmissible will take still firmer root in the minds of peoples. The new balance of forces will be so evident that even the most die-hard imperialists will clearly see the futility of any attempt to unleash war against the socialist camp. Relying on the might of the socialist camp, the peace-loving nations will then be able to compel the militant circles of imperialism to abandon plans for a new world war.

Thus, there will arise a real possibility of excluding world war from the life of society even before the complete triumph of socialism, even with capitalism existing in part of the world.

It may be said: 'But capitalism will still exist, hence there will still be adventurers who might start a war.' That is true and it must not be forgotten. As long as capitalism exists there may always be people who 'in the face of common sense' will want to plunge into a hopeless venture. But by doing so, they will only bring nearer the ultimate downfall of the capitalist system. Any attempt at aggression will be stopped short and the adventurers put where they belong.

*

The doctrine of peaceful co-existence between socialist and non-socialist states was unlikely to make much appeal to the Chinese who had no diplomatic relations with the United States and who were kept out of the United Nations. Moreover, American forces kept Chiang Kai-shek in power on Taiwan, an area legally part of China. For three years Chinese and American forces fought against each other in Korea: at no time have Americans and Russians fought against each other.

This speech by Khrushchev expresses rather well his commitment to the policy of peaceful co-existence and his irritation and impatience with the unrealistic position towards nuclear weapons taken by the Chinese. The speech was made at a critical time. On 20 July 1963 Sino-Soviet talks aiming at reconciliation were suspended after a fortnight of negotiations. A week earlier the Soviets had put forward their case in a strongly worded 'open letter' which the Chinese did not answer until September. On 25 July the Partial Test Ban Treaty was initiated in Moscow, an act which the Chinese regarded as a betrayal of the cause of socialism.

DOCUMENT 7. EXTRACT FROM KHRUSHCHEV'S SPEECH OF 19 JULY 1963 (*SN*, 24 JULY 1963)

The great Lenin and the Bolsheviks founded a militant revolutionary party of the proletariat, and, under the guidance of this party, roused, rallied and organized the working class and the people to resolute struggle against the old rotten landlord-capitalist system. The party of the great Lenin led the working class and the peoples of Russia to the revolution and to the establishment of the power of the people. We did not carry through the socialist revolution in order to wage wars, but in order to live in peace and to build a new life on earth—to build socialism and communism, for the people to glorify the great country of the October revolution with their labour, to multiply the gains of socialism, and to show all mankind what successes can be achieved by a people who have broken forever the fetters of capitalism. . . .

When it is said, however, that a people who have carried through the revolution should start a war which will be a world thermo-nuclear war, should unleash such a war in order to build a more prosperous society on the bodies of millions upon millions of people killed in this war, upon the ruins of the world—this cannot be understood, comrades! Who will then remain on this 'prosperous land'? We cannot agree with such assertions.

Do those who reason this way know that if all the existing missile-nuclear charges are exploded the contamination of the earth's atmosphere will be such that nobody can say what the fate of the survivors will be, whether they won't envy the dead? Yes, yes, comrades, that's how things stand!

We say to those who make victory of socialism dependent on such a war that we will never agree with this. . . .

Today the imperialists pretend to be brave—but only in

words; in reality they tremble before the socialist world which is growing and gaining in strength. And let them tremble! So much the better for us!

Is a world war really required for the victory of socialism and communism? Those who suffer from an itch for war, those who claim that a world war is required for the victory of socialism, occupy this position not because of their courage, but because of their lack of faith in the strength of the working class and in the strength of socialism. They do not believe, apparently, that it is possible for the countries where power is in the hands of the people to secure victory over capitalism in the economic, scientific and cultural spheres under the conditions of peaceful co-existence; that it is possible, relying on the economic might of the socialist countries and on their armed forces, to keep the imperialists in fear and not give them an opportunity to unleash a world war.

These comrades declare that it is impossible to preserve peace because of the specific properties of imperialism. It is most true that the rapacious nature of imperialism has not changed, nor can it change. We all say this and are correct to do so. But, comrades, after all, the policy of the imperialist countries is also determined by people. And these people also have a head on their shoulders, and brains. It is another question in which direction their brains are turning. We are communists, and our thoughts are directed in one way, while the imperialists reason in just the opposite way. However, the imperialists as well, discounting the madmen from whom anything can be expected, are forced to take reality, the changed correlation of world forces and the growth of the forces standing for peace and socialism, into account.

If we follow the logic of certain comrades then we should have no dealings with the imperialists at all. Certainly, if everyone acted and thought in the communist way, then there would be no antagonistic classes, and communism would have already been victorious everywhere. However, while there are still two systems, the socialist and capitalist, each system has its own policy, its own course, and we cannot but take into account the fact of the existence of the two systems. A fight is in progress between these two systems, a life-and-death combat. But we communists want to win this struggle with the least losses, and there is no doubt whatsoever that we shall win. This is why we are striving for victory, for the triumph of communism, without unleashing a world thermo-nuclear war.

The question may be asked: why is it that the Russians, Ukrainians, Uzbeks and the other peoples of the Soviet Union —I will not enumerate them all as there are more than 100 nationalities in our country—why is it that the Hungarians and the peoples of the other socialist countries are for socialism and why is it, let us say, that in Britain and the United States the ideas of socialism and communism have not yet been victorious? The following reply can be given to this question: 'Comrades, everything in good time!' The time will come—and we profoundly believe this—when the working class, the working people, in Britain, in France, in the United States and in the other capitalist countries, will rise for the decisive struggle for socialism. We openly speak about this—I also pointed it out when I was in the United States—because we know that the future belongs to the working class of the entire world; the future belongs to communism.

In order to bring this time closer, however, we have to work; we have to show in practice the superiority of the socialist system.

It was only recently, when representatives of the Soviet Union in conversation with representatives of capitalist states told them that our country would definitely overtake the United States in economic competition, that the capitalists scratched their heads and obviously thought: 'Nonsense! Impossible!' But now they say something else: 'We can already feel the breath of the Soviet Union overtaking us.' This is something quite different, of course!

When we say that socialism is better than capitalism not everybody understands this with their minds; some judge life only by the benefits they receive; they understand life, so to speak, with their stomachs. One cannot, of course, approach life in this way. But one should take into account what benefits are really given to the people. We say to the capitalists: 'You have unemployment, and we do not have unemployment.' And they answer: 'Our unemployed receive more than your employed men.' Yes, unfortunately, this was the case when we had just begun to build socialism in countries which were economically backward and undermined by war.

66

Therefore, we have to develop our economy in order to outstrip the capitalist countries economically and to raise the living standards of all the people. But how can this be achieved? By war? No! War only means new losses and destruction. It can be achieved only by work, by using the great advantages of the socialist system which ensure our advance along the path of building socialism and communism. Comrades, all that we have to do is to make capable use of these great advantages of socialism!

The time is not far off when the socialist countries will outstrip the most economically developed capitalist countries. Soviet man will receive more material benefits than the people in the capitalist countries, to say nothing of the moral and cultural benefits, for in this respect the Soviet people have outstripped the whole capitalist world even today.

We have now outstripped imperialism in the military sense. Our enemies know that if they attack us, if they unleash a new world war, they themselves will be destroyed in its flames.

The socialist system has shown its superiority over the capitalist system in the rate of economic development. It is necessary that quantity should go over into quality, that we achieve superiority over the capitalist states in per capita production, and then even the person who understands life only through his stomach will say: 'Communism is a good system, it suits me too, the more so since those building communism are better off than I am.'

Comrades, does the steadily improving living standard in the socialist countries not point to the triumph of socialism? Can anyone object to this? . . .

The more clearly people realize the danger of a thermonuclear war, the more actively and resolutely will they come out against the military adventures of imperialism, and against imperialism itself as the source of war. Fearing precisely such a turn of events, the most aggressive forces of American imperialism are now trying to present a thermo-nuclear war as yet another inevitable human tragedy, of which there have been many in history. It would be unforgivable for communists to side with the imperialists in this deceit and hide the truth from the peoples.

The communists are striving for the complete abolition of capitalism on earth and for the victory of the socialist revolution. We believe that sooner or later all peoples will finish forever with that moribund system. But the question of the victory of socialism in each given country will be decided by the people of that country, by the revolutionary working class and the Marxist-Leninist party, and not by other peoples or other parties, and, moreover, not by unleashing a thermo-nuclear world war.

It follows from the arguments of some people that a certain socialist country and the communist party of that country have the right to unleash a war against this or that capitalist country, inscribing on their banner the claim that this war, which will inevitably flare up into a thermo-nuclear world war, has been started, you see, in order to liberate the working class of the given country from capitalist oppression.

The question arises: 'Who has given these "theoreticians" the right to decide the destinies of the peoples of other countries at their own discretion?' The working people and the working class of those countries will tell them: 'We are fighting, and will continue to fight, for the victory of socialism, but that victory must be won by us in class struggle in our own countries and not by starting a thermo-nuclear world war.'

Moreover, if we accept the view of those 'theoreticians', we must bear in mind the other side of that 'right'. According to this logic, the imperialist states would also have the 'right' to unleash wars against the socialist countries in order to restore capitalist systems in those countries.

Explaining our attitude on these questions, our great teacher Lenin said that we are resolutely opposed to the export of revolution to other countries. We are also resolutely opposed to the export of counter-revolution.

We have faith in the growing superiority of the socialist system over capitalism. We have faith in the mighty strength of the international working class of the national liberation movement and of all who come out against the oppression of capitalism and of colonialism.

Those who deny the possibility of victory for the revolutionary forces of the working class in class struggle in the conditions of peaceful co-existence, do not have faith in the revolutionary energy and determination of the working class; they over-estimate the forces of imperialism and show fear of it.

We have faith in the strength of the working class and the strength of the peoples, in their reason and their striving to defend life on earth, and we are doing our best to mobilize all who cherish the interests of peace in the struggle against aggression and war; we are doing everything in our power to help our class brothers to free themselves from the oppression of imperialists and colonialists; we are doing everything in our power for the victory of socialism all over the world.

Marxist-Leninists are striving for the unity and stronger cohesion of all the forces which come out against imperialism: the world socialist system, the international working class, the national liberation struggle and the broad democratic movement of the masses of the people who uphold peace and progress.

We are well aware that the unity of those forces is the guarantee of success in the struggle against imperialism, for the victory of the ideals of peace, freedom, democracy, and socialism. Those who stand in the way of the unity of those leading forces of our day, regardless of their motives, are undermining the forces of the anti-imperialist front and therefore, objectively speaking, are playing into the hands of imperialism.

We communists of the socialist countries see it as our duty to give every assistance to the struggle of the peoples for their national independence, freedom and a better life. Everyone knows that the Soviet state, since its very inception, has rendered extensive political and other support to the peoples of Asia, Africa and Latin America in their fight against the colonial yoke.

This support assumes special importance today, when socialist countries exist and when the economic, political and military might of the forces of world socialism has grown immeasurably. Today we regard it as an ever more important task to give all-round assistance by every means to the peoples fighting against all forms of national dependence and oppression.

Marxist-Leninists realize that as long as imperialism exists, the danger of war will remain. The Soviet Union and the fraternal socialist countries are strengthening their defence capacity and doing everything possible to ensure that our armed forces would be able to reply to a blow by the aggressors with a devastating blow. We maintain our rockets, equipped with the most powerful thermo-nuclear weapons, in a state of constant readiness for combat.

But the Soviet Union will never be the first to use these weapons or to unleash a world war. We put all our might on the scales of peace, striving to consolidate peaceful co-existence between the socialist countries and the capitalist states. We do not beg the imperialists for peace, but we fight for peace in a practical way, relying on the economic and military might of the socialist countries, on the unity of the international working class, on the national liberation movement and on all the peace-loving peoples.

We have upheld and shall continue to uphold the Leninist principle of peaceful co-existence between states with different social systems as a policy which expresses the vital interests of the peoples.

*

Under Khrushchev the old policy of pretending that the achievement of independence by the nations of Africa and Asia was only 'formal', and did not signify their liberation from subjection to the world system of capitalism, was abandoned and strenuous efforts were made to turn these newly independent nations into friends of Moscow. Of the nations of Asia none was more persistently wooed than India. In June 1955 Nehru visited Moscow, and favourable reviews of Nehru's book were written in the chief theoretical journal of the Party, *Kommunist*. The personality of Gandhi was also subjected to a new and more favourable scrutiny. In November Khrushchev and Bulganin visited India and Burma. The two leaders went out of their way to win the hearts of the Indians—even renouncing for the trip alcoholic beverages in order not to hurt the prohibitionist susceptibilities of their hosts. They also offered economic and technical aid which India gratefully acknowledged.

This is a very typical Khrushchev speech.

DOCUMENT 8. EXTRACT FROM KHRUSHCHEV'S SPEECH IN BOMBAY, 24 NOVEMBER 1955 (*Pravda*, 26 NOVEMBER 1955)

We are convinced that in the present conditions, too, in the peaceful competition between the capitalist and socialist systems, victory will be on our side, on the side of socialism. I once said this publicly at a reception in the Kremlin. The bourgeois correspondents then hastened to inform the whole world that Khrushchev had 'let his tongue run away with him', that the Bolsheviks had not abandoned their political plans. No, it was not a slip of the tongue, and I did not 'let my tongue run away'—I said what I think and what we believe. We have never abandoned and will not abandon our political line charted for us by Lenin; we have not abandoned and will not abandon our political programme.

As our popular saying goes, 'You do not turn from a good life to seek a bad one'.

Why, then, should we renounce what has brought our country from age-old backwardness to the level of the most advanced and industrially and economically developed countries! Why renounce it? For what reason?

That is why we tell the gentlemen who are wondering whether the Soviet Union will change its political programme: 'Wait for the pigs to fly!' And you know when pigs fly.

Thus, there is only one alternative—co-existence. Co-existence of the two systems. Co-existence of the socialist and the capitalist systems.

I personally dislike the capitalist system very much. I speak of co-existence, not because I want capitalism to exist, but because I cannot but admit that this system does exist.

The other side, however, cannot reconcile itself to the existence of the socialist system although we are not the only ones to have built a socialist state and this road has been taken by many other states as well. Socialism is being built by our great friend—the great Chinese people—a state which as the saying goes, cannot be passed over unnoticed. Socialism is being built by a number of nations in Europe and Asia which are coming out together with the Soviet Union.

The prime minister of India Mr Nehru has said that India will also advance along the road of socialism. That is good. Of course, our understanding of socialism differs. But we welcome such a statement and such a programme.

Thus, the socialist system exists without asking anyone's permission. We not only exist, but we are able to defend our existence worthily.

If we had confined ourselves merely to asking for co-existence, we would have been destroyed long ago.

No matter how much our enemies want our ruin, it is beyond their power.

Therefore, no matter whether they want it or not, whether they like it or not, the socialist and the capitalist states have to live side by side on one planet.

(c) THE COLLAPSE OF CAPITALISM

On the fortieth anniversary of the Bolshevik revolution the representatives of twelve communist parties, those of Albania, Bulgaria, Czechoslovakia, China, East Germany, Hungary, Mongolia, Poland, Rumania, Vietnam, Yugoslavia and the Soviet Union met in Moscow. All the party leaders, even Mao Tse-tung, but not Tito, turned up. The meeting came eighteen months after the dissolution of the Cominform and a year after the Polish and Hungarian upheavals. It gave notice that the new relations between socialist states would be conducted not by international organizations of the Comintern or Cominform type but by periodic meetings between government and party leaders. Indeed the only practical measure that the conference took was to establish a new journal, *For a lasting peace, for a People's Democracy*. However, the declaration which emanated from the conference and which was signed by all the participants, with the exception of Yugoslavia, is regarded, together with the statement of eighty-one parties in 1960, as an authoritative, indeed sacrosanct, announcement on ideology and politics.

Tito had planned to go to Moscow but when it became clear that the meeting would come out with propositions that the Yugoslavs could not accept, Tito decided to absent himself. The conference view of the world as divided into two hostile and warring camps attacked the Yugoslav position of non-alignment as indeed did the attack on revisionism. To some extent these were concessions that the Soviets had to make to the Chinese. Their liberal 'hundred flowers' campaign had recently come to an end and they were about to embark on the 'great leap forward', an ambitious plan to build an industrially advanced society and to carry through a leap from a peasant to a communist society.

The 1960 conference was the most important and certainly the largest such gathering in communist history. It witnessed the first major clash between the Chinese and the Soviets. It was a victory for the Soviets and the statement adopted was largely drawn up by them. The Chinese, of course, showed no sign of being prepared to accept the situation. It must be noted particularly that in the extract quoted war, although considered to be inherent in capitalism, is no longer considered inevitable. This was one of the many points on which the Chinese disagreed.

DOCUMENT 9. EXTRACT FROM THE DECLARATION OF TWELVE COMMUNIST PARTIES MEETING IN MOSCOW 14–16 NOVEMBER 1957 (*SN*, 22 NOVEMBER 1957)

In our epoch world development is determined by the course and results of the competition between two diametrically opposed social systems. In the past forty years socialism has demonstrated that it is a much higher social system than capitalism. It has ensured the development of the productive forces at a rate that is unprecedented and impossible for capitalism, and a steady rise in the material and cultural levels of the working people. The Soviet Union's strides in economy, science and technology and the results achieved by the other socialist countries in socialist construction are conclusive evidence of the great vitality of socialism. In the socialist states the broad masses of the working people enjoy genuine freedom and democratic rights, and people's power ensures the political unity of the masses, equality and friendship among the nations, and a foreign policy aimed at preserving world peace and rendering assistance to the oppressed nations in their struggle for emancipation. The world socialist system which is growing and becoming stronger, is exerting ever greater influence on the international situation in the interests of peace and progress and the freedom of the peoples.

While socialism is on the upgrade, imperialism is heading towards decline. The positions of imperialism have been greatly weakened as a result of the disintegration of the colonial system.

The countries which have shaken off the yoke of colonialism are defending their independence and fighting for economic sovereignty, for world peace. The existence of the socialist system and the aid rendered by the socialist nations to these countries on principles of equality and co-operation between them and the socialist countries in the struggle for peace and against aggression, are helping them to uphold their national freedom and facilitate their social progress.

In the imperialist countries the contradictions between the productive forces and production relations have become acute. In many respects modern science and engineering are not being used in the interests of social progress for all mankind, because capitalism fetters and deforms the development of the productive forces of society. The world capitalist economy remains shaky and unstable. The relatively good level of economic activity still observed in a number of capitalist countries is due in a large measure to the arms drive and other transient factors. The capitalist economy is bound, however, to encounter deeper slumps and crises. The temporary high level of business activity helps maintain the reformist illusions among part of the workers in the capitalist countries. In the post-war period some sections of the working class in the more advanced capitalist countries, fighting against increased exploitation and for a higher standard of living, have been able to win certain wage increases, though in a number of these countries real wages are below the pre-war level. However, in the greater part of the capitalist world, and particularly in the colonial and dependent countries, millions of working people still live in poverty. The broad invasion of agriculture by the monopolies and the price policy dictated by them, the system of bank credits and loans and the increased taxation caused by the arms drive, have resulted in the steady ruin and impoverishment of the main mass of the peasantry. There is a sharpening of contradictions not only between the bourgeoisie and the working class but also between the monopoly bourgeoisie and all sections of the people, and between the United States monopoly bourgeoisie on the one hand, and the peoples, and even the bourgeoisie, of the other capitalist countries on the other. The working people of the capitalist countries live in such conditions that, to an increasing extent, they realize that the only way out of their grave situation lies through socialism. Thus increasingly favourable conditions are being created for bringing them into an active struggle for socialism. . . .

DOCUMENT 10. EXTRACT FROM THE STATEMENT OF EIGHTY-ONE COMMUNIST PARTIES MEETING IN MOSCOW, NOVEMBER 1960 (*New Times*, NO. 50, 1960)

The problem of war and peace is the most burning problem of our time.

War is a constant companion of capitalism. The system of exploitation of man by man and the system of extermination of man by man are two aspects of the capitalist system. Imperialism has already inflicted two devastating world wars on mankind and now threatens to plunge it into an even more terrible catastrophe. Monstrous means of mass annihilation and destruction have been developed which, if used in a new war, can cause unheard-of destruction to entire countries and reduce key centres of world industry and culture to ruins. Such a war would bring death and suffering to hundreds of millions of peoples, among them people in countries not involved in it. Imperialism spells grave danger to the whole of mankind.

The peoples must now be more vigilant than ever. As long as imperialism exists there will be soil for wars of aggression.

The peoples of all countries know that the danger of a new world war still persists. US imperialism is the main force of aggression and war. Its policy embodies the ideology of militant reaction. . . . The aggressive nature of imperialism has not changed. But real forces have appeared that are capable of foiling its plans of aggression. War is not fatally inevitable. Had the imperialists been able to do what they wanted, they would already have plunged mankind into the abyss of the calamities and horrors of a new world war. But the time is past when the imperialists could decide at will whether there should or should not be war. More than once in the past years the imperialists have brought mankind to the brink of world catastrophe by starting local wars. The resolute stand of the Soviet Union, of the other socialist states and of all the peaceful forces, put an end to the Anglo-Franco-Israeli intervention in Egypt, and averted a military invasion of Syria, Iraq and some other countries by the imperialists. . . .

The time has come when the attempts by the imperialist aggressors to start a world war can be curbed. World war can be prevented by the joint efforts of the world socialist camp, the international working class, the national liberation movement, all the countries opposing war and all peace-loving forces. . . .

The choice of social system is the inalienable right of the people of each country. Socialist revolution cannot be imported, or imposed from without. It is a result of the internal development of the country concerned, of the utmost sharpening of social contradictions in it.

DOCUMENT II. EXTRACT FROM AN INTERVIEW GIVEN BY KHRUSH-CHEV, 14 NOVEMBER 1957 (N. S. KHRUSHCHEV, *Speeches and Interviews on World Problems, 1957*, FOREIGN LANGUAGES PUBLISHING HOUSE, MOSCOW, 1958, PP. 270–1)

SHAPIRO (of United Press International): You have spoken of contradictions between the capitalist states. Are there such contradictions at present?
KHRUSHCHEV: Of course there are, and it cannot be helped. Such is the nature of capitalism. It is not only impossible to deny contradictions between the capitalist states, but it must be presumed that they will grow more acute. I shall not tell you about the contradictions existing between the United States, Britain and France in the struggle for 'domination' in various areas of Asia and Africa. The economics of Western Germany and Japan are developing rapidly at present and this cannot but alarm the British monopolists. It is difficult to believe that Western Germany's emergence to the fore conforms to the interests of the United States monopolies, because the West German monopolies are compelled to look for markets which are now mostly controlled by the American monopolies. This means that the West German monopolies must fight to seize the American positions. Here the matter cannot be settled amicably. There are many such 'ganglia of contradictions' which I could mention. Only the fear of communism, the fear

of the people's movement for freedom and independence, damps down to a certain extent these contradictions between the imperialists so they do not result in armed clashes. . . .

SHAPIRO : Do you think that the prospects for peace are not so bad?

KHRUSHCHEV : It seems so . . . The situation in Europe and Asia has generally changed substantially. Whereas formerly there was only one socialist state—the Soviet Union—today there is the world socialist system.

Moreover, the Soviet Union has changed beyond recognition since 1941. Its economy, culture, engineering and science have reached great heights and we are pleased to note that the self-same America which had always insisted that her level of science and technology was unattainable for the Soviet Union, now plans to overtake the Soviet Union in scientific development within two years, while some American leaders believe this will take ten years.

Please yourselves, we aren't going to argue. Do it in two years or ten, we shall not grudge it to you. . . .

Who, indeed, can wage a war now, considering the alignment of forces at the two poles, the capitalist and the socialist? The most real force are the West Germans. But the Germans in Western Germany do not want to fight. They have had enough. They still can't get over the Second World War. The lesson they received has not been forgotten—no one wants to fight, neither young people nor old, with the exception of the militaristic circles following in the wake of United States policy. The German militarists realize that should they start a war, a few hours would suffice to suppress all bases of military importance in Western Germany. Such are the conditions obtaining today. We believe, therefore, that even the most warlike of people can be brought to their senses. However eager they may be to fight, they too can be put in a straitjacket.

The 20th Congress of our party pointed out that the present situation is such that the forces of the socialist and neutral countries, and even the progressive forces in the United States and other western countries, can prevent war, provided we pursue a correct policy. . . .

This does not mean that war cannot flare up. As I have said, one cannot vouch for a madman. But the actual correlation of forces is such that the militarists and monopolists would do well to pause and think—and think hard—before starting a war. It is our conviction that if war is started—and only imperialist countries can do this because no socialist state is interested in war—capitalism will be routed and it will be the last suffering that the capitalist world will have inflicted on mankind, for capitalism will be done with once and for all.

DOCUMENT 12. EXTRACT FROM AN INTERVIEW GIVEN BY KHRUSHCHEV, 25 APRIL 1962 (*Pravda, 27 April 1962*)

COWLES: Mr Chairman, I would like to recall now an incident from the past. I want to recall it because I think that the language barrier between us sometimes creates certain difficulties. You once said something that was translated into English as 'We shall bury you'. In America, these words were taken as a military threat. I should like to ask you, therefore, what you meant by saying, 'We shall bury you'?

KHRUSHCHEV: I think that people who translate statements from one language into another, and especially those who spread and interpret them, should always do this with scrupulous honesty. What you speak of happened because some unscrupulous people deliberately twisted a phrase of mine, a very clear statement that capitalism will be buried in the course of the historical development of mankind, that it will inevitably be superseded by communism. In claiming this, I had in mind that society develops according to definite laws—it is changing all the time; the old dies out and the new emerges and develops.

America was once a colony of Britain, but the American people finally rose up in arms and freed themselves from oppression by Britain. The American people, one might say, buried Britain as the colonizer of the United States and achieved independence.

There was a time when the feudal system held sway in the majority of countries in the world. In its day, when this system was just emerging, it was more progressive than the slave-owning system. Conditions more conducive to the development of the productive forces of society gradually developed within the feudal system. The time came when feudalism had outlived its day. A more progressive system, capitalism, was born within it. Capitalism buried, interred feudalism. True, feudal relations still exist in a number of countries, but in general it can be said that feudalism as a system has been buried, interred, and the countries which were the first to begin to 'bury' that system gained in their economic development. Russia, which lingered longer in the stage of the landlord feudal system, lagged behind in the development of her economy in comparison with the other western countries.

But capitalism engendered irreconcilable contradictions, and a new, progressive social system—communism—with social relations between people entirely different from those under capitalism, has appeared to replace it.

We are convinced that communism will triumph because it provides better conditions for the development of the productive forces of society, provides conditions for the fullest and most harmonious development of society in general and for every individual in particular. Capitalism fights against communism, but it is impossible to arrest the process of the development of mankind. Sooner or later communism will win everywhere in the world and, consequently, communism will bury capitalism.

This is how my statement should be understood. It is not a question of someone burying someone in the physical sense, but of a change in the social system in the course of the historical development of society. When we say that communism will bury capitalism, that does not mean, of course, that the Soviet people, the communists of the Soviet Union, will inter the capitalists of some countries.

No, communism is winning in the Soviet Union, and many other countries are now following the road of communist development. Communism is growing out of the dedicated labour and struggle of the peoples of the socialist countries for a new and better life, the most just, creative life on earth. This is the teaching of life, of history: a more progressive social system inevitably comes to replace a system which is outliving its day. A progressive system buries a moribund one.

This is the view we take of the historical process of the

development of society. I have spoken of this more than once. I spoke about it in the United States, too, when I visited your country. We do not impose our communist convictions by force on anybody. We believe that in America, too, mighty forces will grow—they already exist there and are growing and developing all the time. These progressive forces, which are growing within the American people itself, will in the end triumph. In place of the capitalism which holds sway in America today, the American people will itself assert a new social system, and this system will be communism.

Thus, it can be said that one system, asserting itself, buries another system, which is outliving its day. It is not a case of one people burying a section of another—that would be monstrous, that would mean war between states. The question of the victory of one social system over another is one of class struggle. It is a new class, which is developing and growing stronger at the present time, the working class, the people itself, that will, properly speaking, reign in the world, including the United States of America.

DOCUMENT 13. EXTRACT FROM A SPEECH OF LEONID BREZHNEV, 29 MARCH 1968 (*Pravda*, 30 MARCH 1968)

The irremediable flaws in the capitalist economy can be seen particularly clearly against the background of the rapid and steady development of the economy of the socialist countries and the stupendous achievements of the whole socialist system. . . .

At the present time the capitalist economy is experiencing serious shocks in key links—in Britain, the United States and the FRG. Those shocks are certainly not happening by chance. They are a consequence of all the previous developments in the world economy, above all in the USA. Those shocks reflect the growing instability of the capitalist economy, and the exacerbated unevenness of its development.

Production and trade in the capitalist world grew in the post-war period. This is a fact. But this fact certainly cannot be explained by a revival of the 'viability' of capitalism, as bourgeois ideologists claim. It was connected with special features of the present-day revolution in science and technology. This growth has given way to a series of critical slumps whose dimensions exceed anything that has been seen in the past quarter of a century.

The monetary-financial crisis which is now developing has become a concentrated expression of the crisis phenomena within the framework of the capitalist system. The British pound sterling was recently devalued by 14·3 per cent. The magnitude of that event can be judged by the fact that the British pound is used in 30 to 35 per cent of all international transactions. No wonder that the currencies of more than twenty-five capitalist countries were devalued following the pound.

Now it is the turn of the US dollar, and its devaluation has actually started. Compared with its pre-war level, it has been devalued by 60 to 66·7 per cent. In these conditions the possibility of a profound crisis of the capitalist system cannot be ruled out. We can already see a rapid growth of unemployment in America, Britain, France, Italy and the FRG. By the beginning of this year, unemployment in those countries had already reached a total of six million. Behind this figure are living human beings, human tragedies; this is certainly proof of the flaws of capitalism. And we should speak out plainly about this, comrades, for it is the truth and it is an effective weapon in the ideological struggle.

*

If the Soviet Union was going to eschew war in its relations with the capitalist states, communist parties, too, would have to eschew violence in their drive to power. The Russian communists had come to power by armed insurrection. The Chinese communists had come to power after a civil war which had lasted a generation. Yet in the works of Marx, Engels and Lenin plenty of authority could be found for the view that communist parties could seize power by peaceful and parliamentary means.

The Czechoslovak *coup d'état* of February 1948 was much favoured as an example. The communists there carried through a revolution by legal means. With their socialist allies they had a majority in parliament. The threat of force existed, however, in the persons of armed workers' militias and communist-controlled police. For these reasons the Czechoslovak example was not such as to diminish the fears of the western democracies.

This principle that each people could choose the road it wanted to follow on its way to power, depending on the circumstances, was also connected with the further principle that the building of socialism was an independent endeavour which could no longer be dictated from the centre. The goal that is communism, of course remained the same.

The 20th Party Congress was undoubtedly the most important Party Congress held since the 1930s. It mapped a new course for communism in its condemnation of Stalin and all that Stalinism had stood for. It marked an important stage in Khrushchev's rise to supremacy.

Mikoyan had been in the highest ranks of the Party ever since 1926 and was, at this time, a close supporter of Khrushchev. He seems to have belonged to the conspiracy which removed Khrushchev in October 1964.

DOCUMENT 14. EXTRACT FROM A SPEECH OF ANASTYAS MIKOYAN DELIVERED AT THE 20TH CONGRESS OF THE CPSU IN FEBRUARY 1956 (*CDSP*, *VIII*, 8, 4 APRIL 1956, PP. 7–8)

As we now examine the question of the ways of revolution in the contemporary period, we are compelled—as Marx and Lenin were for their time—to proceed from a precise assessment of the correlation of class forces both in each individual country and on a world scale. It is clear to everyone that in our time no country can develop in isolation, without being influenced to some extent by other countries.

Lenin foresaw that in a small bourgeois country, given the existence of a number of socialist countries nearby, the transition to socialism can be effected by peaceful means. Lenin made it understood that not only the correlation of class forces in a single country should be taken into account, but also the presence of victorious socialism in neighbouring countries.

In connection with all this, the conclusion is drawn in the Central Committee's report that the present conditions afford certain countries a real opportunity to effect a peaceful transition to socialism. In other words, the correlation of class forces in the country, coupled with the favourable general situation described above, gives the working class of that country, jointly with the peasantry, an opportunity to unite the majority of the people under its leadership and to gain power by peaceful means, using existing parliamentary institutions, without an armed uprising or civil war. The peaceful development of a revolution is possible, of course, only as a result of the strength, the high degree of organization and the class consciousness of the working class.

But in those cases where the bourgeoisie possesses a strong military and police machine, it will certainly impose an armed struggle upon the proletariat in order to defend its domination, and the proletariat must be prepared for this beforehand.

The theoretical tenets of Marxism-Leninism, which are confirmed by life itself, convince us of the correctness of the Central Committee's framing of the question. Since Lenin's time the socialist revolution has triumphed in more than ten countries. How has this come about?

Take China. A civil war was waged in this great country for decades. Grim and bloody battles were fought there for a long time by the revolutionary armies against foreign imperialists and the counter-revolutionary forces of the landlords and the comprador bourgeoisie. The proletariat and its communist party, having gained a leading position and having been victorious in the armed struggle of the anti-federal and anti-imperialist revolution, ensured the possibility of carrying out a peaceful transition to socialist reforms.

Leninism captured the hearts and minds of millions of China's best people. Pointing out to the Chinese people the true way to socialism, *Leninism blossomed on Chinese soil and was enriched by the experience of the great Chinese revolution.* . . .

The revolution in Yugoslavia followed a singular course. When fascist Germany began the war against the Soviet Union, the Yugoslav Communist Party headed the revolt against the fascist yoke. Some of the Yugoslav bourgeoisie emigrated, withdrawing from the struggle against fascism; the others joined the fascists and collaborated with the occupation regime. Thus the Yugoslav partisan war against fascism merged with the civil war against the bourgeoisie and landlords who had betrayed Yugoslavia. . . .

In Czechoslovakia the revolution took a different course. By virtue of the favourable post-war situation in Czechoslovakia, the socialist revolution was carried out by peaceful means. The communists came to power after concluding an alliance not only with the working people's parties that were close to them but also with the bourgeois parties that supported the common national front. The Czechoslovak people won a peaceful victory in the revolution.

The working class of Bulgaria, Rumania, Hungary, Poland and other people's democracies achieved victory in the socialist revolution in their own way, but also without civil war.

Thus the course of history has proved incontrovertibly the correctness of the teachers of communism who foresaw a peaceful path of development of the revolution in addition to the path of armed uprising.

The fraternal communist parties of the capitalist countries have an inexhaustible treasury of knowledge—the theory o, Marxism-Leninism, their rich school of practical experiencef and the lessons of the historic victories in our country and in China and the other people's democracies.

DOCUMENT 15. EXTRACT FROM KHRUSHCHEV'S REPORT ON THE MEETING OF EIGHTY-ONE COMMUNIST PARTIES, 6 JANUARY 1961 (*Pravda*, 7 JANUARY 1961)

We are convinced that increasingly favourable conditions for socialist revolutions will arise with the growth of the might of the world socialist system and the better organization of the working class in the capitalist countries. The transition to socialism in countries with developed parliamentary traditions may be effected by using institutions conforming to their national traditions. It is not a question of using the bourgeois Parliament as such, but of employing the parliamentary form, making it serve the people and filling it with a new content. It is thus not a matter of electoral combinations or simple skirmishes at the ballot box. Communists leave that sort of thing to the reformists. Such combinations are alien to them. For communists the absolute condition for winning a stable majority in Parliament is to unify and consolidate the revolutionary forces of the working class and of all the working people, and to launch mass revolutionary actions. To win a majority in Parliament and to transform it into an organ of people's power, given a powerful revolutionary movement in the country, means to smash the military-bureaucratic machine of the bourgeoisie and to set up a new, proletarian people's state with a parliamentary form.

(d) NUCLEAR DIPLOMACY AND DISARMAMENT

Soviet space successes were a triumph of human ingenuity. Gagarin and the other astronauts, Soviet and American, are the heroes of our time. To the Soviets this was an indication of the predominance of socialism over capitalism in peaceful competition and also a sign of their coming military superiority. The military means to which space achievements could be put, escaped no one. It also meant that the Soviet armed forces would hasten their transformation from a mass army to an army equipped with nuclear weapons and with the means of delivering them. Yet, in spite of cuts in manpower the Red Army remained a mass army because Soviet military leaders continued to believe that land operations would have to go on after the initial nuclear exchange.

DOCUMENT 16. EXTRACT FROM AN ARTICLE IN *International Affairs* (MOSCOW) IN FEBRUARY 1958 ON THE SIGNIFICANCE OF THE FIRST SPUTNIK

What has been the impact of the sputniks on the world situation, on relations between the socialist and capitalist countries, on foreign policy and international relations?

It is hardly necessary to prove at length that their launching has enhanced the moral and political influence and the role of the Soviet Union in present-day international relations. It has taken the ground from under the feet of malicious propaganda regarding the alleged economic and cultural backwardness of our country. It showed the world the Soviet Union as it really is.

The development and launching of the sputniks are convincing proof of the high level achieved by Soviet science and technology—not simply in individual branches, but in virtually all modern branches of theory and engineering practice. The sputniks are a synthesis, the product of integrated and coordinated labour, the result of the achievements of Soviet physics and chemistry, mathematics, theoretical and applied mechanics, electronics, etc.

It is seemingly now clear to even the most obdurate of our country's opponents that the sputniks would have been impossible without the combined genius of Soviet scientists and the skill of Soviet engineers, without highly qualified workers, good organization, well-equipped laboratories and, finally, without a highly-developed industry. All this underlines the strength of the Soviet Union, its scientific and technical potential, its growing role as an advanced industrial country, and, hence, as a factor in present-day international relations.

But it is not just a matter of an increase in the weight and prestige of one country. It is a question of a change in the balance of forces between socialism and capitalism, of the strengthening of the former and the weakening of the latter.

Any change of this kind is naturally of great importance in international relations.

The socialist world system is now the standard-bearer of peace and progress throughout the world. Scientific success on such a scale reinforces this system as a whole and contributes to the unity of the countries belonging to it, giving their people still greater confidence in their own strength and future. By strengthening the countries of the socialist community, the scientific achievements themselves become factors of progress and peace. They demonstrate that the peace forces throughout the world have become considerably stronger and more stable, and that their development has received a powerful new impetus, a new stimulus for advance.

We have indeed every reason to conclude that the position of those who support co-existence between countries with different social systems has become more stable than ever before. The world has entered a new stage of co-existence, when the violation of this leading diplomatic principle of our time threatens inevitable destruction to the violators, when any attempt by the imperialists to launch a new world will inevitably boomerang against the entire capitalist system and lead to its complete downfall.

DOCUMENT 17. EXTRACT FROM AN INTERVIEW GIVEN BY KHRUSH-CHEV, 22 NOVEMBER 1957 (N. S. KHRUSHCHEV, *Speeches and Interviews on World Problems, 1957*, FOREIGN LANGUAGES PUBLISHING HOUSE, MOSCOW, 1958, PP. 316–17)

I should like to tell you, Mr Hearst, and through you the people of the United States of America, that the Soviet Union stands for peace and peaceful co-existence. Our country will never begin war, if it is not attacked. We do not contemplate war either against the United States of America or against any other country, irrespective of whether that country is near to the Soviet Union or far from it, for that is contrary to the spirit of our ideology. We want to compete in peaceful construction, in constructive work.

I also want to tell you, Mr Hearst, that in the creation of new types of weapons we have outstripped your country. We now possess the absolute weapon, perfect in every respect and created in a short period of time. I am not saying this to intimidate, there is no need for that, I am simply stating a fact: our scientists, engineers, technicians and workers have produced the most up-to-date weapon. The Soviet Union possesses inter-continental ballistic missiles; it has missiles of different systems for different purposes; all our missiles can be fitted with atomic and hydrogen warheads. Thus, we have proved our superiority on this question. And if war now breaks out—and it can be unleashed only by the aggressive circles of the United States of America, because other countries will not dare to unleash it— then this will be a great misfortune for the peoples of these countries on whose territories American bases are situated from which the United States is preparing to strike a blow at the Soviet Union and other socialist countries.

*

The year 1957 was the year of the Sputnik: it was also the year in which the United States offered to place at the disposal of the Supreme Allied Commander in Europe, the American general Norstad, atomic and nuclear warheads. They were to remain the property of the United States government and could be used only with the permission of both the NATO Council and the American president.

The Soviet government, which had always stressed the importance of disarmament, but was not in fact prepared to make the necessary concessions to bring it about, unleashed a propaganda and diplomatic campaign against this strengthening of NATO. In March 1958 the Soviet Union carried out a series of nuclear explosions, and when they were concluded announced the unilateral suspension of tests.

DOCUMENT 18. RESOLUTION OF THE SUPREME SOVIET ON THE UNI-LATERAL TERMINATION BY THE SOVIET UNION OF ATOMIC AND HYDROGEN WEAPON TESTS, 31 MARCH 1958 (*SN*, 1 APRIL 1958)

As time passes, the question of ending atomic and hydrogen weapon tests is assuming ever greater importance for the cause of peace and the welfare of the peoples.

Today the ending of tests is being demanded by the overwhelming majority of the people of the world. Yet although the peoples have been persistently working for the ending of these tests for many years, these weapons are still being manufactured. This has resulted in the creation of ever newer types of death-dealing nuclear weapons, in an increase in the concentration of radioactive elements in the air and the soil, and this is poisoning the human organism and is threatening the normal development of coming generations.

The Soviet Union has been exerting effort steadily and persistently to reach an agreement with the powers possessing atomic and nuclear weapons on an immediate and unconditional termination of nuclear tests. To this end the USSR Supreme Soviet and the Soviet government have in recent years repeatedly put forward concrete proposals to end the tests—proposals which could long ago have served as a basis for agreement on this question.

In its appeal to the United States Congress and the Parliament of Great Britain of 10 May 1957, the USSR Supreme Soviet urged them to work for an agreement between the governments of the USSR, the United States and Britain on the immediate termination of atom and hydrogen bomb test explosions.

At its previous session last December, the USSR Supreme Soviet, expressing the unswerving determination and the unanimous desire of the Soviet people for peace, proposed that the USSR, Britain and the United States pledge themselves to cease all atomic and hydrogen weapon tests as from 1 January 1958.

The United States and Britain, however, failed to react to these proposals of the Soviet Union. As a result, test explosions of atomic and hydrogen bombs are still taking place in various parts of the globe—evidence of the further intensification of the race to create ever more dangerous types of weapons of mass destruction.

Guided by its desire to make a practical beginning to the world-wide ending of atomic and hydrogen weapon tests, which would be the first step towards finally ridding mankind of the threat of devastating atomic war, the Supreme Soviet of the Union of Soviet Socialist Republics resolves:

1 to end all types of atomic and hydrogen weapon tests in the Soviet Union. The USSR Supreme Soviet expects that the Parliaments of other states possessing atomic and hydrogen weapons will do everything to terminate test explosions of these weapons by their countries as well;

2 to empower the USSR Council of Ministers to take the necessary measures to implement Article 1 of this resolution, and to address an appeal to the governments of other states possessing atomic and hydrogen weapons, urging them to take similar steps to ensure the ending of atomic and hydrogen weapon tests everywhere and for all time.

In the event of other nuclear powers continuing these tests' the government of the USSR will naturally act as it sees fit as regards the testing of atomic and hydrogen weapons by the Soviet Union, depending on the aforementioned circumstances and with a view to the interests of the security of the Soviet Union.

The USSR Supreme Soviet sincerely hopes that the Soviet Union's initiative in ending nuclear-weapon tests will meet with due support from the Parliaments of other countries.

The USSR Supreme Soviet is firmly convinced that if in response to the decision of the Soviet Union other nuclear powers similarly end the testing of such weapons, this will be an important practical step towards consolidating peace and strengthening the security of all peoples. Such a step would unquestionably do much to improve the international situation as a whole, and would help to free mankind from oppressive fears for the future of peace and the fate of the generations to come.

*

Military considerations made the moratorium on testing very brief. The tests were resumed in October 1958 but in the same month a further moratorium on testing was agreed upon, which lasted for three years. In October, too, the Geneva Conference on the discontinuance of nuclear-weapon tests opened. In August 1961 the Soviets resumed testing. Presumably the failure of the Paris summit and mounting tensions in Berlin, Laos and the Congo forced the Soviet Union to explode the largest nuclear devices ever tested.

DOCUMENT 19. EXTRACT FROM THE STATEMENT ON THE RESUMP-
TION OF NUCLEAR TESTING IN THE ATMOSPHERE, 31 AUGUST 1961
(*Pravda*, 31 AUGUST 1961)

The peoples are witnessing the ever increasing aggressiveness of the policy of the NATO military bloc. The United States and its allies are spinning the flywheel of their military machine ever faster, fanning up the arms race to unprecedented scope, increasing the strength of armies, making the tension of the international situation red-hot. Things have reached such a point that the leading statesmen of the United States and its allies are resorting to threats to take to arms and to unleash war as a countermeasure to the conclusion of a peace treaty with the German Democratic Republic.

In the face of these facts, which cannot but cause anxiety, the Soviet government considers it its duty to take all measures so that the Soviet Union should be completely prepared to render harmless any aggressor if he tried to launch an attack. The tragedy of the first months of the great patriotic war when

Hitler attacked the USSR, having ensured for himself superiority in military equipment, is too fresh in the memory of people to allow this to happen now.

This is the reason why the Soviet government has already taken a number of serious measures to strengthen the security of the USSR. For the same reason, after a thoughtful and comprehensive consideration of this matter, it has made a decision to carry out experimental explosions of nuclear weapons. . . .

The question of control has for years been a stumbling block on the way to agreement on disarmament. This was so because control has been used by the western powers as a pretext to turn down any proposal on disarmament. . . . In order not to allow the essence of the matter—disarmament itself—to be ruined, the Soviet government has stated openly that it is ready to accept in advance any proposal of the western powers on international control. Only one thing was expected from the western powers and that was to accept our proposals on general disarmament and to submit their proposals on general control. . . .

What can be the explanation for the fact that no specific proposals on that score have yet followed from the western powers? This can be explained only by the fear that the Soviet Union will accept their proposals on control and then the western powers would either have to agree to general and complete disarmament or would expose themselves to the last as opponents of disarmament and as opponents of control over disarmament.

The main thing in our days is disarmament, universal and total, and an agreement on such disarmament would cover the question of nuclear testing. Indeed, when the arms race is stopped and the stockpiled weapons are destroyed, there will be no incentive for its perfection and consequently for the need to carry out our experimental nuclear tests but, on the contrary, merely an agreement to stop nuclear-weapon tests cannot by itself put an end to the arms race.

The states that already possess atomic weapons will in-evitably feel tempted to act violating such an agreement, to seek new ways and loopholes for perfecting weapons, to say nothing of the fact that the tests carried out by three or four powers are quite sufficient for unlimited stockpiling of the most dangerous thermo-nuclear weapons of the existing types.

The states which do not yet possess thermo-nuclear weapons will in their turn try to create them despite the agreement that prohibits atomic tests. . . .

The governments of the western powers . . . demand that a treaty on the discontinuance of nuclear tests should not provide for the prohibition of underground nuclear explosions. Meanwhile, it is obvious to every informed person that the carrying out of such explosions, even if it is claimed that they are conducted for peaceful purposes, is nothing else but a hidden form of perfecting the existing nuclear weapons or putting finishing touches to its new types. . . .

The entire course of the negotiations in Geneva proves that the western powers pursue the aim of actually legalizing those types of nuclear tests in which they are interested and of establishing an international control body which would be an obedient tool in their hands and in fact would be an appendage of the general staffs of western powers. . . .

The Soviet government considers it its duty to draw the special attention of the peoples of the world to the fact that now in the United States there is much ado about projects for developing a neutron bomb which would kill everything living but at the same time would not destroy material things. Only aggressors dreaming of plunder, of capturing foreign lands and foreign property can mobilize the efforts of scientists for the development of such weapons. . . .

It is an open secret that the United States is on the verge of carrying out underground nuclear explosions and only waits for the first suitable pretext to start them. However, it is clear to everybody that since the US government has the intention to resume nuclear-weapon tests, it is only a matter of time.

The Soviet government cannot ignore the fact that France, the ally of the United States in NATO, has been carrying out nuclear tests already for a long time. While the Soviet Union refrained from nuclear tests, trying to achieve agreement with the United States and Great Britain at the negotiating table on their complete discontinuance, France conducted explosions of nuclear devices one after another. It continues to do so in spite of the appeal of the United Nations to all states to refrain from such tests, in spite of the protests of broad public circles in all countries of the world, in spite of the warnings of the Soviet Union that it will be forced to resume tests if France does not stop its experiments with nuclear weapons. . . .

*

The treaty banning nuclear tests in the atmosphere, in outer space and under water, signed in Moscow, was the first concrete result that emerged from disarmament negotiations. The treaty did not cover underground testing because of the inability to agree on acceptable terms and it is subject to the right of any party to withdraw from its undertakings if its supreme interests are considered to be in jeopardy.

This breakthrough, which was followed by other signs of détente, was possible because of the increasing Soviet fear of a Chinese bomb. The Cuban missile crisis may also have put the Soviets into a more pliable mood.

DOCUMENT 20. KHRUSHCHEV'S COMMENTS ON THE CONCLUSION OF THE PARTIAL TEST BAN TREATY, 29 JULY 1963 (*SN*, 29 JULY 1963)

The successful conclusion of the test ban talks in Moscow between the Soviet Union, the United States of America and Great Britain is an event of great international importance. It is common knowledge that, for many years, the Soviet Union has been fighting for the ending of nuclear-weapon tests. The demand for the earliest possible solution of this problem has always been supported, and is supported now, by all peace-loving states and peoples.

It has now been possible to agree on a treaty banning nuclear-weapon tests in the atmosphere, in outer space and under water. We regard this as a good start. I should like to congratulate all the men of goodwill who worked to achieve agreement on the prohibition of nuclear-weapon tests. I should also like to pay due credit to the efforts of the governments of the United States and Great Britain and to their representatives who were authorized to conduct the negotiations by their governments.

The reaching of agreement on the prohibition of nuclear-weapon tests shows that international problems can be successfully resolved on mutually acceptable terms given the desire and effort of the states concerned and given the goodwill of the great powers.

What is more, we hope—and we think that this hope is now shared by all the people of the world—that the conclusion of a treaty to end nuclear-weapon tests will contribute to a general relaxation of international tension, and thereby, to the establishment of a situation favourable to the solution of international problems which is long overdue.

It would, of course, be wrong to flatter oneself as a result of the successes which have been achieved and to relax one's energy and effort in the further struggle to solve the problems on which the safeguarding of world peace depends, for one must be perfectly clear that a ban on nuclear-weapon tests does not yet mean an end to the arms race and, therefore, by itself, cannot avert the danger of war. Neither does this measure remove the burden of armaments on the manufacture of which states are expending tremendous material resources.

The main task, however, is to end the arms race and to achieve disarmament. Only along this road can the threat of war really be eliminated and states relieved of the burden of military expenditure.

This is why the Soviet government believes that now, as a result of the agreement on the prohibition of nuclear-weapon tests, favourable opportunities have arisen which make it possible to achieve further progress in solving the fundamental international problems. For this, however, fresh efforts will be required which will lead, step by step, to the consolidation of peace and to the realization of mankind's age-old dream of general and complete disarmament. It is, especially for the great powers, necessary to start this work at once.

DOCUMENT 21. KOSYGIN'S SPEECH AT THE SIGNING OF THE TREATY ON THE NON-PROLIFERATION OF NUCLEAR WEAPONS, 1 JULY 1968 (*Pravda*, 2 JULY 1968)

Comrades, gentlemen, permit me, on the instructions of the Soviet government, to express profound satisfaction over the fact that the signing of the Treaty on the Non-proliferation of Nuclear Weapons, which is an important international document approved by the overwhelming majority of the UN members, starts today. The conclusion of a treaty of the non-proliferation of nuclear weapons is a major success for the cause of peace. Since the time nuclear weapons first appeared, the Soviet Union has firmly and consistently favoured delivering mankind from the nuclear threat. The Treaty is an important step towards this goal, since it bars the further spread of nuclear weapons, thus reducing the danger of an outbreak of a nuclear war.

The participation of a great number of states in the signing of the Treaty today is convincing proof that states are capable of finding mutually acceptable solutions to complicated international problems of vital importance for the whole of mankind. The preparation of the Treaty required great effort and prolonged negotiations, in which nuclear and non-nuclear, big and small, developed and developing nations, and countries belonging to different social systems, took part. The Treaty reflects numerous wishes and proposals expressed by states and takes into account various points of view on the solution of the non-proliferation problem; under these circumstances, all the states approving it have agreed about the main thing: the need to prevent the further spread of nuclear weapons.

An important supplement to the Treaty is provided by the quite recently adopted Security Council resolution on assurances of security for non-nuclear weapon countries which are parties to the Treaty. As was stated in the Security Council, the Soviet government intends to comply with this decision unswervingly.

Here in Moscow, five years ago, we signed the treaty banning nuclear-weapon tests in three environments. After that the treaty prohibiting the use of outer space for military purposes was concluded. These and the Treaty on the Non-proliferation of Nuclear Weapons are practical steps towards limiting the arms race which create more favourable conditions for progress in disarmament.

DOCUMENT 22. EXTRACT FROM KHRUSHCHEV'S REPORT TO THE SUPREME SOVIET, 14 JANUARY 1960 (*Pravda*, 15 JANUARY 1960)

It is perfectly clear to all sober-minded people that atomic and hydrogen weapons are particularly dangerous to the countries that are densely populated. Of course, all countries will suffer in one way or another in the event of a new world war. We, too, shall suffer much, shall sustain great losses, but we shall survive. Our territory is immense and our population is less concentrated in large industrial centres than is the case in many other countries. The west will suffer incomparably more. If the aggressors start up a new war, it will be not only their last war, but also the end of capitalism, for the peoples will see clearly that capitalism is a source of wars, and will no longer tolerate that system, which brings suffering and calamities to mankind.

(e) COLLECTIVE SECURITY IN EUROPE

Disengagement was a variation of disarmament limited to a certain geographical area. It had the great advantage to the Soviet Union that it would move NATO armaments from central to western Europe and that it would be a possible first stage in the neutralization of Western Germany. The Polish plan envisaged nuclear disarmament as the first stage of a more general disarmament in Central Europe.

The plan was presented in the United Nations by Polish foreign minister Rapacki and an amended version was sent to the interested powers in February 1958. This Polish action shows the interesting way in which the Soviets use other socialist states to propose their ideas. At that time Poland's stock, due to the liberalization process following October 1956, was high in the west.

Had the plan been successful it could have been used as a model in other areas like South-East Asia or Latin America.

DOCUMENT 23. SOVIET REPLY TO THE POLISH MEMORANDUM ON AN ATOM-FREE ZONE IN CENTRAL EUROPE, 3 MARCH 1958 (*SN*, 5 MARCH 1958)

In reply to the memorandum of the government of the Polish People's Republic of 14 February, concerning the establishment of an atom-free zone in central Europe, the Soviet government considers it necessary to state the following:

The Soviet government, as it has repeatedly declared, fully supports the initiative of the government of the Polish People's Republic concerning the establishment in Europe of a zone— including the territories of the Polish People's Republic, the Czechoslovak Republic, the German Democratic Republic and the Federal Republic of Germany—in which atomic, hydrogen and rocket weapons would be neither manufactured nor deployed. The implementation of this proposal would unquestionably be a major contribution to the cause of relaxing tensions and ensuring peace in the heart of the European continent, in one of the tensest areas of the world with an unusual—for peace-time—concentration of the troops of two military groupings and various modern weapons and equipment.

The establishment of an atom-free zone in Europe would fully accord with the vital interests of the peoples of the European states, who have been profoundly alarmed by the danger of a devastating war involving the use of atomic, hydrogen and rocket weapons and who realize the calamities and suffering that would result from the use of such weapons of mass destruction, particularly in the densely populated areas of Europe. The implementation of this proposal would have a most beneficial effect on the international situation as a whole and would lead to the establishment of the necessary confidence in the relations between states.

If such an atom-free zone were to be set up in Europe, all of central Europe, embracing a territory with an area of roughly one million square kilometres and a population of more than 100 million, would be freed from the manufacture and stockpiling of atomic, hydrogen and also rocket weapons, and this would be of inestimable importance to central Europe, where the armed forces of the two military groupings are in contact and where local conflicts can most easily grow into major ones, with all the dire consequences this would entail for the cause of peace.

The Soviet government has carefully studied the memorandum of the government of the Polish People's Republic, which sets forth its considerations concerning both the obligations to be undertaken by the states within the zone as well the obligations to be undertaken by the USSR, the United States, the United Kingdom and France, and also other states whose troops are stationed on the territories of the states within that zone.

The Soviet government fully agrees that the states within the zone should undertake not to manufacture, stockpile or receive for their own purposes, and to prevent the installation on their territories of, devices and equipment to service nuclear weapons, including rocket-launching ramps.

The Soviet government believes, as it has already said in its statement of 19 February, that the effective implementation of the proposal to set up a zone in Central Europe free from atomic, hydrogen and rocket weapons requires, along with the corresponding obligations of the states within this zone, that the powers possessing nuclear and rocket weapons should solemnly undertake to respect the status of the zone and regard the territory of the states within it as one excluded from the use of nuclear and rocket weapons. This would put these powers under the obligation not to equip their troops or the troops of other states stationed on the territory of the zone with atomic and rocket weapons, and not to transfer these weapons to the governments of states within the zone or to the armed forces stationed within it under the command of military groupings, as also not to import or build installations and military equipment to service nuclear weapons, including rocket-launching installations.

Guided by the interests of consolidating peace on the European continent and throughout the world, the Soviet government, for its part, already declared on 19 February that it was ready to assume the aforementioned obligations, provided the governments of the United States, the United Kingdom and France did likewise.

The government of the USSR notes with satisfaction the identity of viewpoints of the Soviet Union and the Polish

People's Republic on this question and expresses its full agreement with the proposal of the Polish People's Republic to the effect that the USSR, the United States, the United Kingdom and France assume the obligation not to use nuclear weapons against the territory of the zone and any objects on it, as well as the obligations:

(a) not to maintain nuclear weapons among the armaments of their troops stationed on the territories of the states of the zone; not to maintain and not to site on the territory of the states of the zone any installations and equipment designed for servicing such weapons, including rocket-launching installations;
(b) not to transfer in any way or under any pretext either nuclear weapons or related installations and equipment to governments or any other agencies on this territory.

The Soviet Union is also in agreement with the considerations set forth in the memorandum concerning control—to be agreed upon by the parties concerned—in the zone, and is ready to take part in effecting such control.

The Soviet government also expresses its full agreement with the proposals of the government of the Polish People's Republic relating to the procedure of preparing and giving form to the agreement on the zone.

The realization of the proposal for setting up a zone free from atomic, hydrogen and rocket weapons would be conducive to the solution of questions relating to the reduction, by agreement between the states concerned, of the strength of foreign troops and conventional armaments in this zone and to the adoption of further broader measures both in the sphere of disarmament and in the solution of other major international problems.

The problem of the establishment in Central Europe of a zone free from the production and stationing of atomic, hydrogen and rocket weapons is one of the most pressing international problems, calling for immediate solution. It is precisely for this reason that the Soviet government has suggested that a conference of leading statesmen, with the participation of the heads of government, should consider the question of establishing a denuclearized zone, among other most important problems of our times.

The Soviet government hopes that the governments of the powers possessing nuclear and rocket weapons, and also the government of the Federal Republic of Germany, will give every support to the proposal for setting up the zone and thus contribute to the achievement of the noble aim of removing the danger of an atomic war and of using atomic energy only for peaceful purposes, for the benefit of mankind.

*

The French Communist Party in 1965 and 1966 called for a meeting of European communist parties to discuss European security. To the Soviets this was a welcome move because European security was high on their list of priorities. A preparatory meeting was held in Warsaw in February 1967 and the meeting itself took place in Karlovy Vary in April 1967, adjourning one day earlier than expected. Although twenty-four communist parties attended, those of Albania, Rumania, Yugoslavia, Iceland, the Netherlands, Norway and Turkey refused to attend, while the Swedes sent only an observer. In most cases the parties attending were represented by their leaders and Brezhnev's speech formed the foundation of the statement issued by the conference, called 'For Peace and Security in Europe'. The violence of Brezhnev's language was, however, much modified in this document. The document hoped to persuade western public opinion to agitate for an end to NATO whose twentieth anniversary came up in 1969. The conference also issued documents on the Greek colonels' regime and on Vietnam. The Chinese question was mentioned only once, in Brezhnev's speech.

DOCUMENT 24. EXTRACT FROM THE STATEMENT OF COMMUNIST PARTIES MEETING IN KARLOVY VARY IN CZECHOSLOVAKIA IN APRIL 1967 (*Pravda*, 27 APRIL 1967)

The European communist and workers' parties are submitting, for consideration by public opinion and by all the political and public forces concerned, a programme of activities in the interests of creating a system of collective security, based on peaceful co-existence.

This requires primarily that all states should recognize the actually existing situation as it has developed in Europe in the post-war period. This means:

Recognition of the inviolability of the existing frontiers in Europe, particularly on the Oder and the Neisse, and also of the borders between the two German states;

recognition of the existence of two sovereign and equal German states, the German Democratic Republic and the Federal Republic of Germany, which requires that the latter renounce its claim to represent the whole of Germany;

exclusion of any opportunity for the Federal Republic of Germany to gain access to nuclear arms in any form, either European, multilateral or Atlantic;

recognition that the Munich Treaty has been invalid since the moment of its conclusion.

The working-class movement and all the peace and democratic forces of Europe now face the task of ensuring the development of peaceful relations and co-operation among all European states on the basis of respect for their sovereignty and equality. With these aims in view it is necessary to fight for the realization of a number of aims which can be achieved in the new situation, namely:

The conclusion by all European states of a treaty renouncing the use of force or the threat of force in their relations and renouncing interference in internal affairs, a treaty guaranteeing that all disputes shall be solved by peaceful means only, in accordance with the principles of the UN Charter;

the normalization of relations between all states and the GDR, as well as between the two German states and between the GDR and West Berlin as a separate political entity;

the consistent defence and development of democracy in the FRG—the right to demand this is given to the peoples by law, historical experience and postwar international agreements. This envisages universal support for the struggle of the progressive forces in the FRG for the banning of neo-Nazi organizations and all revenge-seeking propaganda, the annulment of the emergency legislation, freedom of activity for the democratic and peace-loving forces and the lifting of the ban on the Communist Party of Germany;

the conclusion of a non-proliferation treaty as an important step towards the stopping of the arms race.

The systems of European security must include the recognition of the principle of neutrality and unconditional respect for the inviolability of neutral states. A more active peace-loving policy on the part of these countries and their contribution to the cause of disarmament would help to establish such a system.

The ending of artificially created barriers in economic relations between the socialist and capitalist states of Europe would be of particular importance for all states and would be conducive to fruitful co-operation, including broad agreements in the sphere of production and scientific research.

Striving to open the way to European security and co-operation, we come out resolutely for the conclusion of agreements on partial solutions, above all in the sphere of disarmament, which would create a favourable climate for more far-reaching treaties. All proposals in this field, advanced by governments, parties, public organizations, political leaders and scientists, deserve thorough examination. Particularly topical among these proposals are those which deal with the withdrawal of foreign troops from the territory of European states, the dismantling of foreign military bases, the establishment of nuclear-free zones in Central Europe, the Balkans, the territory of the Danubian countries, in the Mediterranean and in Northern Europe, and also zones of thinned-out or frozen armaments, and, in general, zones of peace and co-operation in various regions of the continent. These, and other steps, would check the trend towards intensifying the arms race.

The twenty-year period of the validity of the Atlantic Pact expires in 1969, and this presents a clear alternative: a Europe without military blocs. This alternative must be put on the agenda with all earnestness. No effort should be spared in order to develop a broad-scale movement of the peace-loving forces of our continent against the extension or any modification of the Atlantic Pact. This movement is favoured by the constructive attitude of the Warsaw Treaty member-nations who have repeatedly stated, and solemnly confirmed in the Bucharest Declaration, their readiness for the simultaneous disbanding of both military alliances. We second the moves of these states regarding an immediate agreement abolishing the military organizations of the Atlantic Pact and the Warsaw Treaty. We express our readiness to support any initiatives or proposals pursuing the purpose of achieving a détente and strengthening the security of the peoples of our continent.

We fully support the proposals for a conference of all European states on the question of security and peaceful co-operation in Europe. The proposal for a conference of representatives of all the European Parliaments also deserves support.

The consolidation of security and peace will open up new prospects for progress and prosperity before the peoples of our continent.

The peoples of Europe are faced with important social, economic and cultural problems. A Europe, rid of the arms race, which consumes tremendous economic resources and the fruits of the labour of workers, engineers and scientists will be able not only to ensure higher living standards for its population, but also to make a valuable contribution to the development of all mankind.

The struggle for this Europe is closely associated with the struggle for genuine national independence and democracy and against reactionary and fascist dictatorships such as exist in Spain, Portugal and Greece. The fact that the governments of Spain, Portugal and Greece assist American imperialism in building atomic bases in exchange for US support for those discredited regimes shows what a great danger they are to Europe.

*

The Non-aggression Treaty between Bonn and Moscow marked an important stage in the normalization of relations between the two countries. It was a triumph of Soviet policy in that a German government was finally forced to recognize the territorial settlement of 1945. The pact was soon followed by a similar treaty between Poland and Germany.

DOCUMENT 25. EXTRACT FROM THE TEXT OF THE SOVIET-GERMAN TREATY OF NON-AGGRESSION SIGNED IN MOSCOW, 12 AUGUST 1970 (*Pravda*, 13 AUGUST 1970)

The high contracting parties, anxious to contribute to strengthening peace and security in Europe and the world:

Convinced that peaceful co-operation among states on the basis of the purposes and principles of the Charter of the United Nations complies with the ardent desire of nations and the general interests of international peace;

Appreciating the fact that the agreed measures previously implemented by them, in particular the conclusion of the agreement of 13 September 1955 on the establishment of diplomatic relations, have created favourable conditions for new important steps destined to develop further and to strengthen their mutual relations;

Desiring to lend expression, in the form of a treaty, to their determination to improve and extend co-operation between them, including economic relations as well as scientific, technological and cultural contacts, in the interest of both states;

Have agreed as follows

ARTICLE 1 The Federal Republic of Germany and the Union of Soviet Socialist Republics consider it an important objective of their policies to maintain international peace and achieve détente.

They affirm their endeavour to further the normalization of the situation in Europe and the development of peaceful relations among all European states and in so doing proceed from the actual situation existing in this region.

ARTICLE 2 The Federal Republic of Germany and the Union of Soviet Socialist Republics shall in their mutual relations as well as in matters of ensuring European and international security be guided by the purposes and principles embodied in the Charter of the United Nations. Accordingly, they shall settle their disputes exclusively by peaceful means and undertake to refrain from the threat or use of force, pursuant to Article 2 of the Charter of the United Nations, in any matters affecting security in Europe or international security, as well as in their mutual relations.

ARTICLE 3 In accordance with the foregoing purposes and principles the Federal Republic of Germany and the Union of Soviet Socialist Republics share the realization that peace can only be maintained in Europe if nobody disturbs the present frontiers...

They undertake to respect without restriction the territorial integrity of all states in Europe within their present frontiers.

They declare that they have no territorial claims against anybody, nor will assert such claims in the future.

They regard today and shall in future regard the frontiers of all states in Europe as inviolable such as they are on the date of signature of the present treaty, including the Oder-Neisse line which forms the western frontier of the People's Republic of Poland and the frontier between the Federal Republic of Germany and the German Democratic Republic.

ARTICLE 4 The present treaty between the Federal Republic of Germany and the Union of Soviet Socialist Republics shall not affect any bilateral or multilateral treaties or arrangements previously concluded by them.

(f) CONFRONTATION WITH THE UNITED STATES

The second Berlin crisis began on 10 November 1958 when Khrushchev declared that the USSR no longer recognized obligations it had assumed under the Potsdam agreement on Berlin. These views were expressed formally in the note of 27 November. The note, which was regarded as an ultimatum, gave the western powers six months to agree to a Berlin settlement, but it lost much of its force as the six-months' deadline was continuously extended.

One of the results of Khrushchev's action was the foreign ministers' meeting in Geneva in May–June 1959 in which the representatives of the great powers were accompanied by the foreign ministers of the two German states, acting in an advisory capacity.

DOCUMENT 26. EXTRACT FROM THE NOTE TO THE GOVERNMENTS OF THE UNITED STATES, BRITAIN AND FRANCE ON THE QUESTION OF BERLIN, 27 NOVEMBER 1958 (*SN*, 28 NOVEMBER 1958)

The agreement on the quadripartite status of Berlin was once an equal agreement concluded by the four powers for peaceful and democratic goals which were later to become known as the Potsdam principles. At that time, this agreement was in accordance with the exigencies of the day and with the interests of all the signatories—the USSR, the United States, Britain and France. Now that the western powers have begun to arm Western Germany and turn her into an instrument of their policy, spearheaded against the Soviet Union, the very essence of the allied agreement on Berlin has vanished. It has been violated by three of its signatories, who have been using this agreement against the fourth signatory, the Soviet Union. This being the situation, it would be ridiculous to expect the Soviet Union or any other self-respecting state to pretend to ignore the changes which have taken place.

A patently absurd situation has arisen, therefore, in which the Soviet Union supports and maintains, as it were, favourable conditions for activity by the western powers directed against the USSR and its Warsaw Treaty allies. It is clearly obvious that the Soviet Union, and the other parties to the Warsaw Treaty, can no longer tolerate this state of affairs. For the occupation regime in West Berlin to continue would be tantamount to recognizing something like a privileged position for the NATO countries, a privileged position for which, of course, there is no justification.

Can anyone really seriously believe that the Soviet Union will help the forces of aggression to develop subversive activities against the socialist countries, let alone to prepare an attack on them? It must be clear to everyone of sound mind that the Soviet Union cannot maintain a situation in West Berlin which is detrimental to its legitimate interest, to its security and to the security of the other socialist countries. It would be well to remember that the Soviet Union is not a Jordan or an Iran, and that it will never allow methods of pressure to be applied on it, in order to force on it conditions suiting the powers belonging to the opposing NATO military bloc. But this is just what the western powers want from the Soviet Union, since they seek to retain their occupation rights in West Berlin.

Can the Soviet government afford to disregard all these facts, which affect the basic security interests of the Soviet Union, and its ally, the German Democratic Republic, and of all the signatories of the Warsaw Defence Treaty? Why, of course not! The Soviet government can no longer consider itself bound by that part of the Allied agreements on Germany which has assumed an unequal character and is being used for the maintenance of the occupation regime in West Berlin and for interference in the domestic affairs of the German Democratic Republic.

In view of this, the government of the USSR hereby notifies the government of the United States that the Soviet Union regards as null and void the 'Protocol of the Agreement between the Governments of the Union of Soviet Socialist Republics, the United States of America and the United Kingdom, on the Occupation Zones of Germany and on the Administration of Greater Berlin' dated 12 September 1944; and the associated supplementary agreements, including the Agreement on the Control Mechanism in Germany concluded between the governments of the USSR, the United States, the United Kingdom and France on 1 May 1945—that is, to say, the agreements which were to be effective during the first years following the surrender of Germany.

It is not difficult to see that all the Soviet government has done by this statement is to acknowledge the real state of affairs, which rests in the fact that the United States, Britain and France have long since abandoned the essentials of the treaties and agreements concluded during the war against Hitler's Germany and following her defeat. The Soviet government is doing no more than drawing conclusions which, the Soviet Union finds, follow inevitably from the actual state of affairs. In connection with the foregoing, and also proceeding from the principles of respect for the sovereignty of the German Democratic Republic, the Soviet government will enter into negotiations with the government of the German Democratic Republic at an appropriate moment, with a view to transferring to the German Democratic Republic the functions which the Soviet authorities have exercised temporarily in accordance with these Allied agreements, and also in accordance with the agreement between the USSR and the German Democratic Republic of 20 September 1955. . . .

The most correct and natural way to solve the problem would, of course, be for the western part of Berlin, which is virtually detached from the German Democratic Republic, to be reunited with its eastern part and for Berlin to become a single united city within the state on whose land it is situated.

However, the Soviet government, taking into account the present unrealistic policy of the United States, and also of the United Kingdom and France, with regard to the German Democratic Republic, cannot fail to see the difficulties the western powers have in contributing to such a solution of the Berlin problem. At the same time it is guided by concern to prevent the process of abolishing the occupation regime from involving anything like a painful disruption of the ways which have become entrenched in the life of the population of West Berlin.

One cannot, of course, fail to take into account the fact that the political and economic development of West Berlin, during its occupation by the three western powers, has differed from that of East Berlin and the German Democratic Republic, with the result that the way of life in the two parts of Berlin is entirely different at the present time. The Soviet government considers that upon the ending of foreign occupation, the population of West Berlin should be given the right to establish a way of life of its own choosing. Should the inhabitants of West Berlin desire to preserve the present way of life, based on private capitalist ownership, it is up to them to do so. The USSR, for its part, will respect any choice the West Berliners may make.

On the strength of all these considerations, the Soviet government finds it possible for the question of West Berlin to be settled for the time being by making West Berlin an independent political entity—a free city—without any state, including either of the existing German states, interfering in its life. It might be possible, in particular, to agree on the territory of the free city being demilitarized and having no armed forces on it. The free city of West Berlin could have its own government and could run its own economy and its administrative and other affairs.

The four powers, which shared in the administration of Berlin after the war, could, as could the two German states undertake to respect the status of West Berlin as a free city, just as has been done by the four powers, for instance, with regard to the neutral status which has been adopted by the Austrian Republic.

For its part, the Soviet government would have no objection to the United Nations also sharing, in one way or another, in observing the free-city status of West Berlin.

It is obvious that, taking into consideration the special position of West Berlin, which lies in the territory of the German Democratic Republic and is cut off from the outside world, the question would arise of some kind of arrangement with the German Democratic Republic concerning guarantees of unhindered communications between the free city and the outside world—both eastward and westward—with the aim of free movement for passenger and freight traffic. In its turn, West Berlin would commit itself not to tolerate on its territory hostile subversive activity directed against the German Democratic Republic or any other state. That solution to the problem of the status of West Berlin would be an important step towards normalizing the situation in Berlin, which, instead of being a hotbed of unrest and tension, could become a centre for contacts and co-operation between the two parts of Germany in the interests of Germany's peaceful future and the unity of the German nation.

The establishment of the status of a free city for West Berlin would make it possible to safeguard firmly the expansion of the economy of West Berlin, owing to its all-sided contacts with the eastern and western countries, and proper living standards for the population of the city. For its part, the Soviet Union declares that it will do its utmost to promote the attainment of these aims, especially by placing orders for an amount of manufactured goods that will fully ensure the stability and prosperity of the economy of the free city and also by regular systematic supplies of the necessary raw materials and foodstuffs to West Berlin on a commercial basis. Thus, West Berlin's population of over two million, far from suffering from the abolition of the occupation regime, would, on the contrary, have every possibility of raising their living standards.

If the government of the United States, as well as the governments of the United Kingdom and France, expresses its consent to examine the question of abolishing the present occupation regime in West Berlin by setting up a free city on its territory, the Soviet government would be willing, on behalf of the four powers, to enter into official contact on this question with the government of the German Democratic Republic, with which it has already held preliminary consultations before the despatch of the present Note.

It should, of course, be borne in mind that the consent of the German Democratic Republic to the setting up of such an independent political organism as the free city of West Berlin within its territory would be a concession, a definite sacrifice by the German Democratic Republic for the sake of strengthening peace in Europe, for the sake of the national interests of the German people as a whole.

The Soviet government, for its part, has resolved to carry out measures designed to abolish the occupation regime in Berlin, guided by the desire to normalize the situation in Berlin, in the interests of European peace, and in the interests of the peaceful and independent development of Germany. It hopes that the government of the United States will show a proper understanding of these motives and adopt a realistic attitude on the Berlin issue.

At the same time the Soviet government is ready to open negotiations with the governments of the United States and other countries concerned, on granting West Berlin the status of a demilitarized free city. If this proposal is not acceptable to the United States government, there is no topic left for talks on the Berlin question by the former occupying powers.

The Soviet government strives for the necessary changes in the position of Berlin to be made in a calm atmosphere, without haste and unnecessary friction, with the maximum account being taken of the interests of the sides concerned.

It is obvious that some time is needed for the powers that occupied Germany after the defeat of the Nazi *Wehrmacht* to agree on proclaiming West Berlin a free city, provided, of course, that the western powers take a proper interest in this proposal. It should also be taken into consideration that the necessity may arise of talks between the city authorities of both parts of Berlin and also between the German Democratic Republic and the Federal Republic of Germany for a settlement of the issues that may arise.

In view of this the Soviet government proposes to make no changes in the present procedure for military traffic of the United States, the United Kingdom and France from West Berlin to the Federal Republic of Germany for half a year. It regards this period as quite adequate for finding a sound basis for a solution to the problems connected with the change in the position of Berlin and for preventing the possibility of any complications if, of course, the governments of the western powers do not deliberately work for such complications.

During this period the parties will have the possibility of proving, by settling the Berlin issue, their desire for a relaxation of international tension.

If the above period is not used for reaching an appropriate agreement, the Soviet Union will effect the planned measures by agreement with the German Democratic Republic.

It is envisaged that the German Democratic Republic, like any other independent state, must fully control questions concerning its space, that is to say, exercise its sovereignty on land, on water and in the air. At the same time, there will be an end to all the contacts still maintained between representatives of the armed forces and other officials of the United States, the United Kingdom and France on questions relating to Berlin.

*

The Berlin crisis continued to worry Europe. The exodus of people from the German Democratic Republic, mainly the young and the qualified, weakened the Ulbricht regime. In July 1961 alone, 30,000 citizens of the GDR fled to the west. Nearly all of these used the escape hatch of Berlin. In a speech of 10 August Ulbricht had announced that the GDR government had decided to take measures to stop the 'traffic in human beings'. In the night of 12 to 13 August troops of the GDR, strengthened by police and workers' militias, closed the sector borders. On 13 August the statement of the Warsaw Treaty powers was published. It had clearly been drawn up two weeks earlier because the Warsaw Treaty conference had met in Moscow from 3 to 5 August. Two days later the building of the wall commenced.

DOCUMENT 27. EXTRACT FROM A STATEMENT BY WARSAW TREATY MEMBER STATES, 13 AUGUST 1961 (*Pravda*, 15 AUGUST 1961)

The western powers, far from having made any efforts to normalize the situation in West Berlin, on the contrary continue to use it intensively as a centre of subversive activities against the German Democratic Republic and all other countries of the socialist commonwealth. In no other part of the world are so many espionage and subversion centres of foreign states to be found as in West Berlin and nowhere else can they act with such impunity. These numerous subversion centres are smuggling their agents into the German Democratic Republic for all kinds of subversion, recruiting spies and inciting hostile elements to organize sabotage and provoke disturbances in the German Democratic Republic.

The present situation with regard to movement on the borders of West Berlin is being used by the ruling circles of the Federal Republic of Germany and intelligence agencies of the NATO countries to undermine the economy of the German Democratic Republic. Government bodies and military concerns of the Federal Republic of Germany, through deceit, bribery and blackmail, are making some unstable elements in the German Democratic Republic leave for Western Germany. These deluded people are compelled to serve with the *Bundeswehr* and are recruited into the intelligence agencies of various countries to be sent back to the German Democratic Republic as spies and saboteurs. A special fund has even been instituted for such subversive activities against the German Democratic Republic and other socialist countries. Recently the West German chancellor, Adenauer, asked the NATO governments to augment this fund.

It is highly significant that the subversive activities directed from West Berlin have greatly increased recently, immediately after the Soviet Union, the German Democratic Republic and other socialist countries put forward proposals for an immediate peace settlement with Germany. This subversive activity not only does harm to the German Democratic Republic but also affects the interests of other countries of the socialist camp.

In the face of the aggressive aspirations of the reactionary forces of the Federal Republic of Germany and its NATO allies, the Warsaw Treaty member states cannot but take the necessary measures to ensure their security, and primarily the security of the German Democratic Republic in the interests of the German people themselves.

The governments of the Warsaw Treaty member states address the People's Chamber and the government of the German Democratic Republic and all working people of the German Democratic Republic with a proposal that a procedure be established on the borders of West Berlin which will securely block the way to the subversive activity against the countries of the socialist camp, so that reliable safeguards and effective control may be established round the whole territory of West Berlin, including its border with democratic Berlin. It is understood that these measures must not affect the existing order of traffic and control on the ways of communication between West Berlin and Western Germany.

The governments of the Warsaw Treaty member states realize, of course, that protective measures along the borders of West Berlin will somewhat inconvenience the population. But the entire responsibility for the existing situation rests exclusively with the western powers, and with the Federal Republic of Germany in the first place. If the borders of West Berlin have so far remained open, this has been done in the hope that the western powers would not abuse the good will of the government of the German Democratic Republic. But, disregarding the interests of the German people and the population of Berlin, they have used the procedure now operating on the border of West Berlin for their own perfidious, subversive ends. Stronger protection and control on the border with West Berlin must put an end to the present abnormal situation.

At the same time the governments of the Warsaw Treaty member states find it necessary to emphasize that this necessity will disappear when a peace settlement with Germany is achieved and the questions awaiting a solution have been settled on this basis.

*

Khrushchev's reaction to the U-2 incident as portrayed in this speech is an example of his brilliant oratorical talent and his dramatic sense. He had previously, on 5 May, announced that a US reconnaissance plane had been brought down on Soviet territory thus giving Washington the opportunity to concoct its fantastic tale of which Khrushchev made such sport.

A month later both he and Marshal Malinovsky announced that the USSR would strike, if need be with nuclear weapons, on those countries that permitted overflights of Soviet territory. Thus the Soviets promised military protection to all the countries of the socialist camp—a promise that they were unable to honour in the case of either Cuba or Vietnam. To the Chinese this was another example of Khrushchevian bluff.

The U-2 incident was the cause, real or ostensible, for the failure of the Paris summit meeting with Eisenhower later in the month.

DOCUMENT 28. EXTRACT FROM A SPEECH BY KHRUSHCHEV TO THE SUPREME SOVIET CONCERNING THE VIOLATION OF SOVIET AIR SPACE BY A U-2 SPY PLANE, 7 MAY 1960 (*SN*, 9 MAY 1960)

Comrades, Deputies, the act of aggression against the Soviet Union committed by the American Air Force, has justly angered the Deputies and all the Soviet people. Many inquiries and appeals are being received by the session and by the Soviet government. In view of this, permit me once again to dwell on this question, and to furnish certain new information.

After the report I made to the Supreme Soviet in which I dwelt on this incident, the US State Department claimed, in an official press statement, that the point in question was the violation of the Soviet state frontier by an American aircraft of the Lockheed U-2 type, which was allegedly studying weather conditions in the upper layers of the atmosphere in the area of the Turkish-Soviet frontier. This plane, allegedly, had strayed from its course because the pilot had oxygen trouble. The State Department asserts that the pilot lost consciousness and that the plane, steered by its automatic pilot, flew into Soviet territory. According to the State Department, the pilot only had time to report the failure of his oxygen equipment back to the Turkish airfield at Adana from which he had flown—an airfield which,

allegedly, belongs not to the military but to the National Aeronautics and Space Administration.

Soon after that, the National Aeronautics and Space Administration issued a statement with a view to confirming the State
Department's version. Here is what the statement said: 'One of
the N.A.S.A.'s U-2 research airplanes, in use since 1956 in continuing the programme to study gust-meteorological conditions
found at high altitude, has been missing since about nine o'clock
on May 1 (local time) when its pilot reported he was having
oxygen difficulties over Lake Van, Turkey.'

Comrades, I must tell you a secret. When I was making my
report, I deliberately did not say that the pilot was alive and in
good health and that we have got parts of the plane. We did
this deliberately, because if we had told everything at once, the
Americans would have invented another story.

And now, just look how many silly things they have said—
Lake Van, scientific research, and so on and so forth. Now that
they know that the pilot is alive they will have to invent something else—and they will do it.

Then their statement goes on to say: 'The airplane had taken
off from Incirlik air base, Turkey. The flight plan called for
the first checkpoint to be at 37° 25′ North, 41° 23′ East, and for
a left-hand turn to Lake Van beacon, thence to Trabazon
beacon, thence to Antalya and return to Adana.'

This is the 'precise' information they have given. In a little
while I shall tell you how matters stood in reality.

The flight schedule was estimated at 3 hours 45 minutes for a
total of 1,400 nautical miles. Take-off was at 8 a.m. local
time. About one hour after take-off, the pilot reported difficulties with his oxygen equipment. Using emergency radio
frequency, he reported he was heading for Lake Van beacon
to get his bearings, and that he would return to Adana.

As has already been indicated, the statement goes on to say
that his flight plan called for him to make a left turn at Lake
Van beacon. 'His last report indicated he was attempting to
receive that beacon. It is believed that he was probably on a
north-easterly course, but there was no further word. Aerial
search was begun soon after the receipt of the last communication. The Lake Van area is mountainous and very rugged.'

The statement about the mountainous nature of the Lake Van area is quite correct. 'No evidence has been cited of an aircraft having crashed.' This is also correct, because this plane could not have crashed there.

Then the statement describes in detail the instrumentation carried by the plane and the 'peaceful' purposes of its flight. Permit me to give one more quotation: 'The instrumentation carried by the U-2 permits obtaining more precise information about clear air turbulence, convective clouds, wind shear, jet stream and such widespread weather patterns as typhoons.' The State Department indeed launched a 'typhoon'.

'The airplane has also been used by N.A.S.A. to obtain information about cosmic rays and the concentration of certain elements in the atmosphere, including ozone and water vapour.'

These are the official versions put into circulation by American officials to mislead public opinion in their country and throughout the world. I must declare, comrade Deputies, that these versions are completely untrue and aimed at simple-minded people. The authors of these accounts assumed that if the plane had been shot down the pilot had most probably perished as well. So there would be nobody who could be asked how everything had actually happened and there would be no way of checking what kind of plane it was, and what instruments it carried.

In the first place, I wish to announce that the pilot of the shot-down American plane is alive and in good health. He is now in Moscow. The remains of this plane and its special instrumentation, discovered during the investigation, have also been brought here.

The name of the pilot is Francis Harry Powers. He is thirty years old. He says he is First Lieutenant of the United States Air Force, in which he served until 1956—that is to say, until the day on which he went over to the Central Intelligence Agency.

Francis Powers reported, incidentally, that while serving with the American Air Force he used to get 700 dollars a month, but when he went over to the Intelligence Service and started carrying out spying assignments to glean secret information, he began receiving 2,500 dollars a month. That is how capital buys lives, buys people. The pilot has testified that he experienced no dizziness, nor did his oxygen apparatus fail. He was flying along his assigned course, accurately carrying out the orders of his chiefs, switching his equipment on and off over the pre-selected targets, to glean intelligence of the Soviet Union's military and industrial establishments; and he flew on until the very moment that his piratical flight into the interior of this country was cut short.

I want to tell you something about the results of the examination of the shot-down plane and of its equipment, as well as about the results of the interrogation of the pilot. The inquiry is still going on, but the picture is already fairly clear.

To start with, this was indeed a high-altitude low-speed Lockheed U-2. They banked on its high altitude and believed that this plane could not be brought down by any fighter or anti-aircraft artillery. That is why they thought it could fly over Soviet territory with impunity. In fact the plane did fly at a great altitude, and it was hit by the rocket at an altitude of 20,000 metres. And if they fly higher, we shall also hit them! The plane was in no way equipped for 'upper atmosphere research', or for taking 'air samples' as official American spokesmen assert. Not at all. This was a real military reconnaissance aircraft, fitted with various instruments for collecting intelligence and, among other things, for aerial photography.

The competent commission of experts which examined the wrecked plane has established from documentary evidence that this American plane is a specially prepared reconnaissance aircraft. The task of the plane was to cross the whole territory of the Soviet Union from the Pamirs to the Kola Peninsula to get information on our country's military and industrial establishments by means of aerial photography. In addition to aerial cameras, the plane carried other reconnaissance equipment for spotting radar networks, identifying the location and frequencies of operating radio stations, and other special radio engineering equipment.

Not only do we have the equipment of the plane, but we also have the developed film showing a number of areas of our territory. Here are some of these photographs.

Here are the photos of these airfields. Here are two white lines. They are lines of our fighters. Here is another airfield, also with planes on it. All these films we developed ourselves.

I am handing these photographs to Comrade Lobanov—let him examine them.

Here are the photographs of petrol stores. It must be said that the camera is not a bad one, and the photograph is very accurate. But I must say that our cameras take better pictures and are more accurate, so that we have gained little in this respect.

These photographs here show industrial enterprises. Comrade Chairman, please take these photos too.

There is also a tape-recording of the signals of a number of our ground radar stations. These are incontestable evidence of the espionage carried out by the American plane—shot down in the neighbourhood of Sverdlovsk.

These are the kind of 'air samples' the American reconnaissance plane took—and it took them, not over Lake Van in Turkey, but at quite another spot.

The story that the airman was suffering from dizziness owing to a failure in the oxygen equipment had its origin, apparently, in the US State Department and the Pentagon, as a result of the sudden shock caused there because the unsuccessful piratical flight over Soviet territory had become known to the entire world. And the men who were accessories to this marauding flight could not invent anything but the stupid story that it was, so they said, a meteorological plane, and when the oxygen equipment failed, and the pilot lost consciousness, his plane, like a horse out of control, against the pilot's will, dragged him into Soviet territory. What naiveté!

The only thing that is true is that this plane was stationed at the American Turkish air base at Incirlik, east of Adana. As the pilot Powers testifies, he was serving with the 10-10 unit which —just for the sake of camouflage—comes under the control of the National Aeronautics and Space Administration, but which is in reality conducting high-altitude military reconnaissance.

In his depositions, Powers has mentioned the names of several officers he served with at the American military base in Turkey. According to Powers's testimony, the commander of the American 10-10 unit is Colonel William Shelton, and his deputy is Lieutenant-Colonel Carol Funk.

Before his flight, Powers had long trained himself for flying deep into this country and, as he himself said, he had flown along the Soviet frontier many times in order to study the radar system of the Soviet Union.

On 27 April Powers, the spy, on orders from his superiors, flew over from the Turkish city of Adana to the Peshawar airfield in Pakistan. It was, therefore, from Pakistan's territory— that is to say, from the Peshawar airfield and not from the Turkish airfield outside Adana, as was stated in the account given by the State Department of the United States—that Powers took off on 1 May, with instructions to fly along the course indicated on his map over the Aral Sea, Sverdlovsk and other points, to reach Archangel and Murmansk before landing at the Budoe airfield in Norway.

We can now say where he was flying to. I must admit that we knew it already when I was reporting this event. We did not say anything at that time, in order to see what the Americans would invent. Now that they have made their invention, we are reporting how everything really happened.

This is what Powers said when questioned about the task of his flight over Soviet territory.

I was to take off from the Peshawar airfield in Pakistan, cross the national frontier of the USSR and fly across Soviet territory to Norway (the Budoe airfield). I was to fly over certain points in the USSR, of which I remember Murmansk and Archangel. During my flight over Soviet territory I was to switch the equipment on and off over certain points indicated on the map. I believe my flight over Soviet territory was intended to collect information on Soviet guided missile and radar stations.

I want to ask the gentlemen of the State Department: Was it such 'air samples over Lake Van' that the pilot Powers, the spy, was to take?

I will say nothing of the fact that, in flying along this course, the American reconnaissance plane has grossly violated the national sovereignty of Afghanistan by flying across that country's territory without permission. But there is, perhaps, nothing out of the ordinary in that for the morals of the American militarists. Such actions of theirs have long been known. It is sufficient to recall the flights of American military aircraft over Austrian territory when aggression was being prepared against Iraq, where a revolution had just taken place. The Austrian government protested against the treacherous violation of Austria's sovereignty by American military aircraft and against that blatant act of disrespect for her neutrality, sealed by the signatures of the United States among others.

If one is to believe the account that the pilot lost consciousness owing to oxygen trouble and that the aircraft was subsequently controlled by the automatic pilot, you must also believe that the aircraft controlled by an automatic pilot flew from Turkey to Pakistan, touched down at Peshawar airport, stayed there three days, took off early on the morning of 1 May, flew over the territory of Afghanistan, crossed the Soviet frontier and flew more than 2,000 kilometres over our territory for a total of some four hours. Throughout the time of the flight over our territory the aircraft was under observation, and it was brought down as soon as the order was given.

When our anti-aircraft rocket battery intercepted the plane and brought it down, the pilot, it must be believed, soon 'regained consciousness', because he baled out by parachute; he was not, please note, ejected by the automatic device, but left through the upper cover, designed for getting into the plane. The question arises, why did he do this, when there are devices for rapid ejection?

Possibly he did it because there was an explosive charge in the aircraft, which was to have blown up the plane as soon as the pilot had been ejected. The pilot knew this and was possibly afraid that he would be killed in the explosion. He was quite right!

But the installation of the explosive charge was not the only precaution taken. To cover up the tracks of the crime, the pilot was told that he must not fall into the hands of the Soviet authorities alive. For this reason he was supplied with a special needle. He was to have pricked himself with this poisoned needle, resulting in instantaneous death.

What barbarism! Here is this instrument—the latest achievement of American technology for killing their own people.

But everything alive wants to live and when the plane was brought down the pilot baled out by parachute. And when he landed he did not follow the advice of those who had sent him on his predatory anti-Soviet assignment, but remained alive.

It is alleged that the flight was made for scientific purposes, to investigate the upper layers of the atmosphere. Why, then, the question arises, did the pilot have to be armed with a silenced pistol? He was given it for some emergency, not for taking air samples but for blowing people's brains out. All this we shall present to the public as material evidence. This, you may say, is what such Christians are like! He was given this pistol after making low bows as they do in churches. And yet they call us godless atheists. But we have never committed such crimes against humanity and never will. If the pilot was given a pistol with which to defend himself against wild beasts in the event of a forced landing, the question arises, why a pistol with a silencer? This also shows what so-called scientific purposes the plane was pursuing.

The pilot, who was supposed to explore the atmosphere, was given 7,500 roubles in Soviet currency. The question arises, when and where was he to have spent them, and for what purposes? Surely he did not fly in order to exchange old roubles for the new ones?

The pilot was also given French gold francs. I have seen these gold francs with my own eyes. And you can see them here in the photograph. They are covered with cellophane on both sides of the coins. Done in a cultured American way. But what did the pilot need those francs for? He also had West German, Italian and other currency. Besides his own watch, he was also given for his trip two other gold watches and seven ladies' gold rings. Why was all this necessary in the upper layers of the atmosphere? Or perhaps the pilot was to have flown still higher, to Mars, and was going to lead Martian ladies astray?

You see with what careful consideration American pilots are equipped before setting off on a flight to take samples of air in the upper layers of the atmosphere.

No concocted story, therefore, can save the reputation of those who bear the responsibility for this treacherous act.

They have been caught red-handed as the organizers of an incursion into the air space of the Soviet Union such a short time before the meeting of the heads of government in Paris, such a short time before the visit to the Soviet Union of the president of the United States. I believe that this is a bad preparation for serious talks on easing international tension.

I am now reading in the western press comments on these

events, and there are some people who actually accuse nobody else but us! Khrushchev, they say, wants to undermine the summit meeting, because otherwise he would not have brought up this incident at the session of the Supreme Soviet but would have raised it through some other channels.

But what did you expect, gentlemen? You are used to making mischief, and some people regard this almost as a good thing and keep silent! No, we are not people of that kind! If you have made mischief, bear the responsibility for it openly. They live according to the law: if you are rich, you will not be sent to prison. This is true for the capitalist, because he can always buy himself off. But there is another country, there are the countries of socialism, where the law, the state, society, protect everyone living in that state.

What could be the reason for such a reckless step? It was evidently taken because someone in the United States was obsessed with the idea of intelligence. The United States 'open skies' proposal is well known. We rejected that proposal and the American military then decided to 'open' the Soviet sky by themselves. But there are rules of international law, there are national frontiers and no one has the right to disregard those laws or to cross the frontiers of other countries.

DOCUMENT 29. EXTRACT FROM KHRUSHCHEV'S PRESS CONFERENCE IN MOSCOW, 3 JUNE 1960 (*SN*, 7 JUNE 1960)

SHAPIRO (United Press International): What is your attitude to the statement made by Marshal Malinovsky ... on the order issued to the commander of the rocket forces to strike at the take-off bases of aircraft if the airspace of the Soviet Union and other communist countries is violated?

KHRUSHCHEV: I ask you to understand it literally, as Marshal Malinovsky, the minister of defence put it. He has said clearly enough that planes intruding into our air space, enemy planes, will be shot down and crushing blows by rocket forces will be struck at the bases from which they have taken off. The government has issued instructions to this effect to the minister of defence and the minister has issued an order to the commander of the rocket forces.

Why did we do this? Because the leaders of the United States have insisted, and still say, that they reserve the right to fly over our territory for reconnaissance purposes. They explain this right by the necessity for safeguarding the defence of the United States and its allies—its satellites . . .

TATU (*Le Monde*): Does it mean . . . that the Soviet Union will strike with rockets at bases where aircraft take off carrying atomic or hydrogen weapons? . . .

KHRUSHCHEV: What weapons will strike at bases which are used against the Soviet Union—this is a detail which falls within the competence of Marshal Nedelin, the commander-in-chief of the rocket forces. And we have an adequate assortment of rockets. He will find appropriate means to strike the enemy and to discourage the provocateurs from attacking our country.

Each country has the full possibility of avoiding such retaliation. This calls for very little: not to allow the American aggressors to use their land for military bases against the Soviet Union. But above all it would be better to abolish these bases and then the question would no longer arise. The Soviet Union threatens no one. We only warn that we will defend ourselves against aggression by all available means.

*

In spite of persistent rumours of a missile build-up on Cuba, American reconnaissance planes were only to find concrete evidence of this on 14 October 1962 when they photographed a launching pad and intermediate-range missiles. President Kennedy was informed of this discovery on 16 October after his advisers had convinced themselves that there was no mistake. It took the administration nearly a week to decide whether it was going to wipe out this danger by military action or by instituting quarantine round Cuba. Fortunately, for the peace of the world, the second course prevailed, and Kennedy was skilful enough to allow the Soviets to extricate themselves from the adventure without too much loss of prestige.

The crisis did however weaken Khrushchev personally both as regards his Chinese critics and his internal critics. This was evident in the beginnings of an internal neo-Stalinist course which has continued under his successors. Khrushchev began attacking the very limited freedom that Soviet intellectuals enjoyed, going into an obscene tantrum about abstract paintings at a Moscow art exhibition. The attack on art was soon extended into an attack on Yugoslav revisionism.

DOCUMENT 30. ROBERT KENNEDY'S ACCOUNT OF THE MEETING BETWEEN PRESIDENT KENNEDY AND THE SOVIET FOREIGN MINISTER, ANDREI GROMYKO, ON THURSDAY, 18 OCTOBER 1962 (R. F. KENNEDY, *Thirteen Days: The Cuban Missile Crisis*, MACMILLAN, 1969, PP. 43–6)

In the midst of all these discussions, Andrei Gromyko came to see the President. It was an appointment made long before the missiles were uncovered, and the President felt it would be awkward to cancel it. He debated whether he should confront the Soviet Foreign Minister with our knowledge of the missiles' presence and finally decided that, as he had not yet determined a final course of action and the disclosure of our knowledge might give the Russians the initiative, he would simply listen to Gromyko.

They met late Thursday afternoon in the President's office in the White House. Gromyko began the conversation by saying the United States should stop threatening Cuba. All Cuba wanted was peaceful co-existence, he said; she was not interested in exporting her system to other Latin American countries. Cuba, like the Soviet Union, wanted only peace. Premier Khrushchev had instructed him, Gromyko said, to tell President Kennedy that the only assistance being furnished Cuba was for agriculture and land development, so the people could feed themselves, plus a small amount of defensive arms. In view of all the publicity in the American Press, he said, he wanted to emphasize that the Soviet Union would never become involved in the furnishing of offensive weapons to Cuba.

Gromyko said he wished to appeal to the United States and to President Kennedy on behalf of Premier Khrushchev and the Soviet Union to lessen the tensions that existed with regard to Cuba.

President Kennedy listened, astonished, but also with some admiration for the boldness of Gromyko's position. Finally, but with great restraint considering the provocation, he told Gromyko that it was not the United States which was fomenting discord, but the Soviet Union. The USSR's supplying of arms to Cuba was having a profound effect on the people of the United States and was a source of great concern to him. Because of the personal assurances he had received from Khrushchev, he had been taking the public position that no action was required against Cuba, and yet the situation was becoming steadily more dangerous.

Gromyko repeated that the sole objective of the USSR was to give bread to Cuba in order to prevent hunger in that country. As far as arms were concerned, the Soviet Union had simply sent some specialists to train Cubans to handle certain kinds of armament, which were only 'defensive'. He then said he wished to emphasize the word 'defensive' and that none of those weapons could ever constitute a threat to the United States.

The President replied that there should be no misunderstanding of the position of the United States—that the position had been made clear to the Soviet Union in meetings between the Attorney General and Ambassador Dobrynin and in his own public statements. To avoid any misunderstanding, he read aloud his statement of 4 September, which pointed out the serious consequences which would arise if the Soviet Union placed missiles or offensive weapons within Cuba.

Gromyko assured him this would never be done, that the United States should not be concerned. After touching briefly on some other matters, he said goodbye.

I came by shortly after Gromyko left the White House. The President of the United States, it can be said, was displeased with the spokesman of the Soviet Union.

DOCUMENT 31. EXTRACT FROM KHRUSHCHEV'S REPORT TO THE SUPREME SOVIET CONCERNING THE CUBAN MISSILE CRISIS, 12 DECEMBER 1962 (*SN*, 13 DECEMBER 1962)

Comrade Deputies, everyone still remembers the tense days of October when mankind was anxiously listening to the news coming from the Caribbean. In those days the world was on the brink of a thermo-nuclear catastrophe.

What created this crisis? How did it develop? What lessons must be learned from it? These questions call for a penetrating analysis which will help the peace forces better to understand the resulting situation and to define their tasks in the struggle for the further maintenance and consolidation of peace. . . .

The victory of the revolution in Cuba and her success in building a new life gave rise to an outburst of malice among the imperialist circles of the United States of America.

The imperialists are frightened of Cuba because of her ideas. They do not want to reconcile themselves to the idea that little Cuba has dared to live and develop independently, as her people want to, and not in the way which would please the American monopolies. But the question of how people are to live, what road they are to take, is an internal matter for each people!

Flouting the generally accepted standards of international relations, the United States reactionary forces have been doing everything from the first day of the victory of the Cuban revolution to overthrow Cuba's revolutionary government and to restore their domination there. They broke off diplomatic relations with Cuba, have conducted and are conducting subversive activity and established an economic blockade of Cuba.

Threatening to apply sanctions, the United States began to press its allies not only to stop trading with Cuba, but even not to make ships available to carry food to Cuba from the socialist countries which came to the assistance of their brothers. This is an anti-human policy—a desire to starve a whole nation.

But even this seemed insufficient to them. Assuming the functions of a policeman, they decided to take the path of military suppression of the Cuban revolution. In other words, they wanted to usurp the right to export counter-revolution.

United States policy *vis-à-vis* Cuba is the most unbridled, reactionary policy. To declare that Cuba threatens America, or any other country, and on this plea to usurp a special right to act against Cuba, is just monstrous.

Seeking to justify its aggressive actions, American reaction is repeating that the crisis in the Caribbean was created by Cuba herself, adding that blame also rests with the Soviet Union which shipped rockets and IL-28 bombers there.

Yet is this so? It is true that we carried weapons there at the request of the Cuban government. But by what motives were we guided in doing that? Exclusively, humanitarian motives— Cuba needed weapons as a means of deterring the aggressors, and not as a means of attack. For Cuba was under a real threat of invasion. Piratical attacks were repeatedly being made on her coasts; Havana was shelled, and airborne groups were dropped from planes in order to carry out sabotage.

A large-scale military invasion of Cuba by counter-revolutionary mercenaries was launched on Cuba in April of last year. This invasion was prepared and carried out with full support on the part of the United States.

Further events have shown that the failure of the invasion did not discourage the United States imperialists in their desire to strangle Cuba. They began preparing another attack. In the autumn of this year a very alarming situation was created. Everything indicated that the United States was preparing to attack the Cuban Republic, with its own armed forces.

Revolutionary Cuba was compelled to take all measures to strengthen her defence. The Soviet Union helped her to build up a strong army standing guard over the achievements of the Cuban people. In view of the mounting threat from the United States, the government of Cuba, in the summer of this year, requested the Soviet government to render further assistance.

Agreement was reached on a number of new measures, including the stationing of a couple of score of Soviet IRBMs [Intermediate Range Ballistic Missiles] in Cuba. These weapons were to be in the hands of Soviet military men.

What were the aims behind this decision? Naturally neither we nor our Cuban friends had in mind that this small number of IRBMs sent to Cuba would be used for an attack on the United States or any other country.

Our aim was only to defend Cuba. Everybody saw how the American imperialists were sharpening their knives and threatening Cuba with a massed attack. We could not remain impartial observers in face of this bandit-like policy which was contrary to all the standards governing relations between states and contrary to the United Nations Charter. We decided to extend a helping hand to Cuba. We saw a possibility of protecting the freedom-loving people of Cuba by installing rockets there so that the American imperialists, if they really decided to invade, would realize that the war which they threatened to start stood at their own borders, so that they would realize more realistically the dangers of thermo-nuclear war. . . .

Some people pretend that the rockets were supplied by us for an attack on the United States. This, of course, is not wise reasoning. Why should we station rockets in Cuba for this purpose, when we were and are able to strike from our own territory, possessing as we do the necessary number of intercontinental missiles of the required range and power.

We do not in general need military bases abroad. All people who have any understanding of military matters know that in the age of intercontinental and global rockets, Cuba—that small far-away island which is only fifty kilometres wide in some places—is of no strategic importance for the defence of the Soviet Union. We stationed rockets in Cuba only for the defence of the Cuban Republic, and not for an attack on the United States. Such a small country as Cuba cannot, naturally, build up forces such as could launch an offensive against so big a country as the United States.

Only people who have taken leave of their senses can claim that the Soviet Union chose Cuba as a springboard for an invasion of the American continent—of the United States or countries of Latin America. If we wanted to start a war against the United States, we would not have agreed to dismantle the rockets installed in Cuba, which were ready for launching, for battle. We would have used them. But we did not do that, because we did not pursue such aims.

Thus, all the talk about Cuba being converted into a base for an attack on the United States of America is a vicious lie. The purpose of that lie was to cover up the plans for aggression against Cuba. We are loyal to Lenin's principles of peaceful co-existence and we consider that all disputes among states should be settled by peaceful means, by means of negotiations.

Developments in the Caribbean confirmed that there was a threat of such aggression. In the last ten days of October, a large-scale build-up of US naval and air forces, paratroopers and marines began in the south of the United States, on the approaches to Cuba. The US government sent reinforcements to its naval base at Guantanamo, lying on Cuban territory. Big military manoeuvres were announced in the Caribbean. In the course of those 'manoeuvres', a landing was to be made on the island of Vieques. On 22 October, Kennedy's administration announced a quarantine of Cuba. The word 'quarantine', by the way, was merely a fig-leaf in this case. Actually it was a blockade, piracy on the high seas.

Events developed rapidly. The American command alerted all its armed forces, including its troops in Europe, and also the Sixth Fleet in the Mediterranean and the Seventh Fleet based in the area of Taiwan.

Several airborne infantry and armoured divisions, numbering about 100,000 men, were set aside for an attack on Cuba alone. Moreover, 183 warships with 85,000 naval personnel were moved to the shores of Cuba. The landing on Cuba was to be covered by several thousand military planes. Close to 20 per cent of all the planes of the US strategic air command were kept in the air round the clock, carrying atom and hydrogen bombs. Reservists were called up.

The troops of the United States NATO allies in Europe were also put on the alert. A joint command was set up by the United States and Latin American countries, and some of these countries sent warships to take part in the blockade of Cuba. As a result of these aggressive steps on the part of the US government there arose a threat of thermo-nuclear war.

In the face of these intensified military preparations, we, for our part, had to take appropriate measures. The Soviet government instructed the USSR minister of defence to alert all the armed forces of the Soviet Union, and above all the Soviet intercontinental and strategic rocket forces, the rocket anti-aircraft defences and the fighter command, the strategic air command, and the navy. Our submarine fleet, including atomic submarines, took up assigned positions. A state of increased military readiness was announced in the ground forces, and the discharge of servicemen of senior age groups from the strategic rocket forces, the anti-aircraft defence forces and the submarine fleet was halted.

The armed forces of the Warsaw Treaty countries were also fully alerted.

In these conditions, if one or the other side had not shown restraint, had not done everything necessary to avert the outbreak of war, an explosion would have followed with irreparable consequences.

Now, when the tension caused by the events in the Caribbean has been reduced, when we are in the last stage of settling the conflict, I should like to report to the Deputies of the Supreme Soviet what the Soviet government did to extinguish the approaching flames of war.

On 23 October, immediately after the United States had proclaimed the blockade of Cuba, the Soviet government, besides taking defensive measures, issued a statement resolutely warning that the United States government was assuming a grave responsibility for the fate of the peace and was recklessly playing with fire. We frankly told the United States president that we would not tolerate piratical actions by United States ships on the high seas and that we would take appropriate measures with this object in view.

At the same time the Soviet government urged all peoples to bar the road to the aggressors. Simultaneously it took certain steps in the United Nations. The peaceful initiative of the Soviet government in settling the Cuban crisis met with full support from the socialist countries and the peoples of most other United Nations member states. The United Nations secretary-general, U Thant, made great efforts to settle the conflict.

However, the government of the United States of America continued to worsen the situation. Militarist forces in the United States were pushing developments towards an attack on Cuba. On the morning of 27 October, we received informations from the Cuban comrades and from other sources which bluntly said that the invasion would be carried out within the next two or three days. We assessed the messages received as a signal of the utmost alarm. And this was a well-founded alarm.

Immediate action was needed to prevent an invasion of Cuba and to preserve peace. A message proposing a mutually acceptable solution was sent to the United States president. At that moment it was not yet too late to extinguish the fuse of war which had already been set alight. In sending this message we took into consideration the fact that the messages of the president himself had expressed anxiety and a desire to find a way out of the existing situation. We declared that if the United States undertook not to invade Cuba and would also restrain other states allied with it from aggression against Cuba, the Soviet Union would be willing to remove from Cuba the weapons which the United States described as 'offensive'.

The United States president replied by declaring that if the Soviet government agreed to remove these weapons from Cuba the American government would lift the quarantine, i.e. the blockade, and would give an assurance on renunciation of the invasion of Cuba both by the United States itself and other countries of the western hemisphere. The president declared quite definitely, and this is known to the whole world, that the United States would not attack Cuba and would also restrain its allies from such actions.

But we shipped our weapons to Cuba precisely for the purpose of preventing aggression against her. That was why the Soviet government reaffirmed its agreement to remove the ballistic rockets from Cuba.

Thus, briefly speaking, a mutually acceptable solution was achieved, which meant a victory for reason, a success for the cause of peace. The Cuban question entered into the stage of peaceful talks and, as regards the United States, was, so to speak, transferred from the generals to the diplomats. . . .

Which side triumphed? Who won? In this connection it can be said that it was reason, the cause of peace and the security of peoples, that won. The two sides displayed a sober approach and took into account that unless such steps were taken as could help to overcome the dangerous development of events, a Third World War might break out. . . .

Now let us imagine for a minute what could have happened had we copied diehard politicians and refused to make mutual concessions. It would have been like the two goats in the folk tale who met on a footbridge over a chasm and having locked their horns refused to make way for each other.

As is well known, both crashed into the chasm. But is this a reasonable course for human beings?

Among the ruling circles of the United States there are some politicians who are rightly called 'madmen'. The 'madmen' insisted and continue to insist on starting war as soon as possible against the Soviet Union and the countries of the socialist camp. Is it not clear that if we had taken an uncompromising position, we would only have helped the camp of the 'madmen' to take advantage of the situation in order to strike a blow at Cuba and touch off a world war?

In justice, it should be noted that among the leading circles of the United States, there are also some people who take a more sane view of the situation and, considering the present balance of forces in the international arena, realize that, if the United States touched off a war, it would not win it, and would fail to achieve its purpose. . . .

Why do I recall such rather unpleasant things as intercontinental missiles and atomic submarines? Merely because we are compelled to do this by the irresponsible statements of certain leaders of the United States and their allies.

When the events around Cuba were at their height, and danger was crackling in the air, many people in the west said it was necessary to seek a reasonable solution of disputes in order to prevent war. But now, when the shock has passed, so to speak, some of them are beginning to say that disputes should be settled on the basis of concessions by one side. This is an unwise and dangerous policy.

We are not surprised that the tune in the discordant choir of advocates of a 'tough line' is called by Adenauer and his like.

The West German revenge-seekers have for many years served the sinister cause of fanning military conflicts and are always ready to rush with inflammable materials where a crisis situation was developing. They cannot wait to add fuel to the flames in order to cause the conflagration of war. Adenauer dreams of revenge, and this is why he regards all international developments from the standpoint of how to secure more weapons for the *Bundeswehr* under the pretext of the need to resist the Soviet Union and the socialist camp, and how to set the Soviet Union and the United States on a collision course. Still I should like to tell Herr 'Cold War' Chancellor that there was no cause for him to rejoice at the 'toughness' of the west which allegedly forced us to withdraw rockets from Cuba. I can assure you, Herr Chancellor, that when we decided to install forty rockets in Cuba, we did not touch the 'share', so to speak, reserved for you, should you start aggression in Europe.

Now, when our rockets have returned from Cuba—to your 'satisfaction'—we have added them to the defensive means protecting our western frontiers.

Why then do you rejoice, Herr Adenauer? It would appear that you have forgotten the elementary rule of arithmetic that the sum total—in this case, the power of Soviet retaliation— does not depend on the order of the items.

It should be said that now the situation has become calmer in the world, 'toughness' is advocated not only by Adenauer, but by some other leaders as well.

Thus, the British foreign minister, Lord Home, said the other day that there are some signs that following the sobering experience of Cuba the Russians might possibly reconsider their role in the international community, that is to say, might begin to yield to the NATO bloc in everything. He said this is how the Soviet Union should 'apply' the lessons of Cuba now.

The British foreign minister should know that the Soviet Union always considers the lessons of international events. Those, however, who now advocate a 'tough policy' with regard to the Soviet Union, would do well to consider that if such a crisis recurs, and if this time it proves impossible to arrest the dangerous drift of events, Britain, together with her allies, would be plunged directly into the vortex of a catastrophe, and it would then be too late to do anything.

Warlike calls for 'toughness' have again begun to be made in the United States, too. What can we say of such imprudent boasters? They remind me of the hero of a certain hunting tale.

A man once went hunting with his dogs. The dogs started a hare. The hare kept ahead of the dogs for some time, but finally they began to overtake him. Suddenly the hare saw a hole in the ground and dived into it. Oh horror! . . . he found himself in a fox hole, and there were cubs there. The hare was very frightened, and asked in a tiny, timid voice:

'Little foxes, where is your mother?'

'Our mother went to get a chicken to feed us,' the cubs replied.

The hare then recovered some of his courage and said, in a gruff voice this time:

'Pity. I'd have shown her.'

In the same way, some western politicians now say: 'Pity, we would have shown the Soviet Union.' Well, gentlemen, try it!

It is not precluded that some madmen may start a war. But if they start it, then even a thousand wise people will be hard put to stop it. This is known from history. . . .

*

The improvement in Soviet-American relations continued after the fall of Khrushchev in spite of the Vietnamese war. The American involvement there had begun after the Geneva settlement of 1954 but it was not until the 1960s that it reached massive proportions. In 1965 the Americans launched a bomber offensive on North Vietnam, dropping more explosives there in three years than had been dropped on Germany throughout the Second World War. They believed that such hammering would bring the North Vietnamese to their knees, or at least to the negotiating table. In the event the North Vietnamese did come to talks in Paris but only after the bombing had ceased.

To the Soviets the escalation of war was both a danger and an opportunity. The danger lay in an extension of the war but they soon found it possible to give massive military aid to the North and yet keep on good terms with the Americans. The opportunity lay in the fact that the United States was involving much of its manpower in a war which it could not win and from which it could derive little credit. Moreover the protest movement against the war in America together with the re-newed activism of the Negroes gave hope of a permanent weakening of American society and of bringing along the conditions for that revolution which Marxists have so impatiently been waiting for.

It is, however, safe to say that the Vietnam war which has excited so many people in the west has had no popular resonance in the Soviet Union.

DOCUMENT 32. EXTRACT FROM BREZHNEV'S REPORT TO THE 23RD CONGRESS OF THE CPSU RELATING TO VIETNAM, 29 MARCH 1966 (*23rd Congress of the Communist Party of the Soviet Union*, NOVOSTI PRESS AGENCY, MOSCOW, 1966, PP. 43–5)

In speaking of mounting world tension and of the threat of a world war, special mention must be made of US imperialist aggression against Vietnam. In flagrant violation of the Geneva Agreements, the USA has piratically attacked the Democratic Republic of Vietnam and is waging a barbarous war against the people of South Vietnam. This imperialist power, which styles itself a champion of freedom and civilization, is using almost all the known means of destruction and annihilation against a peace-loving country situated thousands of miles away from America, a country that has never harmed US interests. More than 200,000 US troops, US aircraft carriers, huge bombers, poison gases and napalm are being used against the heroic patriots of Vietnam. Irresponsible statements threatening to escalate military operations still further are being made in Washington. Recently the US State Department officially declared that there is a 'programme' of destroying vegetation and crops in Vietnam with chemicals in order to deprive the Vietnamese of food sources. Such is the real face of US imperialism. Through its aggression in Vietnam the US has covered itself with shame which it will never live down.

But no matter what outrages the aggressors commit they can never break the will of the Vietnamese people who have risen in a sacred struggle for the freedom of their country, for their life and honour, for the right to order their own destiny. Their heroic, just struggle will go down in history as a splendid example of unyielding courage, staunchness and determination to achieve victory.

A powerful movement in support of Vietnam is mounting throughout the world. Moral and political isolation of the US aggressors is being intensified. The Vietnamese people enjoy the assistance of the Soviet Union and other socialist countries and the sympathy and support of the broad masses of all countries. Indignation against the war in Vietnam is growing among the American people as well. All this is promoting the best internationalist traditions of the world working class.

The Soviet Union and the peace-loving peoples of the whole world demand that the USA stops its aggression against Vietnam and withdraws all interventionist troops from that country. Continuation of this aggression, which the American military are seeking to extend to other South-East Asian countries, is fraught with the most dangerous consequences to world peace.

We categorically declare that if the aggressors escalate the shameful war against the Vietnamese people they will have to contend with mounting support for Vietnam from the Soviet Union and other socialist friends and brothers. The Vietnamese people will be the masters of their country and nobody will ever extinguish the torch of socialism, which has been raised on high by the Democratic Republic of Vietnam.

As a consequence of US aggression in Vietnam and other aggressive acts of American imperialism our relations with the United States of America have deteriorated. The US ruling circles are to blame for this.

*

Foreign danger has not brought the two communist giants closer together. On the contrary, the Vietnam war has given them another cause of dispute. The Chinese do not believe that the Soviets are doing enough to help Vietnam. They want a direct military involvement of Soviet troops there. Instead the Soviets have accused the Chinese of preventing the transport of war material to Vietnam through China by rail. Clearly the Chinese hoped it would go by sea and present the Americans with a temptation to seize Soviet ships.

The war in south-east Asia has enabled the Soviets to make their presence felt in areas which had been in the Chinese sphere of influence. This Chinese version of events has been neither confirmed nor denied by the Soviets.

DOCUMENT 33. EXTRACT FROM THE *People's Daily* OF 11 NOVEMBER 1965 ON SOVIET ATTEMPTS TO ACT AS MEDIATORS IN VIETNAM (*Peking Review*, 12 NOVEMBER 1965)

In January 1965 the US imperialists asked the Soviet government to use its influence to have the government of the Democratic Republic of Vietnam accept two conditions: (1)

stop supporting South Vietnam, and first of all stop supplying it with guns; and (2) stop the attacks on cities in South Vietnam. Faithfully obeying the orders of the US imperialists, the new leaders of the CPSU officially transmitted to the Democratic Republic of Vietnam these preposterous demands, which were aimed at forcing the Vietnamese people into unconditional surrender.

The new leaders of the CPSU have been busy running errands for the US aggressors, who are anxious to find a way out of their predicament in Vietnam. When Kosygin, chairman of the Council of Ministers of the USSR, passed through Peking on his visit to Vietnam in February 1965 and exchanged views with Chinese leaders, he stressed the need to help the United States 'find a way out of Vietnam'. This was firmly rebutted by the Chinese leaders. We expressed the hope that the new leaders of the CPSU would support the struggle of the Vietnamese people and not make a deal with the United States on the question of Vietnam. Kosygin expressed agreement with our views and stated that they would 'not bargain with others on this issue'. However, the new leaders of the CPSU soon went back on their promise.

Johnson wanted to play his fraudulent game of 'unconditional discussions'. So the new leaders of the CPSU put forward the idea of 'unconditional negotiations'. On 16 February this year, the day after Kosygin's return to Moscow, the Soviet government officially put before Vietnam and China a proposal to convene a new international conference on Indo-China without prior conditions, which in fact was advocacy of 'unconditional negotiations' on the Vietnam question. On 23 February, disregarding the stand which the Vietnamese government had taken against this proposal and without waiting for a reply from China, the new leaders of the CPSU discussed the question of calling the above-mentioned international conference with the president of France through the Soviet ambassador to France.

Johnson's fraud of 'unconditional discussions' met with a stern rebuff from the government of the Democratic Republic of Vietnam. The new leaders of the CPSU then began publicly to insinuate that negotiations could be held if only the United States stopped its bombing of North Vietnam. They engaged in vigorous activities in the international field with a view to putting this project into effect. In communications to certain fraternal parties, they said explicitly that they favoured negotiations with the United States on condition it stopped bombing North Vietnam. They also said that ways and means should be sought to settle the Vietnam question through negotiations. And sure enough, not long afterwards Johnson came out with the manoeuvre of 'the temporary suspension of bombing'.

After these plots of 'unconditional negotiations' and of 'stopping the bombing and holding negotiations' were foiled, the new leaders of the CPSU began to collaborate with the Indian reactionaries and the Tito clique—both lackeys of US imperialism—as brokers on the question of Vietnam. In their prescription for this question there was only mention of the cessation of US bombing of North Vietnam, only abstract talk about the implementation of the Geneva agreements, but no mention of the fact that the crucial point in the implementation of these agreements is the complete withdrawal of the US aggressor troops from Vietnam. In addition, the new leaders of the CPSU have been engaged in secret diplomatic activities. In a nutshell, their purpose is to help the United States to bring about 'peace talks' by deception, 'peace talks' which could go on indefinitely and also allow the United States to hang on in South Vietnam indefinitely. . . .

DOCUMENT 34. STATEMENT ON VIETNAM, 5 APRIL 1968 (*SN*, 9 APRIL 1968)

On 3 April the government of the Democratic Republic of Vietnam made a statement in view of US President Johnson's order of 31 March for a partial cessation of bombing raids against North Vietnam.

The government of the Democratic Republic of Vietnam stated that it was ready to appoint a representative for contacts with a representative of the United States to discuss the question of the unconditional cessation of American bombing and all other acts of war against the Democratic Republic of Vietnam, so as to make possible the opening of talks.

The Soviet government fully supports this statement of the government of the DRV in the belief that it indicates a realistic way towards ending the war in Vietnam and towards a political settlement in the interests of the Vietnamese people and in the interests of restoring a normal situation throughout south-east Asia.

The war of aggression launched by the United States of America against the heroic Vietnamese people is a serious source of tension in south-east Asia and throughout the world. It is emphatically condemned and arouses angry protests among all decent people, including those in the United States.

The US government, encountering powerful and ever-growing resistance from the Vietnamese people, who have the active support and all-round assistance of socialist countries and all the progressive forces of the world, and being faced with the prospect of a hard and onerous war, is compelled to limit its bombing of North Vietnam. Aggression, however, does not cease to be aggression because not the whole of the Democratic Republic of Vietnam but only part of its territory is being bombed. Bombing is continuing over nearly half the territory of the DRV.

The further development of events depends on whether the United States of America takes the next step—on whether it stops the bombing and other acts of war against North Vietnam completely and unconditionally and whether it takes a positive view of the well-known proposals of the government of the Democratic Republic of Vietnam and the National Liberation Front of South Vietnam on the ways of settling the Vietnam conflict. In the opinion of the Soviet government those proposals provide a good basis for a lasting settlement in Vietnam.

The Soviet government expresses the hope that the government of the United States will seriously consider the present situation and take such further steps as will actually lead to the ending of the war and a political settlement. This is demanded by the interests of peace in Asia and throughout the world.

DOCUMENT 35. EXTRACT FROM THE SPEECH BY BREZHNEV TO THE INTERNATIONAL CONFERENCE OF COMMUNIST PARTIES IN MOSCOW, 7 JUNE 1969 (*Pravda*, 8 JUNE 1969)

The antagonisms between imperialism, which intensifies social oppression and rejects democracy, and the masses of people, who are fighting for their vital rights and striving for freedom and democracy, is growing sharper. In some countries the discontent among the people is so great that sometimes as little as a spark is enough to set off a powerful social explosion. Such explosions are becoming ever more frequent everywhere, including the United States, where the most acute social contradictions, the struggle against the war in Vietnam and the fight for negro civil rights, are tangled in a tight knot. It is a long time since imperialism has been confronted with such violent forms of social protest and with general democratic action of the present scale and pitch. Ever more frequently broad masses of peasants, intellectuals, white-collar workers, students and middle strata of the urban population join with the working class in this struggle.

*

In May 1970 South Vietnamese troops supported by American troops moved into neutral Cambodia in order to destroy North Vietnamese bases there, or as American military jargon would have it, to 'deny them sanctuary'. A similar move took place in February 1971 against Laos.

DOCUMENT 36. EXTRACT FROM KOSYGIN'S STATEMENT ON AMERICAN INTERVENTION IN CAMBODIA, 4 MAY 1970 (*Pravda*, 5 MAY 1970)

In connection with the serious aggravation of the situation in south-east Asia caused by the aggressive actions of the United States against Cambodia, the Soviet government has considered it necessary to make the following statement. By order of the president of the United States, Mr Richard Nixon, American armed forces invaded the territory of neutral Cambodia on the night of 30 April–1 May. This was announced in a radio and television address by the United States president. According to news-agency reports, the United States forces, including tanks and aircraft, are moving deep into Cambodian territory, sowing death among the Cambodian population. In these aggressive operations, the United States command is also using sizeable contingents of troops of the South Vietnamese puppet regime.

A new seedbed of war has now been created in the territory of south-east Asia. Besides Vietnam and Laos, its flames have also enveloped Cambodia.

Having carried the fighting over to another state of Indo-China, the United States president voiced in his statement a threat levelled against all states that might decide to come out in support of the victims of American aggression. What is more, in the last few days, the United States has been undertaking massive air raids on some areas of the Democratic Republic of Vietnam (DRV). Thereby, it has crudely violated the obligation it assumed in accordance with the understanding which formed the basis for the four-power negotiations in Paris.

The United States administration is evidently guided by an aggressive line in policy, proceeding from the assumption that a strong power cannot act in international affairs otherwise than through the use of force. It is presumptuously believed in Washington that the United States of America merely has to use force wherever it chooses for a government that does not suit it to be removed and for its *Diktat* to be established. This course, followed in the past, has led and continues to lead the United States foreign policy to failures. That is well known and one example is the war against the Vietnamese people.

Having unleashed war in Cambodia and resumed the large-scale barbarous bombing of inhabited areas of the DRV, President Nixon is in effect also tearing up the decision of his predecessor, President Johnson, to end as of November 1968, all aerial bombing and other action involving the use of force against the DRV.

In the above-mentioned statement of the United States president, an attempt is made to justify the aggression against Cambodia, and, with this in view, arguments are marshalled whose aim is to mislead public opinion in the world and in America itself.

Washington is attempting to motivate the decision on a military invasion of Cambodia by alleging that it was necessary to save the lives of United States soldiers in South Vietnam. This logic is more than strange.

The aggressor, having first invaded the territory of one country, argues that somebody is threatening the lives of his soldiers, that is foreign invaders, and this, from the aggressor's standpoint, is an adequate pretext for invading the territory of another country, neighbouring on the first one.

And so for the United States the frontiers and the sovereignty of states, and the inviolability of their territory, lose all their meaning. But such a policy constitutes the most flagrant arbitrariness in international affairs and it must be resolutely condemned.

It is clear to everyone that with the expansion of United States aggression in Indo-China, the danger for the lives of its soldiers has not diminished at all.

The deeper the United States gets bogged down in its military gambles on the soil of Vietnam, in Laos, and now in Cambodia, the more of their kith and kin will American families lose. If the United States government was really pre-occupied with protecting the lives of tens and hundreds of thousands of Americans, there has always been a simple way out: not to send American soldiers to Vietnam, Cambodia or Laos, but to bring them back home.

Even further away from the truth are allegations that the transfer of hostilities to the territory of Cambodia would bring the end of the war in Vietnam closer. It is made to appear as if the expansion of the theatre of war in Indo-China serves almost to reduce the scale of the fighting rather than to increase it.

As is evident from the statement of the United States president, the real meaning of the statement, and indeed of the entire policy of the United States in south-east Asia, is to eliminate progressive regimes in the countries of the region, to stifle the national liberation movement, to hamper social progress of the peoples and, through colonialist methods, to subordinate the foreign and domestic policies of the states of Indo-China to its military and strategic interests and to draw them into its military bloc.

Such are the major goals of the United States in this region. They are well known to all peoples. These are imperialist, aggressive goals alien to the interests of the peoples, and therefore they are inevitably doomed to failure.

The policy of neutrality and the peace-loving line followed by Cambodia until recently do not suit those who determine United States policies. After the American invasion of Cambodia, the connection between the subversive activities of the relevant United States services and the *coup d'état* in Phnom Penh which resulted in the removal from office of Prince Norodom Sihanouk, the legitimate chief of state, has become all the more evident.

These services and their agents in Cambodia are trying to sow enmity between the Khmer people and the people of Vietnam. They have staged a bloody massacre of Vietnamese living in the territory of Cambodia, and they have set up concentration camps where peaceful inhabitants of the country are being brutally murdered.

They resort to all possible methods to set the peoples of Asia against one another. Fratricidal wars are being imposed on the countries of the region. An example of this is the United States president's doctrine of the 'Vietnamization' of the war. It is clear that any government which would allow the United States to use it as an accomplice in the policy of aggression would brand itself as an enemy of the peoples.

It would be in order to ask who gave the United States the right to be the judge of what is good and what is bad for other peoples. On what grounds does the United States assume a role that cannot be qualified otherwise than that of an international policeman? No one has given it that right and it neither had nor has any grounds for it.

The American military invasion of Cambodia arouses the indignation of all peace-loving forces throughout the world. The Soviet government believes that the expansion of the United States aggression in Indo-China makes even more pressing the need for the unity and greater cohesion of all socialist, all anti-imperialist and peace-loving forces in the struggle against aggression.

In the existing situation, all states which cherish the interests of peace and freedom of the peoples are called upon to display a high sense of responsibility for the further course of events and determination to assist in rebuffing the aggressor.

The result of the invasion of Cambodia by American troops may well be the further complication of the general international situation. In this light the question arises: how should the repeated statements of the United States president in favour of passing from an era of confrontation to an era of negotiation be understood?

Is it possible to speak seriously about the desire of the United States president for fruitful negotiations to solve pressing international problems while the United States is grossly flouting the Geneva agreements of 1954 and 1962, to which it is a party, and undertaking one new act after another undermining the foundations of international security?

What is the value of international agreements which the United States is or intends to be a party to if it so unceremoniously violates its obligations?

It is impossible not to give serious thought to the fact that President Nixon's practical steps in the field of foreign policy are fundamentally at variance with those declarations and assurances that he repeatedly made both before assuming the presidency and when he was already in the White House.

He promised the American people and the world public to do his utmost to end the war in Vietnam, to bring the American soldiers back home and to save their lives. Reality has shown that all those assurances remain meaningless phrases since in actual fact the United States government is intensifying still further its bellicose aggressive line. . . .

Whatever trumped-up pretexts are used to cover it, it is quite clear that cynical contempt for the inalienable right of the peoples of Indo-China to be the master in their own house and a crude American *Diktat* remain the basis of United States foreign policy in that region of the world, while conspiracies, military interventions and aggression remain the instruments of its realization.

There is no doubt that the expansion of American aggression in south-east Asia will meet with an even more resolute and effective rebuff on the part of the peoples that have fallen victim to the imperialist attack, and on the part of all those who cherish the interests of peace and freedom of the peoples.

Responsibility for the aggression against the people of Cambodia has now been added to the heavy responsibility which the United States bears for the war against the Vietnamese people. The Soviet government will naturally draw the proper conclusions for its policy from this course of action of the United States in south-east Asia.

PART II

The Socialist Commonwealth

(a) RECONCILIATION WITH YUGOSLAVIA

The visit of Khrushchev, accompanied by Bulganin, Mikoyan and other members of the Praesidium of the Party, to Belgrade, was intended to be the first public stage of an attempt to bring Tito back into the Soviet fold. Tito heard Khrushchev's speech with much annoyance and Khrushchev was equally astonished at the coolness of Tito. The visit was preceded by a preparatory correspondence between the Soviet and Yugoslav parties, extending over several months. In the course of these exchanges Khrushchev suggested that each side should accept responsibility for the split of 1948, the Yugoslavs blaming Djilas who had already been expelled from the Party, and Khrushchev blaming Beria. Tito turned down this suggestion, but Khrushchev went on with his role, presumably unaware of Tito's decision.

DOCUMENT 37. SPEECH BY KHRUSHCHEV AT BELGRADE AIRPORT, 26 MAY 1955 (*SN*, 27 MAY 1955)

Dear comrade Tito, dear comrades, members of the government and leaders of the League of Communists of Yugoslavia, dear comrades and citizens.

In the name of the Praesidium of the Supreme Soviet of the USSR, of the government of the Soviet Union and of the Central Committee of the Communist Party of the Soviet Union, on behalf of the Soviet people, I extend cordial greetings to you and to the working people of the glorious capital of Yugoslavia, Belgrade, to all the fraternal peoples of Yugoslavia.

The Soviet delegation has arrived in your country in order to determine, together with the Yugoslav government delegation, the future course for the development and consolidation of the friendship and co-operation between our peoples, to discuss our common tasks in the struggle for the progress of our countries, for relieving international tension and strengthening general peace and the security of the nations.

The peoples of our countries are bound by ties of an age-old fraternal friendship and joint struggle against common enemies. This friendship and militant co-operation has been especially strengthened in the hard trials of the struggle against the fascist invaders, in the years of the Second World War. In those hard years, all the Soviet people reacted with deep sympathy to the heroic struggle of their Yugoslav brothers, under the leadership of the communists, and welcomed wholeheartedly the courageous military exploits of the People's Liberation Army of Yugoslavia under the leadership of Marshal Tito. Our peoples will remember for ever that it was here, in Belgrade, that the Yugoslav and Soviet soldiers together struck at the enemy and liberated this ancient Slav city from the Hitler invaders. The foundation of the Federal People's Republic of Yugoslavia was warmly acclaimed by the people of the Soviet Union.

It will be remembered that those years witness the development of the best relations between the peoples of the Soviet Union and Yugoslavia, between our states and our parties. But those good relations were disturbed in the years that followed.

We sincerely regret that, and we resolutely sweep aside all the bitterness of that period.

On our part, we have no doubt about the part played in provoking that bitterness in the relations between Yugoslavia and the USSR by Beria, Abakumov and other exposed enemies of the people. We have thoroughly investigated the materials upon which the grave accusations against and insults to the leaders of Yugoslavia were based at that time. Facts indicate that those materials were fabricated by the enemies of the people, the contemptible agents of imperialism who had fraudulently wormed their way into the ranks of our party.

We are deeply convinced that the cloudy period in our relations is past. We, on our part, are prepared to take all the necessary steps in order to remove all the obstacles to making the relations between our states completely normal, to the promotion of friendly relations between our peoples.

Now that definite headway has been made in making our relations normal, the Soviet delegation voices the conviction that the coming talks will lead to the development and strengthening of political, economic and cultural co-operation between our peoples. All the conditions for this co-operation exist: the age-old historic friendship of the peoples of our countries, the glorious traditions of the revolutionary movement, the necessary economic foundation and community of ideals in the struggle for the peaceful progress and happiness of the working people.

True to the teachings of the founder of the Soviet state, Vladimir Ilyich Lenin, the government of the Soviet Union bases its relations with other countries, big and small, on the principles of the peaceful co-existence of states, on the principles of equality, non-interference, respect for sovereignty and national independence, on the principles of non-aggression and recognition that any encroachments by states upon the territorial integrity of other states are impermissible.

We hope that the relations between our countries will in the future, too, develop on the basis of these principles, for the good of our peoples. And that will be another major contribution to the efforts to ease international tension, to sustain and strengthen general peace.

We fully appreciate Yugoslavia's desire to promote relations with all states, in the west and in the east. We believe that greater friendship and contact between our countries will help to improve relations between all countries, irrespective of social system, and to advance the cause of general peace.

The Praesidium of the Supreme Soviet of the USSR, the Soviet government and the Central Committee of the Communist Party of the Soviet Union have commissioned our delegation to hold a fraternal discussion of all pressing problems with you.

As representatives of the Communist Party of the Soviet Union, the Party founded by great Lenin, we consider it desirable to establish mutual confidence between our parties as well. The most enduring bonds develop between the peoples of those countries where leadership is given by the parties which base all their work on the teachings of Marxism-Leninism. The parties which rely for guidance upon Marxist-Leninist theory achieve complete mutual understanding because they have a common aim—the struggle for the interests of the working class and of the working peasantry for the interests of the working people. It was for the triumph of socialism that the finest sons and daughters of the peoples gave their blood and, fighting against internal and foreign enemies, discarded the yoke of capitalism and won their freedom and independence. Steering the new socialist course, the peoples of these countries are strengthening their forces through enduring unshakable friendship.

We would have failed in our duty to our own peoples and to the working people of the whole world, if we had not done all that we could possibly do to promote mutual understanding between the Communist Party of the Soviet Union and the Union of Communists of Yugoslavia, on the basis of the teachings of Marxism-Leninism.

In the interests of the workers and peasants, in the interests of the international labour movement and of the common aims of the struggle for strengthening peace, for mankind's better future, the leaders of the Communist and Workers' parties must develop mutual confidence between these Parties, on the basis of the principles of Marxism-Leninism.

Long live stable peace among nations!

Long live the fraternal friendship and close co-operation between the peoples of the Soviet Union and Yugoslavia!

Long live the peoples of Yugoslavia!

*

The second Soviet-Yugoslav dispute began at the time of the Polish and Hungarian upheavals. In his speech at Pula on 11 November 1956 Tito tried to square the circle. He said that Soviet intervention in Hungary was both necessary and an error. For a time, however, relations improved until the Moscow communist party summit in November 1957 when Tito cancelled his visit and the Yugoslav representatives refused to sign the declaration. In April 1958 the Yugoslavs published their programme for the 7th Party Congress which was attacked in the Soviet press and resulted in Soviet economic sanctions against Yugoslavia. At the Bulgarian Party Congress Khrushchev expressed his opinions about the Yugoslavs in his usual colourful way.

In the vocabulary of communism an 'honest communist' is an orthodox communist.

DOCUMENT 38. EXTRACT FROM A SPEECH OF KHRUSHCHEV AT THE BULGARIAN COMMUNIST PARTY CONGRESS, 3 JUNE 1958 (*SN*, 6 JUNE 1958)

I don't want to offend anyone, but at the same time I cannot help asking a question which is worrying honest communists everywhere. Why do the imperialist leaders, who seek to wipe the socialist states from the face of the earth and to crush the communist movement, at the same time finance one of the socialist countries, give it credit on easy terms and free handouts? No one will ever believe that there are two socialisms in the world: one socialism that is viciously hated by world reaction, and another socialism acceptable to the imperialists, to which they render assistance and support.

Everyone knows that the imperialists have never given anyone money for nothing, simply because they like his 'beautiful eyes'. They invest their capital only in enterprises from which they hope to get good profits.

If the imperialists agree to render 'aid' to a socialist state in this way, they do so, of course, not in order to strengthen it. The monopoly circles of the United States can by no means be suspected of being interested in strengthening socialism and developing Marxist-Leninist theory. Representatives of this particular country allege that we are deviating from Marxism-Leninism, but claim that they themselves are taking a correct stand. We get quite a curious situation—the imperialists want to 'develop' Marxism-Leninism through this country. . . .

The Communist parties safeguard and preserve the unity of their ranks like the apple of their eye. They wage an irreconcilable struggle against revisionism and dogmatism. In this struggle the main fire of the communist parties is naturally directed against the revisionists, as scouts of the imperialist camp. The ancient legend of the Trojan Horse is widely known. . . .

Modern revisionism is a kind of Trojan Horse. The revisionists are trying to undermine the revolutionary parties from within, to undermine their unity, to sow disorder and confusion in Marxist-Leninist ideology. . . .

I recall a conversation I had with the Yugoslav leaders in 1956, when we were exchanging views in a friendly talk. Speaking of our disagreements, I drew Comrade Tito's attention to the need for a deeper analysis of the events and our mutual relations, for a correct appraisal of the situation that had developed, in order the more rapidly to secure unity of views on a basis of principle. In this conversation I reminded them of the well-known popular saying: 'The whole company is marching in step, and only one soldier is out of step', and I asked who must change—the company or the soldier.

Koca Popovic, who was present during the conversation, asked: 'And who is the company, and who is the soldier?' To that retort I replied: 'Ask yourself who is the company and who is the soldier.'

'At any rate,' I said, 'every soldier knows that a company is a company and that a soldier is only part of the company, and therefore it is not the company that must get into step with the soldier but the other way round. If you take a different attitude, then say plainly that you are not a soldier of this communist company which is marching together in step, guided by Marxism-Leninism.'

We shall always guard as something sacred the unity of our great Marxist-Leninist international army of fighters for communism.

DOCUMENT 39. EXTRACT FROM A SPEECH BY THE ALBANIAN PARTY LEADER, ENVER HOXHA, ON THE FORTY-FOURTH ANNIVERSARY OF THE BOLSHEVIK REVOLUTION, 7 NOVEMBER 1961 (AS QUOTED BY A. DALLIN, *Diversity in International Communism: A Documentary Record*, COLUMBIA UNIVERSITY PRESS, 1963, P. 113)

Until 1955, all Communist and workers parties were unanimous in condemning the Yugoslav revisionist leaders and in waging a resolute struggle of ideological and political principles against them. However, precisely at this time, N. Khrushchev announced that a great injustice had been done to Yugoslavia and her leaders, that baseless accusations had been made against them 'under the influence of the agent Beria', that in the Yugoslav question J. V. Stalin had also been mistaken. And he immediately took the initiative: he went to Belgrade where he called Tito a 'dear comrade', unilaterally threw the resolution of the Information Bureau into the waste-paper basket, and in a loud voice announced that Yugoslavia was a socialist country and that the Yugoslav leaders, although they displayed certain waverings, were in general Marxist-Leninists.

(b) POLAND AND HUNGARY IN 1956

On 28 June 1956 workers in Poznan went on strike as a protest against a fall in wages. The strike developed into a riot in which the workers made political demands. By the evening of the next day the riots were suppressed. Fifty-three had been killed, 300 wounded and 323 arrested. All this took place under the eyes of foreign visitors attending the Poznan international trade fair.

The reaction of the Polish government was one of concern and understanding. No such understanding was shown by the Soviets, as this *Pravda* article shows.

Poland was subject to a process of democratization which alarmed Moscow. On 19 October the eighth plenary session of the Central Committee of the Polish Communist Party assembled, when the Party secretary, Ochab, told them that a Soviet delegation headed by Khrushchev, Mikoyan, Kaganovich and Marshal Koniev had flown into Warsaw airport. This attempt at direct and personal pressure failed. Gomulka became Party secretary and the membership of the Politburo was changed by the appointment of four men close to Gomulka and the dismissal of four representatives of Stalinist orthodoxy. Marshal Rokossovski, the Soviet commander of the Polish army, returned to Russia.

On 14 November Gomulka, accompanied by Ochab and the prime minister, Cyrankiewicz, went to Moscow. At these talks the Soviets, having accepted the changes in Poland, proved reasonable. The Poles were granted many concessions. No doubt the Soviets were shaken by the revolutionary turn of the Hungarian events. The meeting laid the foundations of the cordial relations between Warsaw and Moscow and the equally cordial relations of Khrushchev and Gomulka. It was followed by a treaty which dealt with the status of Soviet troops garrisoned in Poland.

DOCUMENT 40. *Pravda* ARTICLE ON THE POZNAN EVENTS, 1 JULY 1956 (*CDSP, VIII*, 26, 8 AUGUST 1956, PP. 10–11)

As has already been reported, hostile agents carried out a crude provocation in Poznan. Imperialist and reactionary Polish underground agents, taking advantage of certain economic difficulties, incited serious disturbances and street disorders in the city. Several public buildings were attacked, resulting in casualties.

It is no accident that Poznan was selected as the place of provocation because of the international fair now in progress there. The enemies of the Polish people tried to cast a shadow on the growing might of People's Poland which the fair clearly reflects, in order to impede the development of peaceful international co-operation between Poland and other countries.

The hostile provocation failed. The politically conscious section of the Poznan working class helped the authorities to gain control of the situation and re-establish order in the city. The Polish Press Agency reports that by 7.00 a.m. on 29 June the majority of the workers from the striking enterprises returned to their jobs. Street car and bus services have been resumed in the city. The workers express their indignation over the infamous activities of the diversionists who tried to organize a demonstration against the people's rule. Preliminary investigation of the case of the arrested saboteurs and bandits reveals their ties with the reactionary underground.

On 29 June Jozef Cyrankiewicz, chairman of the Council of Ministers of the republic, who is in Poznan, delivered a radio address to the Poznan workers. He stated that the bloodshed in Poznan lies on the imperialist centres and the hostile reactionary underground, the direct organizers of the events. However, Jozef Cyrankiewicz stressed that the Poznan events will not impede or weaken the efforts of the Party and government toward a further democratization of our life, toward a better fulfilment of our tasks, toward development of the economy and national culture, toward a further rapid improvement in the workers' living conditions.

The Polish working class and all the workers of the country express decisive indignation over the insolent imperialist attack in Poznan. Mass meetings and open party gatherings are taking place in enterprises of Warsaw, Lodz, Lublin, Silesia, the Baltic coast area, and other regions of the country at which the workers are holding up to shame the organizers and inspirers of the provocation against the people.

Such a mass meeting took place at the Warsaw Dimitrov Plant. Worker Hauser stated: 'Imperialist provocateurs tried to cast a shadow on our achievements. They wanted to destroy the peaceful life of the Polish people. Our people paid too dearly for the victories achieved under a people's democratic system. We demand severe punishment for the organizers of the provocation.' The participants of the meeting adopted a resolution expressing profound indignation over the imperialist agents' provocation.

The workers of the Warsaw Automobile Plant state in a resolution adopted at a meeting: 'We will not permit a split in the unity of the working class and its party in the struggle for further democratization of our lives.'

The collective of the Kedzierzyn Nitrate Fertilizer Combine adopted a resolution which states: 'We will not permit the forces which detest whatever is our weal and our hope to try to destroy all the fruits of the constant labour of our workers and engineers, dedicated to the prosperity of our people's motherland.'

Expressing the opinion of all the workers of the country, the newspaper *Trybuna Ludu* writes:

We will defend our greatest blessing, Poland, which we raised by the tremendous labour of all the people from the abyss of military destruction, against the hostile plans of native and foreign reaction. We will incapacitate the criminal hand which is trying to strike a blow for which all the people must pay. But, so that this hand will not be able to strike a blow against Poland, vigilance, common sense, and action must be mobilized. The party, the working class, and the public must be consciously opposed to the provocateurs.

Trybuna Ludu states:

No provocation will succeed. The party, government, and the entire country will not leave the path upon which we have embarked. We will not reduce but, on the contrary, will increase efforts to improve our economy, to increase industrial and agricultural production. This is the only way to improve each person's life, the only path to strength and prosperity in People's Poland.

The newspaper *Życie Warszawy* writes:

Today we all recognize how much we need peace and solidarity, unity of action under the leadership of the Polish United Workers Party, and vigilance against enemy intrigues.

In an official statement on the Poznan events, the Polish United Workers Party Central Committee expressed assurance that every attempt to incite disorders and demonstrations against the people's rule would be duly rebuffed by all workers and Polish citizens.

All Polish people unanimously support this conviction. The workers and employees of enterprises and institutions are sending letters to the Party Central Committee stating their desire to rally further around the Polish United Workers Party and the people's government and their readiness to defend with all their might the achievements of the people's democratic system.

DOCUMENT 41. EXTRACT FROM THE COMMUNIQUÉ ON TALKS HELD BETWEEN THE SOVIET AND POLISH DELEGATIONS, 18 NOVEMBER 1956 (*Pravda*, 19 NOVEMBER 1956)

In the course of their friendly negotiations both delegations examined and discussed in detail all aspects of the relations between the Soviet and Polish states, as they developed up to the present. Both parties are of the opinion that the declaration of the Soviet government of 30 October 1956, on the 'principles of development and further strengthening of friendship and co-operation between the Soviet Union and other socialist states' is of great importance for the development and consolidation of friendship between socialist countries. Both parties are of the opinion that the principles laid down in this declaration conform to the decisions adopted on this question by the eighth plenary session of the Central Committee of the Polish United Workers Party and to the policy of the Polish government. During the talks both parties devoted particular attention to the further development and strengthening of the friendship between the peoples of the Soviet Union and the Polish People's Republic and expressed confidence that the indestructible union and fraternal friendship between the USSR and the PPR will widen and consolidate, developing on the basis of complete equality, respect for territorial integrity, national independence and sovereignty, and of non-interference in internal affairs. The Soviet-Polish alliance, in which both the Soviet and Polish peoples are equally interested, is a reliable guarantee of their security. This alliance is a most important factor for the strengthening of the independence of the Polish People's Republic and the inviolability of her frontier on the Oder and Neisse, the frontier of peace.

The parties express profound confidence that the consistent realization of the above-mentioned principles of co-operation between the Soviet Union and the Polish People's Republic will contribute to further consolidate the alliance between the two states, to strengthen the unity of the socialist camp and peace in Europe.

During the talks questions of economic relations between the Soviet Union and Poland in the light of the Soviet government declaration on the 'principles of development and further strengthening of friendship and co-operation between the Soviet Union and other socialist states' were examined in detail. Both parties are determined to develop and strengthen economic co-operation between the two countries on the basis of equal rights, mutual benefit and fraternal mutual help.

In the course of the negotiations the existence of certain outstanding financial accounts for previous years between the parties was determined.

Both parties, on the basis of mutual interest, agreed to regard as settled as of 1 November 1956 the Polish debts arising out of the use of credits granted by the Soviet government to Poland in payment of the full value of coal delivered by Poland to the

Soviet Union in 1946–53 on the basis of the agreement of 16 August 1945. Agreement was also reached on the settlement of financial accounts in connection with railroad transport and non-commercial payments, etc.

The Soviet government is ready to deliver to the Polish People's Republic 1,400,000 tons of grain in 1957. The above grain deliveries will be made on credit.

The Soviet government has also agreed to grant to the Polish People's Republic long-term credits to the amount of 700,000,000 roubles for the payment of commodities delivered by the Soviet Union to Poland in accordance with a mutually agreed list.

The parties discussed problems connected with the temporary stationing of Soviet troops in Polish territory.

The parties declare that until now agreed decisions have not been reached which could provide European states with sufficient guarantees against the rebirth of German militarism. The constant objections by revanchist forces to the correct and existing frontiers between European states and, in the first place, to the established and existing western frontier of Poland also constitute a material reason hampering the normalization of relations in Europe.

Both sides reached the conclusion that this state of affairs, as well as the existing international situations, continue to make the temporary presence of Soviet troops on Poland's territory necessary. This is also connected with the necessity of the presence of Soviet troops in Germany on the basis of international treaties and agreements.

It was settled that both sides would, in accordance with the development of the international situation, consult on problems connected with the stay of Soviet military units on Polish territory, their number and their composition.

At the same time both parties accept the following principles determining the status of these units on Polish territory:

The temporary presence of Soviet troops in Poland can in no way affect the sovereignty of the Polish state and cannot lead to their interference in the internal affairs of the Polish People's Republic.

The disposition and number of Soviet troops is to be determined by special agreements between both sides.

The movement of Soviet military units outside their stationing areas requires the agreement of the government of the Polish People's Republic or other competent Polish authorities.

Soviet military units located in the territory of the Polish People's Republic and their personnel, together with their families, are obligated to respect and adhere to the provisions of Polish law. The limits of Polish and Soviet jurisdiction with regard to the personnel of Soviet military units in Poland will be settled by special agreement.

The times, routes and orders of transit of Soviet troops across Polish territory are to be settled by definite agreements between both sides.

Appropriate agreements determining the legal status of Soviet troops during the time of their temporary stay on Polish territory will be concluded in the near future.

*

The procession to lay a wreath on the statue of General Bem, a Polish officer who fought with the Hungarians in 1848, showed the extent to which the Polish events had excited Hungary. The procession turned into a demonstration and then became a revolution. Soviet troops intervened in the fighting in Budapest but on 28 October Hungary's reforming communist premier Nagy negotiated a withdrawal of Soviet troops from the capital. Two days later the Soviets issued the declaration 'On Friendship and Co-operation between the Soviet Union and other Socialist States'. This was meant as a conciliatory gesture to Hungary and also to Poland. Suslov and Mikoyan visited Budapest only to find that Nagy was presiding over what seemed to them to be a liquidation of communism. A multiparty system was restored and Nagy announced that he wanted to begin negotiations to withdraw Hungary from the Warsaw Pact. The Soviet answer was to create a counter-government headed by Kadar and to impose his rule by force.

Premier Nagy's appeal to the United Nations could not be discussed in the Security Council because the Soviet delegate imposed the veto. The General Assembly, on 4 November, on 10 November and after Shepilov's speech on 20 November voted that the Soviet Union withdraw its armed forces. In January 1957 the General Assembly set up a five-nation Special Committee on Hungary. The Committee was refused entry into Hungary. In its report it stated that the events of 1956 were a spontaneous national revolution and that the Kadar regime had been imposed on the people of Hungary by the Red Army. The Hungarian question remained on the agenda of the General Assembly for a number of years.

DOCUMENT 42. TELEGRAM FROM THE PRIME MINISTER OF HUNGARY, IMRE NAGY, TO THE SECRETARY-GENERAL OF THE UNITED NATIONS, HAMMARSKJÖLD, 1 NOVEMBER 1956 (UN DOCUMENT A/325)

Reliable reports have reached the government of the Hungarian People's Republic that further Soviet units are entering Hungary. The President of the Council of Ministers in his capacity of Minister of Foreign Affairs summoned M. Andropov, Ambassador Extraordinary and Plenipotentiary of the Soviet Union to Hungary, and expressed his strongest protest against the entry of further Soviet troops into Hungary. He demanded the instant and immediate withdrawal of these Soviet forces. He informed the Soviet ambassador that the Hungarian government immediately repudiates the Warsaw Treaty and at the same time declares Hungary's neutrality, turns to the United Nations, and requests the help of the four great powers in defending the country's neutrality. The Government of the Hungarian People's Republic made the Declaration of Neutrality on 1 November 1956; therefore I request your Excellency to put on the agenda of the forthcoming General Assembly of the United Nations the question of Hungary's neutrality and the defence of this neutrality by the four great powers.

DOCUMENT 43. EXTRACT FROM A SPEECH BY FOREIGN MINISTER SHEPILOV IN THE GENERAL ASSEMBLY OF THE UNITED NATIONS, 19 NOVEMBER 1956 (GENERAL ASSEMBLY, ELEVENTH SESSION, PLENARY MEETING)

The Soviet delegation opposed the inclusion of the item on the situation in Hungary in the agenda of the General Assembly.

We still consider that this question is one within the domestic jurisdiction of the Hungarian People's Republic. There had already, as you know, been attempts, at the second emergency special session of the General Assembly, to make use of the United Nations for the purpose of interference in Hungary's internal affairs. . . .

The persistent endeavour to keep the question of the situation in Hungary on the General Assembly's agenda is certainly not explained by any concern for the interests of the Hungarian people, but by the intention of certain groups, on the one hand to distract people's attention from the aggressive actions of the United Kingdom, France and Israel in Egypt and, on the other hand, to encourage the members of the reactionary underground in Hungary by promising them the support of the United Nations.

As for the draft resolution submitted by the Cuban delegation —it reeks of provocation. It contains slanderous inventions, alleging that the Government of the Soviet Union is forcibly deporting Hungarian 'prisoners' to places outside Hungary. It must be said that even in the worst periods of the 'cold war' it would have been difficult to find a document which ignored the basic requirements in the way of substantiation of charges made to such an extent as this one does.

In an effort to give their slanderous assertions an appearance of probability, the authors of the Cuban draft resolution unjustifiably referred, yesterday and the day before (they have not done so today) to mythical reports from the 'official Budapest radio'. An investigation has, however, shown that no such reports were put out by the Budapest radio. It is only natural, therefore, that the representative of Cuba should no longer, today, have referred to that source. As another source of information, the draft resolution—I am thinking of the text which was brought out a few days ago before the draft was brought up to date—speaks of reports from 'the Press throughout the world', refers to those newspapers which, obediently carrying out the orders of reactionary circles, make up all kinds of stories about the situation in Hungary. But today the representative of Cuba, speaking from this platform, was compelled to withdraw his reference to this course, too, for the 'Press throughout the world' gives no authenticated facts of such a kind.

On what grounds then, did the Cuban representative base his provocative allegations? On none whatever. He ignored the law of evidence and employed slanderous insinuation instead of arguments.

The reference in the revised draft resolution to alleged violations in Hungary of the Convention on the Prevention and Punishment of the Crime of Genocide was made with the object of giving this provocative document an appearance of legal validity. It is obvious, however, that this Convention, which condemns acts committed with the intention of destroying people solely because they belong to a certain national, ethnic, racial or religious group, has no connexion whatever with the situation in Hungary.

If the Cuban delegation were seriously concerned with the prevention of genocide, it should take an interest in the situation in those countries where this monstrous practice does in fact obtain.

I might refer, for instance, to those incidents in Kenya about which we all know. According to a Reuter's report, the Church Missionary Society stated, on 19 June 1955, that the authorities in Kenya had arrested and detained over 500,000 Negroes. The American writer, John Gunther, speaking about an operation with the expressive title, 'Anvil', which was carried out by the British authorities in Kenya against the Kikuyu tribe, described it as one of the most effective manhunts in history. A whole army of gaolers, some 14,300 men, is maintained to look after the gaols and concentration camps in Kenya, in which many thousands of innocent people, including women and children, are languishing.

I should also like to recall certain facts about Algeria, whose people are fighting manfully for their freedom in spite of brutal repression. On 6 April 1956, Mr Edouard Depreux, leader of the socialist group in the French National Assembly, made public a terrible figure: he revealed that, according to official information, since the beginning of the struggle in Algeria French troops had wiped out 48,000 Algerians. The *Times of India* rightly observed in that connexion that if we agree that the figures given by the French Government are obviously an underestimate, then the slaughter must be regarded as reaching virtually the proportions of a massacre.

These are the activities against which the Cuban delegation should raise its voice if it really wants to combat genocide, actual genocide and not mythical genocide, as it has done, much to its dishonour. . . .

What has really happened in Hungary, according to the information available to the Soviet Union?

The facts show that the former leaders of Hungary were responsible for grave mistakes and deviations, both in general political matters and in their economic policies. These mistakes, and the economic difficulties that arose in Hungary during the period of the reconstruction of the national economy, caused justified discontent among a section of the population, which demanded that these shortcomings and mistakes be eliminated. These demands were endorsed by many of Hungary's leading figures.

The action of the popular masses who, on 23 October, came out in protest against the grave mistakes and errors committed by the former leaders of Hungary, was quite justified. However, reactionary fascist elements who were endeavouring to undermine and overthrow the popular democratic order soon tried to turn this healthy movement to their own ends. As early as 23 October, during a demonstration in Budapest, attended by a large number of well-intentioned workers, the leaders of the counter-revolutionary underground brought armed gangs which had been previously assembled out into the open. They provoked mass disturbances in Budapest, which later developed into a rising of anti-popular forces.

Desirous of bringing this rising to an end as quickly as possible, the Hungarian Government requested the Government of the Soviet Union to agree to the use of Soviet military units, stationed in Hungary under the Warsaw Treaty, in helping the Hungarian authorities responsible for maintaining order and tranquillity in Budapest. The telegram received by the Council of Ministers of the USSR from the Prime Minister of the Hungarian People's Republic on 24 October 1956 stated:

On behalf of the Council of Ministers of the Hungarian People's Republic, I request the Government of the Soviet Union to send Soviet troops to Budapest to put an end to the disturbances that have taken place in Budapest, restore order quickly and create conditions favourable to peaceful and constructive work.

This request reflected the desire of the Hungarian people to have order quickly restored in their country. Even Imre Nagy, who later gave way to the reactionary forces by yielding ground on certain principles of the socialist state, stated on 25 October that the participation of Soviet troops in the struggle against counter-revolutionary forces was necessary to the vital interests of the socialist order.

The Soviet Union could not, of course, refuse to respond to the request of a friendly State for help. In a few days, however, realizing that the continued presence of Soviet military units in Budapest might lead to a further deterioration of the situation, the USSR Government, in agreement with the Hungarian Government, ordered the withdrawal of its troops from the Hungarian capital.

What happened then? After Soviet troops had withdrawn from Budapest, the reactionary forces cast aside their masks and launched a brutal campaign of reprisal against the democratic leaders of Hungary, against honest Hungarian patriots. During those dark days for Hungary, the fascists hanged honest patriots from lamp-posts along the streets of Budapest. They broke into hospitals and shot the wounded out of hand. They destroyed factories, and set fire to theatres and museums. After the rioters had set fire to the National Museum building in Budapest, they used automatic rifles and machine-guns to shoot firemen and soldiers who tried to save the museum's art treasures. As in the accursed days of Hitler, the streets of Budapest were aglow with the sinister light of bonfires, on which burnt the paraffin-soaked bodies of Hungarian patriots. Nearby—again as in Hitler's time—there was a bonfire of books, the immortal works of the progressive writers and thinkers of mankind.

Thus those counter-revolutionary forces whose object was to overthrow the popular democratic order in Hungary were coming increasingly to the forefront. These forces were trying to wipe out the achievements of the socialist revolution. They raided nationalized enterprises and State shops, and disrupted transport and communications. As each day passed, they grew bolder; Imre Nagy's government, which had lost control of the situation, was pushed by them further and further along the path of complicity with the rioters. Former Horthyist and police officers became increasingly active.

The true nature of the counter-revolution was revealed to all during the white terror. Counter-revolutionary gangs, well-organized and armed, brutally murdered hundreds of workers, peasants, intellectuals and progressives who had fallen into their hands. . . .

Who was immediately responsible for organizing all these crimes? The workers? The peasants? The intellectuals? No. Those responsible for all these crimes were the representatives of the former upper class of exploiters. The *New York Times*, analysing the class composition of the rebels, stated quite openly that they belonged to the remnants of the overthrown classes—rich people impoverished by the Communists, former landowners and rich peasants, persecuted clergymen and the like.

Remnants of the fascist groups that had been crushed during the Second World War and had taken refuge for the time being in Western Germany were sent across the frontier to assist them. Thus, according to an Italian report, during the night of 30 October units of Hungarian fascist *émigrés* who had formerly served in Horthy's army, entered Hungarian territory through Austria from Western Germany. They were armed with American weapons. These are the elements who are now represented as the champions of freedom and democracy!

A so-called 'Hungarian Committee' was established in Vienna to help the rioters. Otto Hapsburg, the sons of Horthy and Gömbös—Hitler's puppets in Hungary—and other representatives of the dark forces of reaction crawled forth from their holes to encourage those who were organizing the counter-revolutionary *putsch*. In the words of the Austrian newspaper, *Salzburger Volksblatt*, the seed sown by the *émigrés* living in the West, who had for many years been tempting Hungary with the vision of liberation by the West, was now producing a harvest of blood.

The fearful phantom of the fascist beasts thus appeared over the peaceful field of Hungary. The lives of millions of Hungarians, their fundamental civic rights, their homes, property and security were threatened.

The government of Imre Nagy not only proved itself incapable of repelling the attack by reactionary forces, but under their pressure gradually eliminated from its midst the representatives of the nation's democratic forces. Finally, the Nagy government fell to pieces, and yielded to the forces of reaction which were trying to establish a fascist dictatorship in the country. Chaos enveloped Hungary.

Faced by this difficult situation, that part of the working class which had at first failed to understand what was happening, and in one way or another had succumbed to the provocative appeals of those who had fomented the rising, began to take a more sober view of events. The national and democratic forces in Hungary began to organize resistance to fascism. Honest statesmen left the Nagy government, convinced that it was only a screen for the forces of fascist reaction that were beginning to dominate the country. Janos Kadar, a Deputy Prime Minister in the Nagy government, formed a new Hungarian Revolutionary Workers' and Peasants' Government. This government set itself the task of preserving the democratic achievements of the Hungarian people, and defending the popular democratic order. This would have been an impossible task without the defeat of the reactionary fascist gangs, which sought to restore the old Horthyist fascist regime.

The new government applied to the Soviet Union for assistance in beating off the attack by the forces of fascism and in restoring order and normal life in the country. Let me admit openly that this was not an easy problem for the Soviet Government to deal with. We fully realized the difficulties which inevitably arise when the armies of one country are being used in another. The Soviet Government, however, could not remain indifferent to the fate of friendly Hungary.

It is common knowledge that the Soviet people had sacrificed the lives of millions of their sons in the struggle for the liberation of Europe, including Hungary, from fascist tyranny. Now the threat of enslavement by fascist reaction was again hanging over the Hungarian people. History would never have forgiven the Hungarian workers and the Soviet people, who had made enormous sacrifices for the liberation of Hungary from fascist oppression, if now, twelve years after the collapse of the Hitlerite hordes in the Second Word War, the Hungarian and

Soviet people had retreated in the face of a counter-revolutionary *putsch* and permitted the re-establishment of a breeding ground for fascism in the centre of Europe.

The Soviet people could not but carry out their duty towards the Hungarian People's Republic, the more so as the Peace Treaty with Hungary, which was signed, let us remember also by the United States and the United Kingdom, not only provides for the dissolution of all organizations of a fascist type on Hungarian territory, but imposes the obligation on Hungary not to permit in future the existence or activities of such organizations.

Lastly, we could not overlook the fact that Hungary is a neighbour of the Soviet Union and that the USSR is linked with Hungary by the Warsaw Treaty of friendship, co-operation and mutual assistance which unites a group of States. A victory of reactionary forces in Hungary would have converted that country into a new jumping-off ground for an aggressive war not only against the Soviet Union but also against the other countries of Eastern Europe. We are convinced that no democratic government, linked by ties of friendship with a neighbouring country, would have been able to disregard an appeal for assistance such as we received from Hungary.

With the help of units of the Soviet army, the Hungarian revolutionary forces did not require long to put down the rebels. In the execution of the democratic programme it has proclaimed, the Government of Hungary is now guiding the life of the country back to normal. . . .

I should now like to turn to another aspect of the question under review.

We have factual information demonstrating convincingly that the events which occurred in Hungary would have taken on quite a different character, not involving any bloodshed, if the action of counter-revolutionary forces inside the country had not been backed from the very outset by foreign instigators who had long been preparing a fascist *putsch* against the people's democratic regime in Hungary. These activities of foreign subversive centres are not exactly a secret. They are carried out, not by any private groups or organizations, but by State agencies subordinate to the highest government organs and financed out of the national budget. . . .

For a long time, many Western agencies have been using all means of propaganda to publicize appeals for the overthrow of the existing political system in the democratic countries; they are setting up special 'centres' on the territory of the Federal Republic of Germany and in Austria, from which planned subversive activities against the Eastern European States are being carried on, including the dispatch of spies and diversionist groups to the territories of those States.

It is no accident that, since the middle of 1955, the interference of ruling circles of the United States in the domestic affairs of Hungary has been noticeably intensified. Messages from leading official personalities of the United States to the Hungarian people containing appeals for the overthrow of the legally constituted authority; the adoption, on 16 April 1956, of a resolution by the House of Representatives openly calling for the so-called 'liberation' of the peoples' democracies; systematic subversive broadcasts by the radio stations of certain Western countries; the mass dissemination of slanderous leaflets by means of balloons; open support for the fascist dregs among the Hungarian emigration; the dispatch of spies and diversionists into Hungary—all this, as has now become plain, is intended to aid the anti-popular conspiracy as an underground movement.

You are perfectly aware that the subversive activity of the United States against the countries of Eastern Europe has been given legal sanction by the United States Congress and, what is more, has been raised to the status of an official policy. You will remember the heated debates here, in the Assembly, when the United States first adopted an Act hitherto unprecedented in political practice enabling the Government to spend $100 million on subversive activities. The Act openly says that the money is intended 'for any selected persons who are residing in or escapees from the Soviet Union, Poland, Czechoslovakia, Hungary, Romania, Bulgaria, Albania' and also the German Democratic Republic and other countries, 'either to form such persons into elements of the military forces supporting the North Atlantic Treaty Organization or for other purposes'.

It should be noted that at the time the United States representatives attempted to show from this rostrum that we had misunderstood this Act, that the appropriations were not intended for subversive work, but for charitable assistance to refugees. The Act, however, from which I have just been quoting, speaks for itself; it tells us what its authors had in mind, namely, the financing of persons chosen by the United States intelligence service, who were living in the territory of socialist States, and their use for subversive work by any methods, including the creation, as it says in the Act, of 'elements of the military forces' from their ranks.

Since that time, similar Acts have been passed in the United States every year, and hundreds of millions of dollars have been poured out to sustain subversive activities. . . .

During the last few years, a large number of subversive groups financed from abroad have been discovered in the Hungarian People's Republic. The Government of the Hungarian People's Republic has, in this connexion, repeatedly protested against the gross interference of certain Western States in the domestic affairs of Hungary.

The counter-revolutionary *putsch* in Hungary had thus been prepared long beforehand systematically and carefully, and not without the active participation of foreign elements. The preparations were, of course, secret, but from time to time some of the initiated gave away the secret. Thus, in an article published in the *Daily Mirror* on 8 November, the well-known American columnist, Drew Pearson, quoted statements from a conversation he had had with Bela Fabian, one of the leaders abroad of the Hungarian reactionary emigrants, who said: 'The Hungarian people will rise up. . . . With a little help from you Hungary will burst into flames. . . . Your balloons have helped.'

It should be borne in mind that, on the eve of the bloody incidents in Hungary, Bela Varga, the leader of the Hungarian emigration centre in the United States, said in New York that underground groups in Hungary were about to start a rebellion. Varga 'predicted' that in a week or two Imre Nagy would return to power and Cardinal Mindszenty would be released from prison.

Even some American newspapers, commenting on the failure of the *putsch* in Hungary, now have to admit that certain reactionary circles must bear a heavy responsibility for starting the bloodshed in Hungary. For instance, the *New York World Telegram and Sun*, in a leading article appropriately headed 'on our conscience', blamed the American instigators for having encouraged what the leading article called 'false hopes' among the Hungarian reactionary underground. American propaganda, said the newspaper, however well-intentioned, had led the Hungarians to believe that the Yanks were coming.

The conspirators who fled from Hungary after the failure of the counter-revolutionary *putsch*, in statements just published, said that, in taking up arms, they had firmly believed that they would receive military assistance. Just listen to what one of these who participated in the *putsch* told the special correspondent of the *Daily News* upon fleeing to Austria. He said that the mighty America had pushed them into taking such action. Complaining that at the decisive moment the United States had failed to send its armed forces to assist the rebels, he said that the United States had lost its best army at Budapest.

The *Christian Science Monitor* published a leading article on 12 November under the heading 'Hungarian rebels reported misled by Western propaganda'. The article stated that: 'Foremost in the thinking of Hungarian insurgents who have reached this country is bitter disappointment in the West.' According to the newspaper, the conspirators had been given far-reaching promises and were convinced that they could 'count not only on words of sympathy, but on hard and fast political and, if necessary, military deeds' (I stress the word 'military').

Now that the fascist adventure has failed, those who are in no small measure responsible for the bloodshed in Hungary hypocritically shed tears over the sufferings of the Hungarian people. They presume to preach to those who helped the Hungarian people to defend their democratic achievements and to save their national independence. This is really being too pharisaical!

It is being proposed here that the United Nations should intervene in the domestic affairs of the Hungarian State. At a time when order is being restored in Hungary and the Government of the Hungarian People's Republic has already started carrying out the comprehensive, constructive programme it has proclaimed, we are in effect being told that we should rekindle the struggle against the people's democratic order in Hungary. That is the only interpretation that can be placed on the irresponsible appeals for the dispatch of a United Nations 'police force' to Hungary. Those who sponsor such proposals apparently do not understand that such measures, far from strengthening peace, can serve only to endanger it. Those who are genuinely interested in Hungary's rapid recovery from its harrowing ordeal and the speedy healing of the wounds inflicted upon it by the fascist rebels should not interfere now in the return to normal public life taking place in that country.

What does Hungary now need most of all? We feel that it needs peace and tranquillity, intensive work to organize and develop its economic life, the restoration of normal administrative and social activities. Can this be achieved by the incitement implicit in the course of action taken by certain circles and reflected both in the Cuban delegation's draft resolution and in some of the speeches made from this rostrum during the past few weeks? No, such a course is obviously designed not to help Hungary but to disrupt its social and economic life.

The Hungarian people now require material aid. The General Assembly has expressed its views on this subject. The Soviet Union and other socialist States have already provided Hungary with assistance on a large scale. Suffice it to say that 700 wagon-loads of foodstuffs, building material and equipment are being sent daily into Hungary from the Soviet Union. As is known, many other countries are also helping Hungary.

The Soviet delegation believes that the main thing to do now is to refrain from stirring up passions over the so-called 'Hungarian question', but rather to make every effort to help restore order, peace and tranquillity in Hungary as soon as possible. The Hungarian Workers' and Peasants' Government is instituting constructive measures on a broad scale. That is the most important pledge that the people's democracy of Hungary, together with the other socialist States, will develop relations of business and friendship with all countries and proceed along the road to peace and progress.

With regard to the Soviet Union's relations with the Hungarian People's Republic, the basic principles governing relations between socialist States are well known. United by common ideals, the socialist States base their relations on full equality, respect for territorial integrity, national independence and sovereignty, and non-interference in each other's domestic affairs. Far from excluding close fraternal co-operation and mutual assistance among socialist States in all fields, it actually promotes these objectives. These principles were restated in the declaration of the USSR Government of 30 October 1956. The Soviet Government is determined to give full effect to the principles set forth in that declaration.

The question of the Soviet troops in Hungary will also be settled in accordance with that declaration. By agreement with the Hungarian Government, the Soviet troops will be promptly withdrawn from Budapest once normal conditions are restored in the Hungarian capital. At the same time the Soviet Government will begin negotiations with the Government of the Hungarian People's Republic, as a party to the Warsaw Treaty, on the question of maintaining Soviet troops on Hungarian territory.

The Soviet Union certainly does not advocate the stationing of troops on foreign soil. We agree with the Prime Minister of India, Mr Nehru, who, a few days ago, reiterated his opposition to military pacts on foreign soil, and to agreements permitting the maintenance of military bases on foreign soil. . . .

The Soviet delegation proposes that the draft resolution presented by the Cuban delegation should be rejected as a slanderous fabrication designed to poison the international atmosphere. The peoples of the world will not forgive us if we follow the lead of those who are seeking, by means of political speculation concerning the so-called Hungarian question, to divert the attention of the United Nations from pressing international problems requiring immediate solution, the most important being the problem resulting from the aggression committed by the United Kingdom, France and Israel against Egypt, as the situation there is still fraught with grave danger.

(c) RELATIONS AMONG SOCIALIST STATES

In the Stalinist era the favourite Soviet means of economic exploitation of the satellites was the joint stock company. Such companies were widely used in those countries that had been enemies in the war, that is Rumania, Bulgaria, Hungary and Eastern Germany. There were sixteen such companies in Rumania, six in Hungary, and seven in Bulgaria, while the uranium mines in Czechoslovakia, Eastern Germany and Hungary were also jointly exploited. The capital was owned on a 50–50 basis, the Soviet half being normally provided by German property seized by the Soviets. Such companies were set up primarily in road, water and aerial transport and the mining and petroleum industries. In 1954 the Soviets sold their share to the recipient countries on unspecified 'favourable terms'. The sales to Eastern Germany were carried out some time later.

DOCUMENT 44. SOVIET-RUMANIAN COMMUNIQUÉ OF 18 SEPTEMBER 1954 ON THE TRANSFER TO RUMANIA OF THE SOVIET SHARE IN MIXED SOVIET-RUMANIAN ENTERPRISES (*Pravda*, 25 SEPTEMBER 1954)

After the end of the Second World War mixed Soviet-Rumanian firms were formed in a number of branches of Rumania's national economy under an agreement reached between the government of the USSR and Rumania. The formation of these firms was aimed at facilitating the restoration and development of Rumania's economy, which had been greatly damaged as a result of the German fascist occupation of the country.

In the course of the firms' existence both parties made big capital investments in the firms' enterprises. The Soviet Union's contributions to the firms consisted chiefly in deliveries of up-to-date equipment and materials necessary for the activities of the firms' enterprises. The Soviet side also gave the firms technical assistance by transferring technical documentation, sending specialists, drafting projects for the construction and reconstruction of enterprises and training skilled Rumanian cadres.

As a result of the capital investments and the implementation of the measures agreed between the parties, the capacity and technical level of the firms' enterprises advanced a great deal, which made it possible to increase output accordingly and to master the production of new types of commodities not previously turned out in Rumania. At the same time much attention was paid to improving the housing, cultural and living conditions of the factory and office workers.

The successful activities of these firms played a positive part in the restoration and development of the national economy of the Rumanian People's Republic and prepared the conditions for the transfer of the direction of the firms' enterprises to the state organizations of Rumania.

In this way the mixed Soviet-Rumanian firms fulfilled the task set them, and in this connection the government of the USSR and the government of the Rumanian People's Republic discussed questions concerning these firms and agreed on the transfer to the Rumanian People's Republic of the Soviet share in twelve firms.

In accordance with this, agreements were signed in Moscow on 31 March and 18 September 1954, on the sale and transfer to the Rumanian People's Republic of the Soviet share in the mixed Soviet-Rumanian firms of Sovrommetall (Soviet-Rumanian metal), Sovromugol (Soviet-Rumanian Coal), Sovromtransport (Soviet-Rumanian Transport), Sovromnefte-mash (Soviet-Rumanian Oil Machinery), Sovromsudostroy (Soviet-Rumanian Shipbuilding), Sovromtraktor (Soviet-Rumanian Tractor), Sovromkhim (Soviet-Rumanian Chemicals), Sovromgaz (Soviet-Rumanian Gas), Sovromles (Soviet-Rumanian Timber), Sovromstroy (Soviet-Rumanian Construction), Sovrombank (Soviet-Rumanian Bank) and TARS (civil aviation).

The agreements provide that the value of the Soviet share in these firms transferred to Rumania will be reimbursed by the Rumanian side on favourable terms, in instalments over a number of years.

These agreements, which are a result of the friendly relations between the USSR and the Rumanian People's Republic, will help further to strengthen the friendship and co-operation between the two countries.

*

The declaration issued at the time when Soviet troops were poised to crush the Hungarian revolt expresses the new relations which the Soviet Union hoped to fashion with the other socialist states. These relations are of course, based on the primacy of the Soviet Union. The declaration was further elucidated in the declarations of the conferences of 1957 and 1960.

DOCUMENT 45. EXTRACT FROM THE DECLARATION OF THE USSR GOVERNMENT ON THE FOUNDATIONS FOR THE DEVELOPMENT AND FURTHER STRENGTHENING OF FRIENDSHIP AND CO-OPERATION BETWEEN THE SOVIET UNION AND OTHER SOCIALIST STATES, 30 OCTOBER 1956 (*Pravda*, 31 OCTOBER 1956, *New Times*, 45, 1956)

The policy of peaceful co-existence, friendship and co-operation among all states has been, and remains, the immutable foundation of the foreign relations of the Union of Soviet Socialist Republics.

This policy finds its most profound and consistent expression in the mutual relations between the socialist countries. United by the common ideals of building a socialist society and by the principles of proletarian internationalism, the countries of the great commonwealth of socialist nations can build their mutual relations only on the principles of complete equality, respect for each other's territorial integrity, state independence and sovereignty, and non-interference in each other's internal affairs. This does not exclude, but on the contrary presupposes, close fraternal co-operation and mutual assistance among the countries of the socialist community in the economic, political and cultural spheres.

It was on this basis that the system of people's democracy in a number of countries of Europe and Asia was formed, gained strength and displayed its great viability after the Second World War and the routing of fascism.

The process of building the new system and implementing the far-reaching revolutionary transformations in social relations met with many difficulties, unresolved problems and downright mistakes, including those in the mutual relations between socialist countries—violations and mistakes which belittled the principle of equality in the relations between the socialist states.

The 20th Congress of the Communist Party of the Soviet Union resolutely denounced these violations and mistakes and set the task of consistent application by the Soviet Union in its mutual relations with the other socialist countries of the Leninist principles of equal rights of the peoples. It proclaimed the need to take full account of the historical past and the distinctive features of each country that has embarked upon the road of building a new life.

The Soviet government is consistently carrying out these historic decisions of the 20th Congress which create conditions for the further strengthening of friendship and co-operation among the socialist countries on the immutable foundation of respecting the full sovereignty of each socialist state.

Recent events have shown that it has become necessary to issue an appropriate statement on the Soviet Union's position with regard to the mutual relations between the USSR and other socialist countries, primarily in the economic and military spheres.

The Soviet government is ready to discuss jointly with the governments of other socialist states measures such as would ensure the further development and consolidation of the economic ties among the socialist countries so as to remove any possibility of violation of the principle of national sovereignty, mutual benefit and equality in economic relations.

This principle must also be applied to the advisers. It is known that in the first period when the new social system was taking shape, the Soviet Union, at the request of the governments of the people's democracies, sent to those countries a certain number of its specialists—engineers, agronomists, scientific workers and military advisers. Recently the Soviet government has more than once raised with the socialist states the question of recalling its advisers.

In view of the fact that by this time skilled national cadres in all spheres of economic and military development have been trained in the people's democracies, the Soviet government considers it as urgent to examine together with the other socialist states the question of the desirability of the further stay of Soviet advisers in those countries.

In military affairs an important foundation for the mutual relations between the Soviet Union and the people's democracies is the Warsaw Treaty, under which the parties to the Treaty undertook appropriate political and military commitments, including the commitment to adopt 'agreed measures necessary to strengthen their defensive power in order to protect the peaceful labour of their peoples, guarantee the inviolability of their frontiers and territories and provide defence against possible aggression'.

It is common knowledge that Soviet units are stationed in the

Hungarian and Rumanian Republics under the Warsaw Treaty and in conformity with government agreements. Soviet military units are stationed in the Polish Republic on the basis of the Potsdam four-power agreement and the Warsaw Treaty. There are no Soviet military units in the other people's democracies.

For the purpose of assuring the mutual security of the socialist countries the Soviet government is ready to examine with the other socialist countries that are members of the Warsaw Treaty the question of the Soviet forces stationed in those countries. In so doing, the Soviet government bases itself on the general principle that the stationing of forces of any state which is a member of the Warsaw Treaty on the territory of another state, party to the Warsaw Treaty, is being done on the basis of agreement between all the parties to the Treaty and only with the consent of the state on whose territory and at whose request those forces have been so stationed or are to be so stationed. . . .

The Soviet government expresses confidence that the peoples of the socialist countries will not allow external and internal reactionary forces to shake the foundations of the people's democratic system, won and reinforced by the selfless struggle and labour of the workers, peasants and intellectuals of each country. They will do their utmost, after removing all obstacles standing in the way of the further strengthening of the democratic foundations, independence and sovereignty of their countries, to develop further the socialist foundations of each country, its economy, and its culture for the sake of the uninterrupted rise in the living standards and cultural level of all the working people, and they will strengthen the fraternal unity and mutual assistance among the socialist countries for the consolidation of the great cause of peace and socialism.

DOCUMENT 46. EXTRACT FROM KHRUSHCHEV'S INTERVIEW WITH TWO POLISH JOURNALISTS (*Pravda*, 10 MARCH 1958)

During the past two years relations between the communist and workers' parties have developed and grown stronger, than hitherto, along the lines of proletarian internationalism. The communist parties are called upon to unite the peoples in the struggle for peace and socialism. That is why the communist parties want to have close bonds with each other, want united action. At the same time every party is absolutely independent politically and in its organization, expressing as it does the interests of the working class and working people, the national interests of its country. The international and national interests of the working class, as of all the working people, do not contradict each other, but blend harmoniously together. The communist parties have always regarded the consolidation of international proletarian solidarity as their sacred duty, and have resolutely been fighting against any attempts to weaken the unity of the international working-class movement. . . .

The enemies of the working class counted on causing 'complications' in relations between the fraternal parties, and particularly between the parties of the socialist states.

With this end in view, they tried to exaggerate difficulties encountered in building socialism and to make use of certain individual misunderstandings and irregularities in relations between the socialist states. These misunderstandings can, of course, take place, inasmuch as an absolutely new type of relations is taking shape—relations which have no precedent in history. As experience shows, however, all the problems concerning relations between the socialist states are solved and can be solved, through friendly discussion on the basis of strict observance of the principles of proletarian internationalism.

This, of course, does not suit our enemies. They would like to see the peoples of the socialist countries at loggerheads. This would make it easier to realize their cherished dream of restoring capitalism in the people's democracies. It is common knowledge, for instance, that the reactionary imperialist forces wanted to cash in on the events in Hungary and also on the difficulties encountered in building socialism in Poland. Moreover, they actively intervened in Hungarian events. The counter-revolutionary forces rushed there to crush socialist Hungary and restore fascism. But the healthy forces of the Hungarian people united to repel fascist reaction and, helped by the Soviet Union and the other socialist states, defeated the counter-revolutionary insurgents. . . .

The enemies of socialism have shouted their heads off, and are continuing their rumpus about some sort of 'special processes' taking place in Poland, about tendencies of some sort showing that Poland has been departing from the socialist path of development. . . .

Can the working people voluntarily forfeit the socialist gains to their enemies, agree that capitalism be restored in the countries of socialism. that the factories and mills be returned again to a handful of capitalists, and that the land be returned to the landowners and *kulaks*?

Can the working people of these countries permit the return of unemployment and cruel exploitation of the workers and peasants, and allow the capitalists and landowners to oppress the working people again?

It is absolutely clear how illusory and impracticable are the dreams of representatives of international reaction about the restoration of capitalism in the socialist states. . . .

The march of a country whose people have chosen the road of socialism and are working to build a new society, without rich or poor, without exploitation of man by man, without unemployment and poverty, cannot be reversed. That is even less possible now that every socialist country relies upon the support and assistance of the whole of the mighty socialist camp.

The working people of every socialist state are deeply interested in everything that happens in the other fraternal, friendly countries.

DOCUMENT 47. EXTRACT FROM THE DECLARATION OF TWELVE COMMUNIST PARTIES MEETING IN MOSCOW, 14–16 NOVEMBER 1957 (*SN*, 22 NOVEMBER 1957)

At the bedrock of the relations between the countries of the world socialist system and all the communist and workers' parties lie the principles of Marxism-Leninism, the principle of proletarian internationalism which have been tested by life. Today the vital interests of the working people of all countries call for their support for the Soviet Union and all the socialist countries who, pursuing a policy of preserving peace throughout the world, are the mainstay of peace and social progress. The working class, the democratic forces and the working people everywhere are interested in tirelessly strengthening fraternal contacts for the sake of the common cause, in safeguarding from enemy encroachments the historic political and social gains won in the Soviet Union, the first and mightiest socialist power, in the Chinese People's Republic and in all the socialist countries, and in seeing these gains extended and consolidated.

The socialist countries base their relations on principles of complete equality, respect for territorial integrity, state independence and sovereignty and non-interference in one another's affairs. These are vital principles. However, they do not exhaust the essence of the relations among them.

Fraternal mutual aid is part and parcel of these relations. This aid is a striking expression of socialist internationalism.

On a basis of complete equality, mutual benefit and comradely mutual assistance, the socialist states have established among themselves extensive economic and cultural co-operation that plays an important part in promoting the economic and political independence of each socialist country and the socialist commonwealth as a whole. The socialist states will continue to extend and improve economic and cultural co-operation among themselves.

The socialist states also advocate all-round expansion of economic and cultural relations with all other countries, provided they desire it, on a basis of equality, mutual benefit and non-interference in one another's internal affairs.

The solidarity of the socialist countries is not directed against any other country. On the contrary, it serves the interests of all peace-loving peoples, restrains the aggressive strivings of the bellicose imperialist circles and supports and encourages the growing forces of peace. The socialist countries are against the division of the world into military blocs. But in view of the situation that has taken shape, with the western powers refusing to accept the proposals of the socialist countries for the mutual abolition of military blocs, the Warsaw Treaty Organization, which is of a defensive nature, serves the security of the peoples of Europe and supports peace throughout the world, must be preserved and strengthened.

The socialist countries are united in a single community by the fact that they are taking the common socialist road, by the common class essence of the social and economic system and state authority, by the requirements of mutual aid and support, identity of interests and aims in the struggle against imperialism, for the victory of socialism and communism and by the ideology of Marxism-Leninism which is common to all.

The solidarity and close unity of the socialist countries constitute a reliable guarantee of the sovereignty and independence of each of them. Stronger fraternal relations and friendship among the socialist countries call for a Marxist-Leninist internationalist policy on the part of the communist and workers' parties, for educating all the working people in the spirit of combining internationalism with patriotism, and for a determined effort to overcome the survivals of bourgeois nationalism and chauvinism. All issues pertaining to relations between the socialist countries can be fully settled through comradely discussion, with strict observance of the principles of socialist internationalism.

DOCUMENT 48. EXTRACT FROM THE STATEMENT OF EIGHTY-ONE COMMUNIST PARTIES MEETING IN MOSCOW, NOVEMBER 1960 (*New Times*, NO. 50, 1960)

All the Marxist-Leninist parties are independent and have equal rights; they shape their policies according to the specific conditions in their respective countries and in keeping with Marxist-Leninist principles, and support each other. The success of the working-class cause in any country is unthinkable without the internationalist solidarity of all Marxist-Leninist parties. Every party is responsible to the working class, to the working people of its country, to the international working class and communist movement as a whole.

The communist and workers' parties hold meetings whenever necessary to discuss urgent problems, to share experiences, acquaint themselves with each other's views and positions, work out common views through consultations and co-ordinate joint actions in the struggle for common goals.

Whenever a party wants to clear up questions relating to the activities of another fraternal party, its leadership approaches the leadership of the party concerned, and, if necessary, they hold meetings and consultations.

The experience and results of the meetings of representatives of the communist parties held in recent years, particularly the results of the two major meetings—that of November 1957 and this meeting—show that in present-day conditions such meetings are an effective form of exchanging views and experience, enriching Marxist-Leninist theory by collective effort and elaborating a common attitude in the struggle for common objectives.

The communist and workers' parties unanimously declare that the Communist Party of the Soviet Union has been, and remains, the universally recognized vanguard of the world communist movement, being the most experienced and steeled contingent of the international communist movement. The experience which the CPSU has gained in the struggle for the victory of the working class, in socialist construction and in the full-scale construction of communism, is of fundamental significance for the whole of the world communist movement. The example of the CPSU and its fraternal solidarity inspire all the communist parties in their struggle for peace and socialism, and represent the revolutionary principles of proletarian internationalism applied in practice. The historic decisions of the 20th Congress of the CPSU are not only of great importance for the CPSU and communist construction in the USSR, but have initiated a new stage in the world communist movement, and have promoted its development on the basis of Marxism-Leninism.

*

From the autmn of 1963 Khrushchev had been attempting to convene a world conference of communist parties. The Chinese would be forced to accept the discipline that such a conference imposed or, if they refused to accede, they would be condemned by it. Not only the Chinese objected to such an approach which ran the risk of splitting the world communist movement. In July 1964 the Soviets announced that they would go ahead with the conference and invited twenty-six members of the drafting committee of the 1960 conference to meet in Moscow in December 1964. The Chinese warned 'that the day you call a schismatic meeting will be the day you step into your grave'. Khrushchev's fall in October 1964 postponed the meeting. A month later, the Soviets, realizing that they could as little agree with the Chinese as could Khrushchev proposed that a meeting take place in Moscow on 1 March 1965. It was described as a 'consultative meeting' and only eighteen parties attended, plus one observer.

Having got a taste for conferences the Soviets resorted frequently to this device, in Karlovy Vary in April 1967 and in Budapest in February to March 1968. It was there decided to hold a conference in Moscow at the end of the year. The invasion of Czechoslovakia forced the Soviets to postpone this meeting to June 1969. If this meeting did anything constructive, which is doubtful, it underlined publicly the divisions in the communist world.

Western observers have always expected that such conferences as those of 1965 or 1969 would result in a formal condemnation of the Chinese. It seems, however, that what little support the Soviets have in the world communist movement would evaporate if this were attempted.

Nineteen parties attended the 1965 meeting, one of them, the Communist Party of USA, as an observer only. The Yugoslavs and the Rumanians were absent. Even the British arrived deliberately one day late. It is likely that a hard line against the Chinese was prevented by the Italian delegate, Enrico Berlinguer.

At the 1969 meeting seventy-five parties were represented— a numerical success. But of these thirty-two were minuscule shadow movements. Fourteen parties expressed objections to the communiqué which the conference issued. Five of the parties which signed, including the Rumanian Communist Party, did so with reservations. The communist parties of Albania, China and Yugoslavia were absent.

DOCUMENT 49. EXTRACT FROM THE COMMUNIQUÉ OF THE CONSULTATIVE MEETING OF COMMUNIST PARTIES IN MOSCOW, 10 MARCH 1965 (*SN*, 10 MARCH 1965)

The solidarity of all the revolutionary forces of modern times— the socialist commonwealth, the national liberation movement and the international working class—has decisive importance for the successful struggle against imperialism. The interests of the solidarity of these forces insistently demand the strengthening of the unity of the world communist movement.

The differences in the communist movement, which weaken

its solidarity, harm the cause of the world liberation movement and the cause of communism.

The participants in the meeting stated the conviction that what unites the communist parties is much stronger than what disunites them at a given moment. Even given the existence of disagreements concerning the political line and many important problems in theory and tactics, it is fully possible and necessary to strive for unity of action in the struggle against imperialism, in the cause of comprehensive support for the liberation movement of the peoples, in the struggle for universal peace and the peaceful co-existence of states with different social systems— regardless of whether the countries involved are large or small —in the struggle for the vital interests and historical tasks of the working class. Joint action in the struggle for these common goals is the most correct path for overcoming the existing differences.

The participants in the meeting emphasized the need for the communist parties to dedicate collective efforts to improving mutual relations among the parties, to strengthening the solidarity of the international communist movement, while observing democratic principles of independence and the equality of all the fraternal parties.

In the struggle for the resolution of the tasks common to the whole communist movement, it is expedient to use all possibilities and paths, bilateral and multilateral meetings of representatives of the fraternal parties and other forms of party communication and exchanges of opinion.

The participants in the meeting held unanimously that in today's conditions, as the 1960 statement points out, international conferences of communist and workers' parties are an effective form for the mutual exchange of opinions and experience, for enriching Marxist-Leninist theory through collective efforts and working out single positions in the struggle for common goals. Such conferences, carried out with the observance of the principles of full equality and the independence of each party, can well serve the cause of overcoming disagreements and consolidating the communist movement on the basis of Marxism-Leninism and proletarian internationalism. Therefore the active and thorough preparation of a new international conference and its convocation at a suitable time, in the opinion of the participants in the meeting, fully answer the interests of the world communist movement.

In order to convene and successfully carry out the new conference, it should be thoroughly prepared both from the standpoint of content and with respect to organization; joint efforts should be actively exerted to create favourable conditions for participation in its preparation by all the fraternal parties, and it is necessary to strive tirelessly to improve the atmosphere in the international communist movement. The conference is called upon to serve the common cause of all communists. The focusing of attention and the concentration of efforts on the urgent tasks now facing the communist movement will best of all serve the *rapprochement* of our positions on the vital questions of the day.

The participants in the meeting expressed the opinion that it would be desirable to hold a preliminary consultative meeting of representatives of the eighty-one parties that participated in the 1960 conference to discuss the question of a new international conference. It is necessary to carry out consultations with all these parties to solve the question of calling such a preliminary meeting.

The parties represented at the present meeting favoured the cessation of open polemics, which have been of a nature that is unfriendly and offensive to fraternal parties. At the same time, they deem it useful to continue the exchange of opinions on important contemporary questions of common interest in a comradely form, without mutual attacks. The participants in the meeting favour strict observance of the norms for relations between parties established by the 1957 and 1960 conferences and oppose the interference of some parties in the internal affairs of others.

DOCUMENT 50. EXTRACT FROM THE STATEMENT ISSUED BY THE INTERNATIONAL COMMUNIST PARTIES CONFERENCE IN MOSCOW, 17 JUNE 1969 (*Mezhdunarodnoe Soveshchanie Kommunisticheskikh i Rabochikh Partii. Dokumenty i Materialy*, MOSCOW, 1969, PP. 326–8)

The participants in the meeting are convinced that the effectiveness of each communist party's policy depends on its successes in its own country, on the successes of other fraternal parties and on the extent of their co-operation. Each communist party is responsible for its activity to its own working class and people and, at the same time, to the international working class. Every communist party's national and international responsibilities are indivisible. Marxist-Leninists are both patriots and internationalists; they reject both national narrow-mindedness and negation or underestimation of national interests and striving for hegemony. At the same time, the communist parties, the parties of the working class and all working people are the standard-bearers of genuine national interests, unlike the reactionary classes, which betray these interests. The winning of power by the working class and its allies is the greatest contribution which a communist party fighting under capitalist conditions can make to the cause of socialism and proletarian internationalism.

The communist and workers' parties are conducting their activity in diverse, specific conditions, requiring an appropriate approach to the solution of concrete problems. Each party, guided by the principles of Marxism-Leninism and in keeping with concrete national conditions, fully independently works out its own policy, determines the directions, forms and methods of struggle and, depending on the circumstances, chooses the peaceful or non-peaceful way of transition to socialism and also the forms and methods of building socialism in its own country. At the same time the diverse conditions in which the communist parties operate, the different approaches to practical tasks and even differences on certain questions must not hinder concerted international action by fraternal parties, particularly on the basic problems of the anti-imperialist struggle. The greater the strength and the unity of each communist party, the better can it fulfil its role both inside the country and in the international communist movement.

Communists are aware that our movement, while scoring great, historic victories in the course of its development, has recently encountered serious difficulties. Communists are convinced, however, that these difficulties will be overcome. This belief is based on the fact that the international working class has common long-term objectives and interests, on the desire of every party to find a solution to existing problems which would meet both national and international interests, and the communists' revolutionary mission; it is based on the will of communists for unity on an international scale.

The communist and workers' parties, regardless of some difference of opinion, reaffirm their determination to present a united front in the struggle against imperialism.

Some of the divergences which have arisen are eliminated through an exchange of opinion or disappear as the development of events clarifies the essence of the outstanding issues. Other divergences may last long. The meeting is confident that the outstanding issues can and must be resolved correctly by strengthening all forms of co-operation among the communist parties, by extending inter-party ties, mutual exchange of experience, comradely discussion and consultation and unity of action in the international arena. It is the internationalist duty of every party to do everything it can to help to improve relations and to promote trust between all parties and to undertake further efforts to strengthen the unity of the international communist movement. This unity is strengthened by a collective analysis of concrete reality.

(d) ECONOMIC AND MILITARY CO-OPERATION

The fact that the Council for Mutual Economic Assistance (Comecon) received its constitution eleven years after it was founded illustrates the small role it played in the politics and economics of the area. It should be particularly noted that Comecon does not envisage the same kind of integration as does the European Economic Community. All members have the right of veto. Moreover, members may declare their lack of interest in a question concerned, thus excluding themselves from a Council recommendation or decision. The organization was at first limited to European socialist states but observers from the Asian socialist states attended Council sessions. In 1962 Mongolia, in order to help her stay out of the clutches of the Chinese, became a member. Meanwhile Albania ceased to attend meetings and may be presumed no longer to be a member. In September 1964 Yugoslavia became associated with Comecon by being admitted to several standing commissions.

DOCUMENT 51. EXTRACTS FROM THE COMECON CHARTER, 1960 (MICHAEL KASER, *Comecon*, OXFORD UNIVERSITY PRESS, 1967, PP. 235–40)

The Governments of the People's Republic of Albania, the People's Republic of Bulgaria, the Hungarian People's Republic, the German Democratic Republic, the Polish People's Republic, the Rumanian People's Republic, the Union of Soviet Socialist Republics and the Czechoslovak Republic:

Considering that the economic co-operation which is being successfully carried out between their countries is conducive to the most rational development of the national economy, to raising the standard of living of the population and to strengthening the unity and solidarity of these countries;

Being fully determined henceforth to develop all-round economic co-operation on the basis of consistently bringing about the international socialist division of labour in the interests of the building of socialism and communism in their countries, and in the interests of ensuring lasting peace throughout the world;

Being convinced that the developments of economic co-operation between their countries promotes the achievement of the purposes defined in the Charter of the United Nations;

Confirming their readiness to develop economic relations with all countries irrespective of their social and political structure on the basis of equality, mutual advantage and non-interference in each other's internal affairs;

Recognising the constantly increasing role of the Council for Mutual Economic Assistance on the organisation of economic co-operation between their countries;

Have agreed for these ends to adopt the present Statutes.

ARTICLE I. PURPOSES AND PRINCIPLES

1 The purpose of the Council for Mutual Economic Assistance is to promote, by uniting and co-ordinating the efforts of the member countries of the Council, the planned development of the national economy, the acceleration of economic and technical progress in these countries, the raising of the level of industrialization in the industrially less-developed countries, a steady increase in the productivity of labour and a constant

improvement in the welfare of the peoples of the member countries of the Council.

2 The Council for Mutual Economic Assistance is established on the basis of the principle of the sovereign equality of all the member countries of the Council.

Economic, scientific, and technical co-operation between the member countries of the Council shall be carried out in accordance with the principles of full equality of rights, respect for each other's sovereignty and national interests, mutual advantage and friendly mutual assistance.

ARTICLE II. MEMBERSHIP

1 The original members of the Council for Mutual Economic Assistance are the countries which have signed and ratified the present Statutes.

2 Admission to membership of the Council shall be open to other countries which share the purposes and principles of the Council and have expressed their readiness to accept the obligations contained in the present Statutes.

3 Any member country of the Council may withdraw from the Council upon giving notice to the depositary of the present Charter to this effect. . . .

4 Member countries of the Council shall agree:

(a) to ensure the fulfilment of the recommendations of the Council organs adopted by them;

(b) to render the Council and its officials the necessary co-operation in the discharge by them of the functions stipulated in the present Charter;

(c) to submit to the Council the materials and information necessary for carrying out the tasks entrusted to it;

(d) to inform the Council about progress in fulfilling the recommendations adopted in the Council.

ARTICLE III. FUNCTIONS AND POWERS

1 In accordance with the purposes and principles laid down in Article I of these Statutes, the Council for Mutual Economic Assistance:

(a) shall organize all-round economic, scientific and technical co-operation between the member countries of the Council with a view to making the most rational use of their natural resources and to accelerating the development of their productive capacities;

(b) shall co-operate in the improvement of the international socialist division of labour by means of the co-ordination of national economic plans, and of the socialization and co-operation of production of member countries of the Council;

(c) shall adopt measures in order to study the economic and scientific-technical problems of member countries of the Council;

(d) shall co-operate with member countries of the Council in elaborating and implementing common undertakings in the fields of:

the development of industry and agriculture of member countries of the Council;

the development of transport so as primarily to satisfy the ever-increasing freight traffic in the imports, exports and transit of member countries of the Council;

the most effective utilization of investment funds allocated by member countries of the Council for the expansion of the extractive and manufacturing branches of industry and for the construction of major projects of interest to two or more countries;

the development of the exchange of goods and services between the member countries of the Council and with other countries;

the exchange of scientific and technical knowledge and advanced production experience;

(e) shall undertake other activities for the achievement of the objectives of the Council.

2 The Council for Mutual Economic Assistance, as represented by its organs, acting within the bounds of their competence, is empowered to make recommendations and decisions in conformity with the present Charter.

ARTICLE IV. RECOMMENDATIONS AND DECISIONS

1 Recommendations shall be adopted on matters of economic, scientific and technical co-operation. Recommendations shall be communicated to the member countries of the Council for consideration.

The recommendations adopted by the member countries of

the Council shall be implemented by decisions of their governments or competent authorities in accordance with their
national legislation.

2 Decisions shall be made on organizational and procedural
matters.

3 All recommendations and decisions by the Council shall be
adopted only with the consent of the interested member
countries of the Council, and each country shall be entitled to
declare its interest in any matter considered by the Council.

The effects of recommendations and decisions shall not
extend to countries which have declared their lack of interest
in the question concerned. Each such country may, however,
accede subsequently to recommendations and decisions adopted
by the other member countries of the Council.

ARTICLE V. ORGANS

1 The Council for Mutual Economic Assistance shall have the
following principal organs for discharging the functions and
powers referred to in Article III of these Statutes:

the Council Session
the Executive Committee
the Standing Commissions
the Secretariat. . . .

ARTICLE VI. THE COUNCIL SESSION

1 The Council Session is the supreme organ of the Council
for Mutual Economic Assistance. It shall be empowered to
discuss all matters coming within the competence of the
Council, and to adopt recommendations and decisions in
accordance with the present Statutes. . . .

ARTICLE VII. EXECUTIVE COMMITTEE

The Executive Committee of the Council shall consist of the
representatives of all the member countries of the Council, on
the basis of one from each country.

1 The Executive Committee is the chief executive organ of
the Council.

The Executive Committee has a Bureau for Integrated Planning Problems in which each country is represented by a
deputy chairman of the state planning organ.

2 The Executive Committee holds its meetings not less frequently than once every two months.

3 The Executive Committee within the sphere of its competence has the right to adopt recommendations and decisions in accordance with this Charter. The Executive Committee may submit proposals to be considered by the Council Session.

4 The Executive Committee:

(a) shall direct the totality of work connected with the execution of tasks posed before the Council in accordance with the resolutions of the Council Sessions, and shall systematically supervise the execution by member countries of the duties which follow from recommendations adopted by organs of the Council;

(b) shall direct the work of co-ordinating plans of national economic development, specialization and co-operation of the production of member countries of the Council and shall organize the elaboration of the basic direction of the national division of labour in the major production branches of those countries;

(c) shall consider proposals of member countries of the Council Standing Commissions, the Bureau of the Executive Committee for Integrated Planning Problems, the Secretariat of the Council, and other organs of the Council concerning questions of economic and scientific-technical co-operation, shall analyse the state of that co-operation and shall elaborate undertakings for its further development;

(d) shall elaborate basic directions and measures for the development of the exchange of goods and services between the member countries of the Council, and of scientific-technical co-operation between member countries of the Council;

(e) directs the work of the Secretariat of the Council and of the Standing Commissions of the Council, and determines the basic lines of activity of those Commissions. . . .

*

Khrushchev's desire to use Comecon as a means of economic and political integration was supported by the industrialized northern tier of eastern Europe, Czechoslovakia, Poland, Hungary and the GDR and was resisted by Rumania which decided that it, too, wanted a highly developed industry, thus depriving the industrialized northern states of both a market and a source of raw material. The Rumanians saw their aspirations for economic and political independence put in jeopardy and made their view public in April 1964. They took the same attitude over the Warsaw Treaty. In these positions they were supported by the Chinese. After 1964 such integrationist plans were abandoned, to be revived, though rather cautiously, after the invasion of Czechoslovakia.

DOCUMENT 52. EXTRACTS FROM KHRUSHCHEV'S ARTICLE, 'VITAL QUESTIONS OF THE DEVELOPMENT OF THE WORLD SOCIALIST SYSTEM', IN *Kommunist*, NO. 12, 1962 (*World Marxist Review*, SEPTEMBER 1962)

The formation in 1949 of the Council for Mutual Economic Assistance marked the beginning of multilateral co-operation, at first in the sphere of trade and afterwards also in the sphere of production. The world socialist system is now beginning to take shape as a single entity, not only politically but also economically. In the course of the twelve years' existence of the Council we have succeeded in creating, at least for the member countries of the organization, a solid basis for joint co-operation and mutual aid.

The functions of the Council in organizing joint economic co-operation do not extend as yet to all the socialist countries. The differences in time in taking the road to socialism prevented them from simultaneously entering into joint economic co-operation. However, the successful economic integration of the member countries will make joint co-operation easier for all the socialist countries. Between the member countries and the socialist countries which do not belong to the Council, broad economic contacts are taking shape, and these are paving the way for still wider economic co-operation.

At present the socialist camp as a whole and most of the countries comprising it have a developed industry and large-scale socialized agriculture. The socialist system, which embraces 26 per cent of the territory of the world, produces, according to incomplete figures, about 37 per cent of the world industrial output. In most of the socialist countries industry accounts for approximately three-quarters of the overall national product.

The socialist world market, in which all the socialist countries are taking part—the Soviet Union, People's China, and the people's democracies in Europe and Asia—has grown stronger.

The socialist countries are now at a stage where the conditions have ripened for raising their economic and political co-operation to a new and higher level. At this level special significance is acquired by co-ordinated national-economic plans, socialist international division of labour, and by co-ordination and specialization of production, which will guarantee the successful organic development of the socialist countries.

The world socialist system is now at a stage where it is no longer possible correctly to chart its development by merely adding up the national economies. The task now is to do everything to consolidate the national economy of each, broaden its relations, and gradually advance towards that single worldwide organism embracing the system as a whole which Lenin's genius foresaw.

With the emergence of socialism beyond the confines of a single country, its economic laws found much greater room for action and the operation of these laws became more and more complex.

For example, the law of planned and proportionate development operating on the scale of the system as a whole calls for planning and definite proportions both in each of the socialist countries taken separately and on the scale of the entire commonwealth. To utilize the economic laws of socialism fully we must take due cognizance of their operation not only at national levels but also on the international plane.

We are now faced with a task of historical significance—to learn how to make the most effective use of the advantages of socialism, that is advantages flowing from the existence of the new world system, to direct the socialist international division of labour, specialization and co-ordination of production, and co-ordination of research and technological work, and to make full use of the possibilities opened up by the socialist world market.

Marx in his time pointed out that even the simple addition of labour greatly increases its productivity. All the greater, then, is the productivity of social labour, given the combined efforts of the socialist countries with their single-type social structure and community of political aims and interests. By co-ordinating the economies of the socialist countries we shall be able to increase tenfold the strength of each and of the system as a whole. We are bringing the forms of our economic co-operation into conformity with our increased productive forces, and we are clearing the way for their further development.

Streamlining the system of co-operation and mutual aid will help to bring the socialist nations closer, make for the evening up of their economic development generally and, at the same time, enhance the sovereignty of each country, since each will have in addition to its own forces the support of the entire socialist community. Not to make use of the advantages deriving from the international division of labour now that we have a socialist system would mean taking the more difficult way in creating modern productive forces, depriving ourselves of the possibility of expanding production in keeping with the latest achievements of science and technology.

It goes without saying that a prerequisite for the continued expansion of the productive forces of the socialist countries and, consequently, of the entire socialist world economy, is the fullest utilization by each country of its internal resources, steady improvement in the forms and methods of economic leadership, and consistent application of the Leninist principles and methods of socialist managements.

The world socialist system, it should be said, can forge ahead only through the all-round co-operation of the countries belonging to it, through their co-ordinated effort, bearing in mind the interests of each country and of the socialist community as a whole. There is no other way. . . .

After the adoption by the 22nd Congress of the Communist Party of the Soviet Union of the programme for building communism in the Soviet Union, the imperialists began to trumpet loudly about the 'economic challenge' of the USSR, and to work feverishly to hold their own in the economic competition between the two systems. The leaders of capitalism and its ideologists forthrightly declared that, in view of the growing threat of an economic offensive on the part of the Soviet Union and the other socialist countries, the capitalist countries should combine their forces. It was not accidental that President Kennedy, in a recent declaration about the so-called interdependence of the western powers, called for a joint effort on the part of the imperialist countries of western Europe and the United States, with a view to establishing an 'Atlantic Partnership'. It goes without saying that Kennedy's plans provide for maintaining and enhancing the leading role of the United States in the capitalist world. These developments show once again that the imperialists dread economic competition every bit as much as they dread our military might, and are trying to counterpose to the socialist countries, to the international communist movement and to the national liberation struggle of the peoples, a solid front of the reactionary forces.

After the Second World War the trend towards integrating the foreign policy and the economies of the capitalist countries became more pronounced. We saw the rise of international organizations such as the European Coal and Steel Community, the Common Market, the Organization for Economic Co-operation and Development and others. The rulers of the western world, notwithstanding all their antagonisms, have partly succeeded in forming inter-state alliances whose activities create difficulties for the newly emergent countries in Asia and Africa and also in Latin America.

How is it that the imperialists, despite their antagonisms, have managed in a measure to co-ordinate on an international scale economic co-operation in a number of important spheres?

First, we see manifested here, although on a contradictory basis, the objective trend towards a greater internationalization of economic life, rendered more pronounced in our days by the rapid scientific and technological advance. State-monopoly capital on its part is anxious to encourage this trend and to use it for its aggressive military-political aims. By forming their inter-state economic associations, the imperialists are trying to counteract the negative consequences of the spontaneous development of the capitalist world economy.

Second, faced with the fact of the growing might of the socialist system and its planned economy, and faced with the fact of the rapid advance of the movement for emancipation of the peoples, the imperialists are forced to find ways and means of easing the antagonisms in their camp. Dreading peaceful economic competition with the socialist countries, they are trying to tone down their internal antagonisms in view of the basic contradiction of our epoch—the contradiction between capitalism and socialism.

The Common Market signifies big advantages for the imperialist monopolies. At the same time it threatens the interests of the working class, the peasantry and the middle sections of the urban population. The small countries will, increasingly, become more dependent on this imperialist alliance, which, in essence, signifies a new form of the division and redivision of the capitalist world market. The aggressive forces want to use the Common Market for the purpose of reinforcing NATO and stepping up the arms race. . . .

The Soviet government, like the governments of the other member countries of the Council, stands for extending the joint financing of industrial construction, transport installations and other enterprises of international significance. Joint financing should be practised first of all in the raw material branches working for export, since these branches are the biggest consumers of capital. In our view the conditions have matured for jointly examining in the Council plans for the more important enterprises of common interest.

Co-ordinating capital construction will ensure a rational distribution of the productive forces on the scale of the entire commonwealth. And should we succeed—and of this there can hardly be any doubt—in agreeing on plans for capital construction between the countries, with the proviso that the new industrial enterprises will cater not only for national but also for common needs, that account will be taken not only of the production capacity of one's own country but also of the others, then it will be possible to release quite substantial funds for other things.

Co-ordination of plans, far from restricting the economic initiative of the countries, will, on the contrary, give free rein to it. The result will be a much better and fuller utilization of the resources for advancing both the economy of each country and that of the socialist as a whole.

In the past the Council was not in a position to revise the system of co-ordinating plans generally, and investment plans in particular, on a new basis, because, first, according to the old statute it did not have the necessary powers, and second, it lacked the necessary planning instruments—material balances, comparable national-economic indices and unified statistics. The decisions of the June meeting will, however, enable the work of the Council to be organized in a new way.

Co-ordinating the national-economic plans together with co-ordinated and specialized production will help to bring the economies of the socialist countries closer together and will add to our common economic potential. What we need are those flexible forms of mutually advantageous and equal co-operation that will best take into account the interests of each country and help them to prosper.

The process of extending the international division of labour is reflected best of all in foreign trade. The overall volume of foreign trade of the member countries of the Council in 1961 exceeded the 1950 volume three-and-a-half times over. The increase in the direct trade between the member countries was approximately the same. True, the volume of industrial production for this period rose in the same proportion. But if we bear in mind that the growth of agricultural output was somewhat slower, it will be found that the growth in trade between the member countries exceeded the growth of their overall national-economic production. This was due partly to the extended division of labour.

The aforementioned figures, while they can be regarded as satisfactory for the previous stage of co-operation, do not correspond to the tasks of today. With the substantial extension of the division of labour and specialization and co-ordination, the growth of the trade between the member countries will noticeably outstrip the growth in their output and the increase in the volume of their overall foreign trade.

Some bourgeois economists delight in stressing the successes of the west European integration, particularly in the sphere of the division of labour. They point out, for example, that the growth of trade between the Common Market countries from

1950 to 1961 was double the rate of growth of their industrial output, that it considerably surpassed the growth of their overall foreign trade.

Comparing the growth of trade in the Common Market countries with that in the Council's member countries, they claim that the international division of labour among the countries belonging to the Council for Mutual Economic Assistance is still at a lower level than in the European Community. But in saying this they ignore the fact that we started out from different levels and that it took the capitalists dozens of years to reach their present level. Long before the integration the 'Six' were highly developed, industrially, and specialization and co-ordination were more widely practised. But we had to begin from scratch. In the early stages the conditions needed for an extensive division of labour did not exist in all the countries of the people's democracy. Some of them had little or no industry, no sources of accumulation and, consequently, lacked the basis without which effective international division of labour is unthinkable.

Now, however, this stage has been passed. All the member countries of the Council have their own industrial basis, which can be extended more rapidly by means of the socialist international division of labour. The higher the level of the productive forces the more insistent the need for greater co-ordination and specialization and the better will be the conditions for their implementation.

The facts show that year by year in the socialist camp the exchange of goods—mainly of raw materials and other items—is growing. This, of course, is a good thing. As for reciprocal deliveries of manufactured goods and of machinery and equipment in the first place, their growth so far has lagged behind the increased output in these branches. For the period from 1955 to 1960 the output of machinery and equipment in the Council's member countries showed a growth of 95 per cent. Moreover, up-to-date machines were exported by former agrarian countries like Bulgaria, Rumania and others, which is proof of their successful industrialization. The reciprocal deliveries between the member countries for the same period showed an increase of 79 per cent. By 1965 the member countries of the Council anticipate that output of machines and equipment will have risen by approximately 50 per cent compared with 1960, while the growth of reciprocal deliveries of this production, in keeping with trade agreements, will be 45 per cent. But the level of the division of labour between our countries no longer corresponds to their economic requirements.

The lag in the reciprocal deliveries of machinery and equipment compared with the general growth of production of these items reflects an insufficient development of the division of labour and of specialization and co-ordination. But there can be no doubt that the lag is only a temporary matter which can, and will, be overcome by our joint efforts.

It should be said that in the sphere of specialization and co-ordination in the manufacturing branches of industry the Council's member countries inherited a very bad 'legacy' from capitalism. The conditions in some of the people's democracies in the past, when they were part of the capitalist world economy, were such that they were left with an economically unjustified universalization of industry based on small-quantity production. The absence of a reliable raw-materials and fuel basis, and above all the economic dependence on the imperialist monopolies of the big powers, deprived the majority of these countries of the possibility of developing large-scale production. This circumstance prevented them from taking part in the international division of labour on any kind of favourable conditions and engendered a tendency for them to produce as many types of manufactured goods as possible. They had no guarantees that they could get the things they needed in exchange for their own products.

The course of the co-operation between the member countries of the Council made it quite clear that this kind of 'universalization' had no justification—it was much too costly.

The tendency for a country to produce as many types of manufactured goods as possible, which derives from the principle of 'having everything of your own' regardless of the cost, generally speaking can arise in our time either as a result of an insufficiently developed economy or for reasons of a non-economic character. We are speaking here not about the big powers, for they can afford to have a more universal industry, thanks to specialization and co-ordination inside their countries and to a relatively big home market. But even for these countries international co-ordination has its advantages.

Under socialism the operation of the law of value does not bear a spontaneous character. Our enterprises do not come under the hammer even when they show a loss. But it goes without saying that we cannot afford to ignore the principle of 'profitability' without which it is impossible to conduct a socialist economy.

The more profitable the socialist enterprises are, the greater the accumulations at the disposal of the state for extended reproduction and for satisfying consumer needs. The profitable enterprise nowadays is the enterprise in which there is mass production and specialization, the enterprise equipped with the latest achievements of science and technology. Hence for the Council's member countries the question stands as follows: either the way of universalization of industry in each country or a resolute advance along the road of co-ordination and international specialization. The member countries hold that only in the latter way will their successful development be assured.

As we know, the expansion of the productive forces under capitalism is associated with a vast concentration and centralization of capital, which makes it possible to engage in mass production. In the developed capitalist countries the ups and downs of the market lead to the abolition of small production. As a rule, the enterprises which come out on top in the competitive struggle are those which engage in mass production and where production costs are low. The capitalists are impelled to division of labour and specialization by the merciless operation of the law of value, according to which any enterprise must be profitable, otherwise it goes to the wall. Mass production is the key to economic successes of capitalism. Why, for example, was Ford able to sell his automobiles on the world market? Because he engages in assembly-line production, which is the cheapest way to produce.

But it is here, too, that we see the weak and vulnerable sides of capitalist production. Concentration of capital and mass production under capitalism are based on private ownership of the means of production. The capitalist produces not for himself but for the market. In the conditions of private ownership and the operation of the blind laws of capitalism, growth of production comes up against the relatively narrow dimensions of the market, making it impossible to foresee for any considerable length of time the requirements of the market. This is one of the sources of the many unpleasant moments encountered by the capitalists, including crises and stagnation in their industry.

The socialist countries, having put an end to private ownership of the means of production, have liberated themselves also from the ills engendered by capitalism. And if we now, on the scale of the entire socialist system, combine our planning with the organization, on the basis of socialist 'concentration of capital' of assembly-line production—the advantages of which were first demonstrated by capitalism—we shall undoubtedly accelerate our victory in the economic competition with the capitalist system. But for this we must widely organize co-ordination and specialization on the scale of the world socialist system. Highly developed production such as that in the socialist countries has nothing in common with autarchy. To cling to the national exclusiveness of the economies of our countries would signify turning our backs on the very great advantages flowing from the socialist system, artificially holding back our advance, thus doing harm to our cause.

The world socialist system is not just a social-political union of countries, it is a world economic system. It follows then that the co-ordination should be pursued not within the restricted limits of each socialist country but on the scale of the socialist world economy, which means overcoming the national exclusiveness inherited from the past. Our planned production will enable us to do this successfully.

We are now advancing towards a much higher level, a level from which it is possible to observe and to take into account much more fully the interests of the entire socialist world economy.

International division of labour and specialization of production offers the best conditions for socialist industrialization, especially in the formerly backward countries. We communists fully understand the strivings of each of the socialist countries for industrialization, since this is a prerequisite for expanding the national economy, raising the culture and evening up the general level of economic development in the socialist community. We fully appreciate the desire of the peoples of these countries to overcome as quickly as possible the legacy of the past and to reach the heights of the developed countries. And we hold that specialization and co-ordination will make possible the construction of bigger and more profitable enterprises equipped with modern technology. Given this approach, the national income will grow rapidly, accumulations will be built up for extended reproduction and better conditions will be created for training highly skilled personnel and for scientific and technological progress.

The big specialized enterprises set up in keeping with the socialist division of labour are guaranteed sales for their products on the socialist world market, and the planned character of the economy ensures a stable demand for them. What is more, since all or many of the socialist countries are interested in these specialized enterprises, this presupposes joint activity and help in building and running them. It follows, therefore, that building a specialized and co-ordinated industry is equally advantageous both for the countries which already have developed industries and for those now advancing along the road of industrialization.

International specialization will benefit not only the small countries—but also such big countries as the Soviet Union. It goes without saying that the home requirements alone of a country like the USSR, with its immense market, enable it to build large enterprises of optimal size. But it, too, can benefit from participation in the socialist international division of labour. The Soviet Union is prepared even to cut down the production of certain types of manufactured goods should it be found more expedient to manufacture them in the other countries belonging to the council.

Co-operation in the council has now reached a point where it is necessary to decide the trend of the specialization in each country, that is, to decide exactly which branches, and in what complex and on what raw-material basis, should be built in each of the countries so as to meet our common needs in the most economic way. The time has come to draw up a balance sheet of production and consumption of the main types of manufactured goods in our countries for a period extending at least up to 1970, and in this way prepare a general scheme for inter-state specialization and co-ordination. The intention for the immediate years is to produce the more important types of manufactured goods on the basis of international specialization and co-ordination.

The programme for promoting the socialist international division of labour should be supplemented by agreed measures for improving organization and planning in the sphere of trade. With the emergence of socialism beyond the confines of a single country there arose the socialist world market—a completely new sphere of international exchange—which, in contrast to the capitalist world market, is governed not by blind laws but by planning. Trade between the socialist countries is ensured by long-term agreements based on planned production.

From the foreign-trade relations which have taken shape, we can see that we are still not making full use of the abundant possibilities for expanding trade among the member countries of the council. It often happens that needed goods are purchased 'on the side' whereas with the proper organization they could be purchased in our own countries. There is hardly any need to say that this state of affairs hampers our economic advance.

The socialist international division of labour can develop successfully only if the mechanism of our foreign trade operates smoothly and without a hitch, if trade ensures the full and prompt realization of the goods created through the division of labour. This explains why the member countries have agreed on a series of measures to improve the system of foreign trade. In particular, a big role will be played by going over to multi-lateral accounting, and also by measures to enhance mutual responsibility for fulfilment of obligations.

Expansion of foreign trade depends on the rate of growth of production, on the level of the international division of labour, and on the state of foreign-trade relations. Until now the expansion of trade on the scale of the member countries has had its source chiefly in the growth of volume of production. The time has now come to make the fullest possible use of all three factors.

A high degree of international specialization and co-ordination provides a sound basis for long-term trade agreements. The council is now faced with the job of drawing up a system which will ensure going over from bilateral to multilateral planning and regulation of trade and accounting between the socialist countries.

*

The Warsaw Treaty was signed on 14 May 1955, one day before the Austrian State Treaty, thus giving Soviet troops the legal right to garrison Hungary and Rumania. Like Comecon the Pact took some time to become active. In 1956 Soviet troops fought in Hungary, in theory at least, as a Warsaw Pact force. From 1961 onwards the role of the Pact in Soviet military and political planning has become ever more important. Their role is that of important auxiliary forces. The GDR actually adhered to the Treaty in January 1956, after establishing an army and a ministry of defence.

DOCUMENT 53. EXTRACT FROM THE WARSAW TREATY, 14 MAY 1955 (*New Times*, NO. 21, 1955)

Treaty of Friendship, Co-operation and Mutual Assistance Between the People's Republic of Albania, the People's Republic of Bulgaria, the Hungarian People's Republic, the German Democratic Republic, the Polish People's Republic, the Rumanian People's Republic, the Union of Soviet Socialist Republics and the Czechoslovak Republic.

The Contracting Parties, reaffirming their desire for the establishment of a system of European collective security based on the participation of all European states irrespective of their social and political systems, which would make it possible to unite their efforts in safeguarding the peace of Europe;

mindful, at the same time, of the situation created in Europe by the ratification of the Paris agreements, which envisage the formation of a new military alignment in the shape of 'Western European Union' with the participation of a remilitarized Western Germany and the integration of the latter in the North-Atlantic bloc, which increases the danger of another war and constitutes a threat to the national security of the peaceable states;

being persuaded that in these circumstances the peaceable European states must take the necessary measures to safeguard their security in the interests of preserving peace in Europe;

guided by the objects and principles of the Charter of the United Nations Organization;

being desirous of further promoting and developing friendship, co-operation and mutual assistance in accordance with the principles of respect for the independence and sovereignty of states and of non-interference in their internal affairs;

have decided to conclude the present Treaty of Friendship Co-operation and Mutual Assistance. . . .

Article 1

The Contracting Parties undertake, in accordance with the Charter of the United Nations Organization, to refrain in their international relations from the threat or use of force, and to settle their international disputes peacefully and in such manner as will not jeopardize international peace and security.

Article 2

The Contracting Parties declare their readiness to participate in a spirit of sincere co-operation in all international actions designed to safeguard international peace and security, and will fully devote their energies to the attainment of this end.

The Contracting Parties will furthermore strive for the adoption, in agreement with other states which may desire to co-operate in this, of effective measures for universal reduction of armaments and prohibition of atomic, hydrogen and other weapons of mass destruction.

Article 3

The Contracting Parties shall consult with one another on all important international issues affecting their common interests, guided by the desire to strengthen international peace and security.

They shall immediately consult with one another whenever, in the opinion of any one of them, a threat of armed attack on one or more of the Parties to the Treaty has arisen, in order to ensure joint defence and the maintenance of peace and security.

Article 4

In the event of armed attack in Europe on one or more of the Parties to the Treaty by any state or group of states, each of the Parties to the Treaty, in the exercise of its right to individual or collective self-defence in accordance with Article 51 of the Charter of the United Nations Organization, shall immediately, either individually or in agreement with other Parties to the Treaty, come to the assistance of the state or states attacked with all such means as it deems necessary, including armed forces. The Parties to the Treaty shall immediately consult concerning the necessary measures to be taken by them jointly in order to restore and maintain international peace and security.

Measures taken on the basis of this Article shall be reported to the Security Council in conformity with the provisions of the Charter of the United Nations Organization. These measures shall be discontinued immediately the Security Council adopts the necessary measures to restore and maintain international peace and security.

Article 5
The Contracting Parties have agreed to establish a Joint Command of the armed forces that by agreement among the Parties shall be assigned to the Command, which shall function on the basis of jointly established principles. They shall likewise adopt other agreed measures necessary to strengthen their defensive power, in order to protect the peaceful labours of their peoples, guarantee the inviolability of their frontiers and territories, and provide defence against possible aggression.

Article 6
For the purpose of the consultations among the Parties envisaged in the present Treaty, and also for the purpose of examining questions which may arise in the operation of the Treaty, a Political Consultative Committee shall be set up, in which each of the Parties to the Treaty shall be represented by a member of its government or by another specifically appointed representative.

The Committee may set up such auxiliary bodies as may prove necessary.

Article 7
The Contracting Parties undertake not to participate in any coalitions or alliances and not to conclude any agreements whose objects conflict with the objects of the present Treaty.

The Contracting Parties declare that their commitments under existing international treaties do not conflict with the provisions of the present Treaty.

Article 8
The Contracting Parties declare that they will act in a spirit of friendship and co-operation with a view to further developing and fostering economic and cultural intercourse with one another, each adhering to the principle of respect for the independence and sovereignty of the other and non-interference in their internal affairs.

Article 9
The present Treaty is open to the accession of other states irrespective of their social and political systems, which express their readiness by participation in the present Treaty to assist in uniting the efforts of the peaceable states in safeguarding the peace and security of the peoples. Such accession shall enter into force with the agreement of the Parties to the Treaty after the declaration of accession has been deposited with the Government of the Polish People's Republic.

Article 10
The present Treaty is subject to ratification, and the instruments of ratification shall be deposited with the Government of the Polish People's Republic.

The Treaty shall enter into force on the day the last instrument of ratification has been deposited. The Government of the Polish People's Republic shall notify the other Parties to the Treaty as each instrument of ratification is deposited.

Article 11
The present Treaty shall remain in force for twenty years. For such Contracting Parties as do not at least one year before the expiration of this period present to the Government of the Polish People's Republic a statement of denunciation of the Treaty, it shall remain in force for the next ten years.

Should a system of collective security be established in Europe, and a General European Treaty of Collective Security concluded for this purpose, for which the Contracting Parties will unswervingly strive, the present Treaty shall cease to be operative from the day the General European Treaty enters into force.

(e) THE SOVIET UNION AND CHINA

Khrushchev's attack on the Albanian leaders at the 22nd Congress of the CPSU made public the differences between the Soviets and the Chinese. For a time the Albanians were the surrogates for the Chinese and received as such the blasts of Moscow. Later, when the dispute became more acrimonious, such subterfuges were dropped. It seems probable that the Albanians whom Khrushchev mentions as having been imprisoned and executed were involved in a plot to overthrow the Albanian Party leadership.

Chou En-lai, the Chinese premier, understood that the criticism was levelled at the Chinese. He defended the Albanians and then left Moscow before the conclusion of the Congress, not forgetting to lay a wreath on Stalin's embalmed body, a few days before it was removed from the mausoleum and buried in the Kremlin walls.

Even before the Congress economic pressure was applied against Albania.

DOCUMENT 54. EXTRACT FROM KHRUSHCHEV'S CONCLUDING SPEECH DEALING WITH ALBANIA AT THE 22ND CONGRESS OF THE CPSU, 27 OCTOBER 1961 (*The Road to Communism: Documents of the 22nd Congress of the Communist Party of the Soviet Union*, FOREIGN LANGUAGES PUBLISHING HOUSE, MOSCOW, 1961, PP. 334–40)

Comrades, the Central Committee Report, as well as speeches by delegates to this Congress, dealt with the erroneous stand of the leaders of the Albanian Party of Labour, who have set out to fight against the course adopted by the 20th Congress of our Party and to undermine the foundations of friendship with the Soviet Union and other socialist countries.

The representatives of fraternal parties who spoke here said that they share our concern over the state of affairs in the Albanian Party of Labour and emphatically condemn the dangerous actions of its leaders, which prejudice the basic interests of the Albanian people and the unity of the socialist commonwealth as a whole. The speeches made by delegates and by the representatives of fraternal parties show convincingly that the Central Committee of our Party was absolutely correct in reporting to this Congress, frankly and from a standpoint of principle, that Soviet-Albanian relations are in an abnormal state.

It was our duty to do so because, unfortunately, our numerous attempts to normalize relations with the Albanian Party of Labour yielded no results. I should like to stress that the Central Committee of our Party has shown the greatest patience and done all in its power to restore good relations between our two parties.

Members of the Praesidium of the CCCPSU made repeated attempts to meet the Albanian leaders to discuss the questions that had arisen. As far back as August 1960 we twice proposed a meeting to the Albanian leaders, but they evaded it. And they just as stubbornly rejected talks with us during the Moscow meeting of the fraternal parties in November 1960.

When a meeting was finally arranged at the instance of the CCCPSU Enver Hoxha and Mehmet Shehu wrecked it, and began actions that may only be described as provocative. The leaders of the Albanian Party of Labour withdrew arrogantly from the November meeting, thus showing that they refused to take the collective opinion of the fraternal parties into consideration. They rudely turned down our subsequent proposals for meeting to exchange views and remove the differences, and stepped up their campaign of slanderous attacks against our Party and its Central Committee.

The leaders of the Albanian Party of Labour do not mind using any methods to conceal from their people the truth as to what our Party and our people are doing. Albania is the only country in the socialist community not to have published the full text of the draft programme of the CPSU. The Albanian press carried only some parts of the draft, deliberately creating a distorted picture of the activities of our Party. That fact speaks for itself. Indeed, even the opponents of communism were unable to keep silent about our programme.

We are aware why the Albanian leaders are concealing the

programme of the CPSU from their Party and their people. They fear the truth like death. The Party programme is our sacred cause, it is our lodestar in communist construction.

Had the Albanian leaders published it in full, Albania's working people would have seen who lies and who speaks the truth; they would have seen that all the activities of our Party, and all its plans, are in keeping with the vital interests of the peoples, including the interests of the Albanian people who are friendly to us.

Our great Party has more than once been a target for bitter and foul attacks on the part of overt and covert enemies of communism. But we must say in so many words that we do not recall anyone passing at so giddy a speed as the Albanian leaders have done from professions and vows of everlasting friendship to unbridled anti-Soviet calumny.

They apparently expect in this manner to clear the ground for winning the right to receive hand-outs from the imperialists. The imperialists are always ready to pay thirty pieces of silver to those who split the communist ranks. But pieces of silver have never brought anyone anything but dishonour and ignominy.

Obviously, the Central Committee of our Party had to tell this Congress the whole truth about the pernicious stand of the leadership of the Albanian Party of Labour. Had we not done so, the Albanian leaders would have continued to insinuate that the Central Committee of the Soviet Communist Party was afraid to inform the Party of the differences it had with the leadership of the Albanian Party of Labour. Our Party and the Soviet people should know about the conduct of the Albanian leaders. And let this Congress, which is entitled to speak on behalf of the entire Party, take its stand on the matter, let it pass its weighty judgment.

This Congress emphasized the readiness there is to normalize relations with the Albanian Party of Labour on the basis of Marxist-Leninist principle. But what was the Albanian leaders' reaction? They came out with a clamorous statement slinging mud at our Party and its Central Committee.

Comrade Chou En-lai, leader of the delegation of the Communist Party of China, voiced in his speech concern over the open discussion, at this Congress, of the issue of Albanian-

Soviet relations. The main point in his statement was, as we see it, the anxiety that the present state of our relations with the Albanian Party of Labour might affect the unity of the socialist camp.

We share the anxiety expressed by our Chinese friends, and appreciate their concern for greater unity. If the Chinese comrades wish to apply their efforts towards normalizing the relations between the Albanian Party of Labour and the fraternal parties, there is hardly anyone who can contribute to the solution of this problem more than the Communist Party of China. That would really benefit the Albanian Party of Labour, and would meet the interests of the entire socialist commonwealth.

It is true, of course, that communists should shape their inter-party relations in such a way as to leave no loophole for the enemy. Unfortunately, the Albanian leaders have grossly flouted this principle. They have long since been openly assailing the policy of the 20th Congress, thereby furnishing the bourgeois press with food for all kinds of speculation. None other than the Albanian leaders have been shouting from the house-tops about their special stand and their special views, as distinct from those of our Party and other fraternal parties. This became evident at the 4th Congress of the Albanian Party of Labour, and has been even more so of late.

Why did the Albanian leaders launch a campaign against the decisions of the 20th Congress of our Party? What is the heresy they espy in those decisions?

To begin with, the Albanian leaders resent the emphatic condemnation of the cult of Stalin's person and its harmful consequences. They disapprove of our having firmly condemned the arbitrary methods and the abuses of power which hit many innocent people, including prominent representatives of the old guard, who together with Lenin founded the world's first proletarian state. The Albanian leaders cannot speak without annoyance and rancour of the fact that we have for ever put an end to a situation in which one man was able to decide at will highly important questions bearing on our Party and our country.

Stalin is no longer among the living, but we considered it necessary to brand the disgraceful methods of leadership that flourished in the atmosphere of the cult of his person. Our Party does this to ensure that such practices never recur.

One would think that the Leninist course adopted by the 20th Congress of the CPSU and supported by the fraternal parties should also have been backed by the leadership of the Albanian Party of Labour, since the cult of the individual is incompatible with Marxism-Leninism. What happened, however, was that the Albanian leaders began to extol the cult of Stalin's person and launched a bitter struggle against the decisions of the 20th Congress of the CPSU in an effort to divert the socialist countries from this correct course. Needless to say that that was no accident. All that was pernicious in our country at the time of the cult of the individual manifests itself in even worse form in the Albanian Party of Labour. It is no longer a secret to anyone that the Albanian leaders maintain their power by resorting to force and arbitrary methods.

The situation in the Albanian Party of Labour has been abnormal and harmful for a long time now. In that situation, anyone whom the leadership does not favour may be subjected to a cruel repression.

Where are the Albanian communists who founded the Party and fought against the Italian and German fascist invaders? Almost all of them have fallen victim to the bloody crimes committed by Mehmet Shehu and Enver Hoxha.

The CCCPSU has received more than one letter from Albanian communists asking us to prevent the Albanian leaders from doing injustice to the finest sons and daughters of the Albanian Party of Labour. Delegates to this Congress can form an idea of the moral make-up of the Albanian leaders by reading some of those letters.

The Albanian leaders accuse us of interfering in the internal affairs of the Albanian Party of Labour. I should like to say what they mean by this so-called interference.

A few years ago the CCCPSU pleaded with the Albanian leaders for Liri Gega, former member of the Political Bureau of the CC of the Albanian Party of Labour, who was sentenced to death together with her husband. For a number of years she had been a member of leading bodies of the Albanian Party of Labour, and had taken part in the liberation struggle of the Albanian people. In appealing at that time to the Albanian leaders, we were prompted by humane considerations, by the desire to prevent the shooting of a woman who, moreover, was pregnant. We considered, and still consider, that as a fraternal party we had a right to express our opinion on the matter. Indeed, even in the blackest periods of reaction the Tsar's satraps, who tortured revolutionaries, could not bring themselves to execute pregnant women. And here is a socialist country where a woman about to become a mother was sentenced to death and executed. It was an utterly unwarranted act of cruelty.

Today honest people are being cruelly persecuted in Albania merely because they make bold to speak out for Soviet-Albanian friendship, of which the Albanian leaders like to talk in such pompous and florid terms.

Comrades Liri Belishova and Koco Tashko, prominent functionaries of the Albanian Party of Labour, were expelled from the Central Committee of the Albanian Party of Labour; what is more, they are now being openly branded enemies of the Party and the people. And this just because Liri Belishova and Koco Tashko had the courage honestly and openly to voice their disagreement with the policy of the Albanian leaders, and called for unity between Albania, the Soviet Union and the other socialist countries.

Those who today advocate friendship with the Soviet Union and the CPSU are regarded as enemies by the Albanian leaders.

How are we to reconcile these facts with the vows and assurances of friendship for the CPSU and the Soviet Union that came from Shehu and Hoxha? It seems that their talk about friendship was so much hypocrisy and eyewash.

That is the situation in the Albanian Party of Labour, and that is why the Albanian leaders are opposing the Leninist course adopted by the 20th Party Congress. For Shehu, Hoxha and others, putting an end to the cult of the individual would mean, in effect, relinquishing key posts in Party and government, and that is something they do not want to do. We are confident, however, that the time will come when the Albanian communists and the Albanian people will have their say, and then the Albanian leaders will have to answer for the damage they have done to their country, their people, and the cause of socialist construction in Albania.

DOCUMENT 55. EXTRACT FROM A SPEECH BY ENVER HOXHA AT THE FORTY-FOURTH ANNIVERSARY OF THE BOLSHEVIK REVOLUTION, 7 NOVEMBER 1961 (A. DALLIN, *Diversity in International Communism: A Documentary Record*, COLUMBIA UNIVERSITY PRESS, 1963, PP. 127–8)

Thus, in the economic field all credits that the Soviet Union had granted to our country for the Third Five Year Plan were cut, and this was done to sabotage the economic plan of our country; all the Soviet specialists who were working in Albania and whom our economy needs and whom we officially asked to stay were withdrawn unilaterally and without any reason; with an ultimatum that, starting this year, we repay old debts (although according to existing documents, this should start after 1970) the Soviet side has broken off almost all trade on a clearing basis; scholarships were taken away from all Albanian civilian and military students in the Soviet Union, etc., etc. Economic pressures have been accompanied with pressures and restrictive measures in the military sphere.

*

There seems little doubt that the Soviets promised to aid China to build its own nuclear armoury. It was a promise that they were to regret. To the Chinese it meant that they were to remain permanently inferior to the Soviets unless they developed their own nuclear programme. This they successfully did and the first Chinese A-bomb was exploded a day after the fall of Khrushchev.

The signing of the Test Ban Treaty was another stage in the ever more bitter confrontation between the two major communist powers. To the Chinese it was clear evidence of Soviet collusion with the west.

DOCUMENT 56. EXTRACT FROM THE *Peking Review*, 16 AUGUST 1963

It is not only at present that the Soviet leaders have begun to collude with US imperialism and attempt to manacle China.

As far back as 20 June 1959, when there was not yet the slightest sign of a treaty on stopping nuclear tests, the Soviet government unilaterally tore up the agreement on new technology for national defence concluded between China and the Soviet Union on 15 October 1957 and refused to provide China with a sample of an atomic bomb and technical data concerning its manufacture. This was done as a presentation gift at the time the Soviet leader went to the United States for talks with Eisenhower in September.

DOCUMENT 57. EXTRACT FROM A STATEMENT IN *Pravda* OF 21 AUGUST 1963, DEALING WITH NUCLEAR WEAPONS

It follows from the Chinese government's statement of 15 August that the Chinese leaders are greatly displeased with the Soviet Union for not giving China samples of atomic weapons. It looks as if annoyance with this policy of the Soviet Union and the other socialist states of not spreading nuclear weapons explains the attacks of the Chinese leaders on the USSR's measures in the field of foreign policy—measures which are aimed at easing international tension and strengthening peace —and especially their attacks on the Nuclear Test Ban Treaty. The Chinese people are experiencing many privations, and that is why such a course in the policy of the Chinese leaders would be more beneficial for the Chinese people, would be more appreciated by them and would be correctly understood throughout the world.

Let us grant that by overstraining its economy the People's Republic of China may finally be able to produce a few atom bombs. Yet how many such bombs would in this case be aimed by the imperialists at the People's Republic of China? Would the Chinese leaders then feel themselves more secure, even though sitting on their own atom bomb? . . .

It is impossible to overlook one more circumstance: the government of the People's Republic of China, disregarding its duty as an ally and abusing the relations of trust existing among the socialist countries, has embarked upon the road of making public classified documents and information relating to the defences of the countries of the socialist community, and, what is more, of presenting the facts tendentiously, in a distorted light. Of course, the Soviet government will not sink so low as to set out on the road of divulging information relating to the defences of socialist states. The Soviet government is compelled to state that after these actions of the Chinese government, there is scarcely anyone who will believe the sincerity of its assurances and trust it with information of defensive importance. It is natural that the Soviet government will draw its own conclusions on this subject. . . .

More than once the Soviet government took steps to convince the Chinese government that preventing the spread of nuclear weapons was in the interest of peace, in the interest of all socialist countries, including the interest of the People's Republic of China. As history would have it the Soviet Union is the only socialist country that produces nuclear weapons. . . .

It would be naïve, to say the least, to assume that it is possible to conduct one policy in the west and another in the east, to fight with one hand against the arming of Western Germany with nuclear weapons, against the spreading of nuclear weapons in the world, and to supply these weapons to China with the other hand. . . .

The position of the Chinese government, set forth in the statement of 15 August, can be understood only as meaning that the Chinese leaders do not care how nuclear weapons spread among the capitalist countries as long as the leaders of the People's Republic of China get a chance to lay their hands on a nuclear bomb and see what it is like.

It must be admitted that being at a definite stage of its economic development and possessing a definite economic potential, the People's Republic of China is as yet unprepared to produce nuclear weapons in quantity. Even if the People's Republic of China were to produce two or three bombs, this would not solve the question for it either, but would bring about a great exhaustion of China's economy. . . .

That is why the most reasonable policy for the People's Republic of China in present conditions—if, of course, its desires and its possibilities are to be made commensurate—would be to devote its efforts to the development of the national economy, science, technology and agriculture, devoting them to improving the well-being of the Chinese people, to meeting their vital needs.

DOCUMENT 58. EXTRACT FROM A STATEMENT OF THE SOVIET
GOVERNMENT DEFENDING ITS POSITION ON THE PARTIAL TEST BAN
TREATY, 4 AUGUST 1963 (*SN*, 6 AUGUST 1963)

The government of the People's Republic of China made a
statement on 31 July concerning the outcome of the Moscow
talks on a nuclear weapon tests ban in the atmosphere, space
and under water.

In this statement the PRC government announces that it is
opposed to the nuclear-weapon Test Ban Treaty and refuses
to accede to it. The PRC government even describes the Treaty
as a 'fraud' which, it alleges, is 'fooling' all the peoples of the
world and which 'contradicts the hopes of the peace-loving
peoples of all countries'.

In this connection the Soviet government considers it necessary to make the following statement:

The Treaty banning nuclear tests is of significance in principle,
from the viewpoint of continuing the search for ways of solving
the outstanding issues that divide the world. The fact that states
with different social systems—great powers, the contradictions
between which have more than once threatened to plunge
mankind into the whirlpool of world war—have been able to
find a mutually acceptable solution to a momentous international problem proves the correctness and viability of the
policy of peaceful co-existence.

The peoples have seen a real possibility of reducing international tension and the possibility of curbing the arms race,
the grave burden of which weighs down on them.

The results of the Moscow talks provide hope that the unsettled international issues, on which the strengthening of the
cause of peace on earth depends, can be settled. It is exactly
this that the Soviet government is working for, having again
advanced, during the Moscow three-power talks, a broad
programme of action aimed at consolidating peace. The programme envisages a number of urgent measures to remove the
danger of a thermo-nuclear conflict, primarily the signing of a
non-aggression pact between the NATO and the Warsaw Treaty
countries. The Soviet government has once more called for
the removal of the vestiges of the Second World War, for the

signature of a German peace treaty, and for the normalization of the situation in West Berlin on that basis.

The programme of struggle to strengthen peace which is advanced by the Soviet Union is in accordance with the fundamental interests of the peoples. It has met with warm support from the governments and peoples of the socialist states, from broad public circles of the countries of Asia, Africa and Latin America, from millions of working people of the capitalist countries and from all the progressive people of the world. . . .

In the atmosphere of this unanimous approval, you can count on the fingers of one hand those who venture openly to oppose the Treaty on the prohibition of nuclear tests. And there is nothing surprising in this: those who oppose the prohibition of nuclear tests, whatever verbal contrivances they may resort to, show themselves to be opponents of peaceful co-existence and opponents of the line of easing world tension and undermining the forces of aggression and war.

The few days since the meeting of representatives of the three powers in Moscow have already clearly revealed those who find the new important success of the forces of peace unpalatable.

They are, primarily, the so-called 'wild men' in the United States who are raising the bogy of 'the menace of communism' and are shouting that the Treaty will not give the United States the possibility of creating still more destructive weapons.

They are the extremists from the camp of the West German militarists and revenge-seekers who are still hatching plans for new military gambles.

They are the extremists from the camp of the French ruling circles who, for some unknown reason, have decided that the grandeur of France does not consist in a contribution to easing international tensions or in friendship with other nations, but in friendship with nuclear bombs, in creating a stockpile of nuclear weapons at any cost.

When such views are expressed by representatives of the most bellicose circles of imperialism, there is nothing surprising in it; but when the Treaty banning nuclear-weapon tests is opposed by communists—and, what is more, by the communists standing at the head of a socialist country—this cannot but arouse well-justified amazement.

How can the leaders of a socialist country reject out of hand an international agreement which serves to strengthen peace, which is in line with the wishes of the peoples and which meets their vital interests?

Only disregard of the vital interests of the peoples who have long been demanding an end to nuclear testing could suggest such an interpretation of the aims and significance of the Treaty as those which the Chinese government seeks to give in its statement.

The government of the PRC claims in its statement that the conclusion of the Treaty has the aim of 'consolidating the nuclear monopoly' of the three powers, and that the Soviet Union's participation in such a treaty is 'capitulation to American imperialism'.

One cannot imagine a greater absurdity. In pressing for the conclusion of a treaty banning nuclear-weapon tests, the Soviet Union and all peace-loving forces see in it an important step to protect mankind from the dangerous consequences of the pollution of the atmosphere, water and outer space by radioactive substances. But those who level accusations against the USSR—capitalist states—seek to present this as an attempt by the Soviet Union to achieve some sort of nuclear monopoly, and even as 'capitulation'.

It follows, therefore, that if nuclear weapons spread throughout the world, if the way is left open for the West German revenge-seekers to get possession of these weapons, if one series of nuclear explosions carried out by scores of states was followed by another, then that would, it appears, meet the interests of peace and would not be capitulation to imperialism!

No, it is just the other way round. That would mean playing irresponsibly with the destinies of millions upon millions of people, and everyone who shows concern for the present and future of his people, for the preservation of peace not only in words but in practical deeds, cannot but realize this.

*

Ever since 1955 the Soviets have regarded India as their major ally among the non-aligned states. The Chinese saw in India just another bourgeois state with whom it happened to have a disputed frontier. In 1959 fighting broke out between India and China, and rather heavier fighting broke out simultaneously with the Cuban missile crisis in 1962. The Indian army was out-manoeuvred and forced on the defensive. The Soviets continued to supply the Indian army and air force with weapons.

For their part the Chinese gave support to the Soviets at the time of the Cuban crisis. To the Soviets this was worthless support. As soon as the Soviets withdrew their missiles from Cuba the scorn of the Chinese knew no bounds. They accused them of 'adventurism' in sending the missiles to Cuba and 'capitulationism' in withdrawing them.

DOCUMENT 59. SOVIET STATEMENT ON THE SINO-INDIAN BORDER DISPUTE, 21 SEPTEMBER 1963 (*Soviet News Booklet*, NO. 122)

No doubt remains now that one of the reasons for the attack by the Chinese leaders on the policy of the world communist movement was the lessening of international tension, which took place in 1959, when there was a definite relaxation in the cold war between the Soviet Union and the United States, especially after Comrade Khrushchev's trip to the USA.

It cannot be considered as accidental that at that actual period the Chinese leaders got themselves involved in an armed clash on the Indian-Chinese border, and this, besides creating an acute situation in that part of the world, was ultimately aimed at torpedoing the relaxation of international tension which had taken place.

Already at the time when the Chinese-Indian conflict began in 1959, the Soviet leaders told the Chinese government frankly that the aggravation of the dispute in connection with frontier territories in the Himalayas, territories inherited by China and India from the old days, and the development of this dispute into a large armed conflict, was undesirable and fraught with negative consequences, not only for Chinese-Indian relations but for the whole international situation.

We consider that in frontier disputes, especially in a dispute of the type of the Chinese-Indian clash, one should adhere to the Leninist views according to which it is possible to settle any frontier problems without resorting to armed force, granted that both sides desire to do so.

Everyone can now see that the Chinese-Indian conflict in the Himalayas had the most negative consequences for the cause of peace, inflicted great harm on the unity of the anti-imperialist front in Asia and placed the progressive forces in India in an extremely difficult position.

As could be expected, China herself did not benefit in any way. And her prestige in the eyes of the peoples of the world and especially of the Afro-Asian peoples, has certainly not grown.

It was with a feeling of bewilderment and bitterness that the peoples saw one of the socialist countries, which had recently become independent and served as a model to them, get itself involved in a military conflict with a young neutralist state and, using its military superiority, endeavour to gain for itself in that way a favourable solution of the problem of a certain part of territory.

The Chinese leaders ignored the comradely advice of other socialist and fraternal countries. Moreover, they saw in this an unwillingness to support them in the international arena and considered this comradely advice a great injury to themselves.

In the article 'What is the Cause of the Dispute?', the Chinese comrades directly link the beginning of their differences with the fraternal parties with the fact that the Soviet Union and other socialist countries failed to give unconditional support to China's stand in the conflict on the Indian-Chinese border.

The actions of the Chinese leaders, which undermine the policy of neutralism, in effect help the imperialist powers to increase their influence in the emancipated countries and especially in India.

All this can, of course, hold up the development of the struggle for national independence and have a negative effect on the balance of forces in the world arena: this attitude to a neutral country is all the more obscure in view of the fact that the government of the People's Republic of China has in every way been making overtures to the blatantly reactionary regimes in Asia and Africa, including countries which belong to the imperialist military blocs.

The Chinese leaders often use the question of the Soviet Union's aid to India for anti-Soviet purposes. However, they do not tell their people the truth of the fact that Soviet aid to the peoples of the emancipated countries is imbued with the desire to strengthen their economic and political positions in their struggle for independence and against imperialism.

That policy is also to be seen clearly in our relations with India. The Soviet Union helped the Indian people, who had shaken off the yoke of British imperialism, to gain a footing in neutral positions and to oppose the attempts of the imperialists to impose an economic yoke on India. We have always considered this policy to be correct, for it conforms to the interests of peace and socialism.

It would not be amiss to recall the fact that before 1959 the People's Republic of China pursued the same kind of policy with regard to India. We were glad to see the development of good-neighbourly relations between Asia's two largest states, their support of one another in the struggle for peace and against the aggressive designs of imperialism. We met with approval the friendly contacts between Chinese and Indian leaders, their joint statement in favour of peace, and especially, the Pancha Shila principles proclaimed by premiers Chou En-lai and Nehru. In the light of all this, the Chinese-Indian armed conflict came as a complete surprise both to the Soviet people and to the whole world public.

The Chinese leaders are now making accusations, stating that India is waging war on China and using Soviet armaments. First of all, this is essentially not true to the facts; secondly, if one were to follow this kind of logic, the Indian government has a great deal more reason to declare that the Chinese troops are waging war on India and are using Soviet armaments—because everyone knows of the tremendous military aid which the Soviet Union gives to China.

In helping socialist China and peace-loving India, we have been prompted by the best of sentiments. We were proceeding from these friendly feelings and in the interests of strengthening the peace and unity of the anti-imperialist forces when we declared that the Chinese-Indian conflict evoked our deep regret. We still consider that the solution of that conflict in a peaceful way, through negotiations, would be in the interests of both the Chinese and Indian peoples and in the interests of world peace. . . .

DOCUMENT 60. EXTRACT FROM KHRUSHCHEV'S REPORT TO THE SUPREME SOVIET DEALING WITH THE CUBAN MISSILE CRISIS, 12 DECEMBER 1962 (*SN*, 13 DECEMBER 1962)

Comrade Deputies, it should be said that during the peaceful adjustment of the conflict in the Caribbean shrill voices of discontent could also be heard from another side, from people who even call themselves Marxist-Leninists, even though their actions have nothing in common with Marxism-Leninism: I mean specifically the Albanian leaders. Their criticism of the Soviet Union in effect echoed that coming from the most reactionary, bellicose circles of the west.

Why is it that the loudest shouts today come precisely from the Albanian leaders? I should like to recount an incident from my life to explain this.

I spent my childhood and youth in the mines. If Gorky's university was his life among the people, my university was the mines. It was a Cambridge of sorts for a working man, a 'university' of the dispossessed people of Russia. My father went there, and so did I in my childhood and youth.

I remember that in mining settlements foul-mouthed people sometimes used to find a small boy who had barely begun to articulate words without yet understanding what they meant, and taught him the most foul language. They would tell him: 'Go to that house and say this to the people there.' Sometimes they did even worse. 'Go to your mother,' they would say, 'and repeat these words to her. Here are three kopecks for you. Afterwards we'll give you five.'

And the child would run to the window, or to his mother, and repeat the foul words, while the 'jokers' would regard this as a kind of show.

The Albanian leaders are like these unreasoning boys. Someone has taught them foul language, and they go about and use it against the Communist Party of the Soviet Union. And yet it is their mother! And for using this foul language they get the promised three kopecks. And if they use stronger and cruder language they get another five kopecks, and praise.

What do they want, these people who call themselves Marxist-Leninists? Why are they pressing for the same thing, in fact, as Adenauer, that is, to push us to conflicts, to an aggravation of the international situation? It is a true saying: If you go to the left, you'll find yourself on the right. Objectively, they acted like people provoking a conflict during the Cuban crisis. They really wanted to set the Soviet Union and the United States on a collision course. But what does it mean to set these two great world powers on a collision course? It means to provoke a world thermo-nuclear war.

It is interesting how they themselves would behave in such a war? I do not think that they would like to take part in it. They obviously would prefer to sit it out. But the question arises: what do they want? Can it be that they want the blood of the peoples of the Soviet Union, Cuba and other socialist countries to flow? . . .

Resting on the assumption that the nature of imperialism has not changed, some people say that it must be exposed and cursed. Imperialism, of course, must be exposed—it is an evil for the peoples of the world, but cursing imperialism alone, no matter how rightly, will not sap its strength.

It is, of course, true that the nature of imperialism has not changed. But imperialism today is no longer what it used to be when it held undivided sway over the world. If it is now a 'paper tiger', those who say this know that this 'paper tiger' has atomic teeth. It can use them and it must not be treated lightly. It is possible in the relations with imperialist countries to make reciprocal compromises, while, on the other hand, having all the means to smash the aggressors should they unleash war. . . .

One must be very cautious and not rush in with irresponsible charges, such as that some carry out an orthodox policy while others pursue a mistaken policy, some are attacking imperialism and do not tolerate it, while others allegedly display liberalism. These questions can be rightly understood, and different actions can be correctly assessed, only if one takes into account the time, place and circumstances in which one has to operate.

India, for instance, achieved the liberation of Goa, Diu and Daman. These were vestiges of colonialism on Indian soil. Even when the British colonialists had been expelled from India, Portugal retained her colonies there, colonies which disfeminated the foul stench of colonialism. India, and her government, showed patience and tolerated this for several years, but then threw out the colonialists. Did they act rightly? Of course, they did! Incidentally, when this question was discussed in the Security Council, the United States and Great Britain tried, in point of actual fact, to have India proclaimed an aggressor. They tried to set the public opinion of the world against India. It was only the veto of the Soviet Union that prevented them from achieving this. . . .

Macao is situated at the mouth of the Chuchiang River, on the coast of China. It is a small territory and not easily to be spotted on the map. It was leased by the Portuguese way back in the middle of the sixteenth century and in 1887 they wrested it completely from China and made it their colony. The British colony of Hong-Kong is there also—it lies in the Delta of the Hsichiang River, literally below the heart of such an important town as Kwangchow (Canton). The odour coming from these places is by no means sweeter than that which was released by colonialism in Goa.

But no-one will denounce the People's Republic of China for leaving these fragments of colonialism intact.

It would be wrong to prod China into actions of some kind which she considers untimely. If the government of the People's Republic of China tolerates Macao and Hong-Kong it clearly has good reasons for doing so. It would, therefore, be ridiculous to levy against it the accusation that these are concessions to the British and Portuguese colonialists, that this is appeasement.

But perhaps this is a retreat from Marxism-Leninism? Nothing of the kind! It means that the government of the People's Republic of China is taking into account reality, the actual possibilities.

And this is by no means because the Chinese are less sensitive to colonialism than the Indians, that they are more tolerant towards Salazar than India is. No, our Chinese friends hate colonialism just as every revolutionary does. But they are clearly basing themselves on their conditions, they are acting in accordance with their own views and are showing patience.

But does this mean that we must condemn them for this, that we must claim that they have retreated from Marxism-Leninism? No, it doesn't! That would be ridiculous.

As a result of a variety of conditions, one sometimes has to live not among fragrant roses but amidst thorns and sometimes even in close proximity to the colonialists' outhouses.

But the hour will come when our Chinese friends will find this position intolerable and will tell the colonialists in a loud voice 'Get out!' And we shall welcome that step. But it is for our Chinese friends themselves to decide when this is to be done.

We are not hurrying them. On the contrary, we say: 'Decide this matter in the way that your country's interests, and the interests of the whole socialist camp demand.'

What would have happened, if, during the events over Cuba, we had failed to display the necessary restraint and had listened to the shrill promptings of the 'ultra-revolutionaries'? We would have entered a period of a new world war, a thermo-nuclear war. Our vast country would have held out, of course, but tens upon tens of millions of people would have perished!

As for Cuba, one result of a thermo-nuclear war would probably be that it would have simply ceased to exist. Other countries involved in the conflict which are densely populated and lack wide expanses would also have perished completely. Further, the consequences of atomic radiation would have brought untold suffering to the survivors and to future genera-tions. . . .

We have said already that it wasn't in the interests of social-ism to allow the crisis over Cuba to develop into a thermo-nuclear world war. Such a war is needed by the aggressive imperialist forces which, frightened by the inevitable historical prospect of the defeat of capitalism in peaceful competition with socialism, are saying: if one has to die, let it be with music, as the saying goes—even if that music be the bursting of nuclear bombs.

And so it happens that, on the one hand, war is eagerly desired by the aggressive adventurist forces of imperialism, the madmen who have lost the hope that capitalism can hold its own in peaceful competition with socialism; and, on the other hand, attempts are being made to push events in the same direction by people who call themselves Marxist-Leninists, but who actually are dogmatists who do not believe in the possi-bility of the victory of socialism and communism, in the condi-tions of peaceful co-existence with capitalism. Both the former and the latter want to prod history on to a new war, to decide the question of the victory of communism or capitalism by means of war, by means of a method in which millions upon millions of men and women would be killed.

These people, it would seem, are poles apart in their thinking, but nevertheless their positions coincide. They hold the same views and act in the same way on this vitally important question.

But for us, people building communism, just as for our brothers who are building socialism, there is no reason to die either with or without music. We must complete the work of building communism.

Why should we invite ourselves to go to the Devil? Why should we hurry to the other world? Nobody has yet returned from there to tell us that it is better there than it is on earth. Are you, comrade deputies, disappointed that you have gathered in this hall to discuss questions concerning the further development of our country in conditions of peace, at a time when thermo-nuclear war has been prevented? No, we all rejoice over this.

A few days ago, members of the Praesidium and secretaries of the Central Committee visited a new textile mill in Novye Cheremushki, in Moscow. We talked to women workers there. I asked one of them: 'How are you getting on?' She replied: 'I am getting on well, Comrade Khrushchev.' 'Have you got a flat?' 'Yes, I have' [she replied]. 'Where?' 'Not far from here,' she said. 'When housing was built near the factory, I was given a flat there.' 'Have you got a family?' 'Yes, I have two boys. One is at a boarding-school. The other is living with me, and is also going to school.'

The woman told me her wages and about the conditions in which she is living and working.

'So you can manage all right?' I asked. 'Yes, Comrade Khrushchev. We all have only one concern, one great wish— that there should be no war.'

That woman voiced the sentiments of all the working people. The same feelings are expressed by the peoples of the Soviet Union, the People's Republic of China, India, Albania, the United States, Britain, France and the other countries of the world.

We do not need war! The Soviet people, who raised the

banner of the struggle for socialism and to whom has fallen the honour of building communism, want peace. We are confident that we are right; we are confident of our strength.

We have travelled a long road in forty-five years. And now we are advancing with even greater strides. What we used to cover in five years we are now covering in a month. Do we have something to treasure? Of course, we have; we have prospects; we have confidence in the ultimate victory of our ideas. We seek these victories, not on the road of war, but on the road of peaceful creation, and peaceful competition with capitalism. We reject not only world thermo-nuclear war, but all wars between states in general, with the exception of a just war of liberation and a defensive war which has to be waged by a people which is the victim of aggression.

Naturally, if a war is imposed on us from whatever quarter, we shall stand up for ourselves and for our allies, and we shall use all the means we have at our disposal.

We shall, however, do everything in our power to avoid a military clash in order to exclude wars altogether from the life of society. Can this aim be achieved given the existence of two systems—the capitalist and the socialist systems—in the world? The balance of forces in the world is now such that the forces of peace and socialism can curb the aggressive forces of imperialism and compel them to heed the will of the peoples.

Imperialism is not all-powerful now, and the developments around Cuba have confirmed this. The imperialists now have to reckon with the might of the socialist countries.

DOCUMENT 61. EXTRACT FROM *Zeri i Popullit,* ORGAN OF THE ALBANIAN WORKERS' PARTY, 20 APRIL 1965 (QUOTED BY A. L. HORELICK AND M. RUSH, *Strategic Power and Soviet Foreign Policy,* UNIVERSITY OF CHICAGO PRESS, 1966, P. 209)

We brothers and comrades-in-arms in socialism and communism have a right to ask of the Soviet brothers and comrades: What security have you for the Soviet Union itself against the imperialist danger? Is it not time to check with the greatest strictness on the activities of your chattering, bluffing, treacherous and Khrushchevite leaders? Khrushchev and his disciples, who are in power at present, not only make false boasts to conceal the abyss, but they give away vital information to the Americans to strip the Soviet Union bare. Soviet brothers, check up a little on these people and see whether the weapons created by your renowned scientists are in safe hands. . . .

The Khrushchevite revisionists have bluffed . . . in international affairs. This is one of their characteristics. It is the way they work. It happened in 1956 in the case of Egypt, and later in the case of Berlin, Cuba and so on. But while the bluff on Egypt had some results at the time the other revisionist bluffs for Berlin and Cuba failed for a very simple reason, the imperialists had seen the cards held by the Khrushchevite revisionists.

*

The Ilyichev report was delivered to a conference sponsored by the Academy of Sciences and the Institute of Marxism-Leninism. It is probable that it put forward the line the Soviets were going to take at the conference of December 1964—which was cancelled after Khrushchev's fall. Ilyichev, an important party ideologist, points out the more absurd of the Chinese claims. Indeed, the unmeasured violence of the Chinese in deed and word, especially at the time of the Great Cultural Revolution, has always accrued to the advantage of the Soviets.

DOCUMENT 62. EXTRACT FROM THE REPORT BY LEONID ILYICHEV *Kommunist*, NO. 11, 1964 (W. E. GRIFFITH, *Sino-Soviet Relations 1964–1965*, M.I.T. PRESS, CAMBRIDGE, MASS., 1967, PP. 359–61)

Nationalism and its poisoned fruits can be discerned lately in many of the political actions of the CCP Central Committee and the Chinese government. The biased evaluation of China's historical past, for example, cannot but attract attention.

It will be recalled that since ancient times the ideologists of China have built up an image of their country as the 'Middle Empire', the oldest civilization, the custodian of world order and spiritual harmony, as the 'Celestial Empire' which wields power on earth. The imperial ideology of China's special role in the history of mankind is to a certain extent influencing the minds of the present Chinese leaders.

It would be unjust, of course, to deny the tremendous contribution made by the Chinese people to the development of world civilization, to underestimate their spiritual influence on the culture of other peoples. But it would be absolutely wrong, while paying due tribute to China's role in history, not to notice the great-power aspirations which thrived in China, to ignore or belittle the role of other countries and peoples in the history of mankind. But it is this chauvinistic and even outright racialist appraisal of China's role that can be frequently found in the writings of Chinese ideologists. According to some Chinese historians, the history of mankind is concentrated in the part of Asia where China is situated. The country's historical past is idealized, the history of other peoples is referred to slightingly and 'Sino-centric' concepts are made the basis of everything. Philosophy and history, literature and art in present-day China are subordinated to substantiating such ideas.

The Chinese historians go to all lengths to extol, to demonstrate China's special role in the destinies of mankind.

If Europe had classical forms of slavery, in China, it turns out, they were 'highly classical'. And the feudal system in China, in contrast to Europe, was also a 'model' one. True, the capitalist system developed earlier in Europe, but because the 'leading position of people of the yellow race from Asia was firmly captured by people of the white race from Europe'. America was discovered by the Chinese. China had Confucius, Europe did not. Europe experienced the fall of the Roman Empire, but in China this did not happen. And so on and so forth. Everyone understands the national pride of the scholar if his people performed an exploit or made a great discovery. National pride is not alien to the peoples. There is nothing wrong in this, but why belittle other peoples, other countries. In China arrogant nationalism comes to the surface not only when hoary antiquity is assessed. It is openly said in China that without reference to Chinese history it is impossible 'to explain the general laws governing the development of human society'.

To achieve their hegemony-seeking schemes, the Chinese leaders are pursuing a thoroughly planned and co-ordinated policy. Its main trends are clear, already now.

First, a struggle against the CPSU and the Soviet Union, because the Chinese leaders see in the high prestige enjoyed by our Leninist Party and the USSR—the first socialist country which is successfully building communism—the main stumbling block to realizing their nationalistic great-power plans.

Second, a struggle against the unity of the socialist camp, the Communist movement, the working people of all countries and continents, because this unity and proletarian internationalism are a major obstacle to the hegemonistic aspirations of the Peking leaders. That is why they have taken the line of forming factions in the Communist movement as a whole and in individual Communist parties, factions which would obediently carry out directives from Peking; the line of forming a grouping of some socialist countries, of setting the peoples of Asia, Africa and Latin America against the peoples who are building socialism and communism and against the working class of the capitalist countries.

It can be considered an accomplished fact that of the two diametrically opposed slogans, political lines and world outlooks—proletarian internationalism and bourgeois nationalism —the Chinese leaders have chosen nationalism. They scorned the warning made by Lenin: 'One who has adopted the standpoint of nationalism naturally arrives at the desire to erect a Chinese Wall around his nationality, his national working-class movement . . . is unembarrassed even by the fact that by his tactics of division and dismemberment he is reducing to nil the great calls for rallying and unity of the proletarians of all nations, all races and all languages. . . .'

Third, a struggle against the policy of peaceful co-existence of states with different social systems and of easing international tensions; this is tantamount to spurring on nuclear armaments and pursuing a line which can lead to atomic war. As time goes on it is becoming increasingly clear that the mainspring of many foreign-policy actions of the Chinese splitters is hidden in the wish for a big military conflict, while they themselves stand aloof 'watching from the mountain top the battle of tigers' and profiting by it.

Fourth, the persistent attempts of the Chinese leaders to dominate the national-liberation movement. To this end they flatter and play up to nationalist circles and declare the national-liberation movement to be the leading element in the world revolutionary process. Hence the theory of the 'storm-centre of the revolution' in the 'three-A zone' (Asia, Africa,

Latin America), hence the political actions aimed at dividing the world revolutionary forces according to national and even racial features.

Fifth, one of the trends of the Chinese leaders' battle for hegemony is to flirt with the imperialist powers behind the cover of talk about the 'intermediate zone'. The political meaning of this strategic 'innovation' is to substantiate the need for separate political co-operation between China and imperialist states—West Germany, Britain, France, Japan—while loudly accusing others of a 'compact with imperialism'.

This is the first time in history that the world Communist movement is faced with such far-reaching efforts by a group of splitters to capture leadership of the revolutionary struggle at all costs and subordinate it to its great-power ambitions.

*

There seems little doubt that this letter sent by the Soviet to other communist parties is genuine. It gives a very good summary of the Soviet case and stresses the various attempts that Moscow has made at conciliation. It must be pointed out, however, that such conciliation could only take place on Moscow's terms.

DOCUMENT 63. EXTRACT FROM THE SECRET LETTER OF THE CPSU TO OTHER COMMUNIST PARTIES REGARDING THE SPLIT WITH THE CHINESE COMMUNIST PARTY, EARLY IN 1966 (*Die Welt*, 21 MARCH 1966, QUOTED IN THE *New York Times*, 24 MARCH 1966)

In endeavouring to create a favourable political atmosphere the CPSU Central Committee has unilaterally discontinued open polemics. We played up the desire of the Chinese leaders and invited a Chinese party-government delegation headed by Comrade Chou En-lai ... to attend the ceremonies of the forty-seventh anniversary of the October revolution in Moscow.

In early February 1965, the Soviet delegation headed by Comrade A. N. Kosygin ... made use of a stay in Peking en route to the Democratic Republic of Vietnam and the Democratic People's Republic of Korea to establish new contacts with the Chinese leaders. We entered the negotiations with complete sincerity. With the aim of conducting them from the outset objectively and in a spirit that would lead us to concrete and positive results.

In the negotiations with the Chinese Party-government delegation headed by Chou En-lai, Comrade L. I. Brezhnev ... states: 'We hold the view that since the October plenum of the CPSU Central Committee, new favourable possibilities have appeared to overcome gradually the difficulties that have developed in the relations between our parties, to normalize the situation in the communist movement, and to achieve its integration in principle on the basis of the ideas of Marxism-Leninism, of the declaration of 1957, and of the statement of 1960. We fully intend to continue consistently on this road and we express the sincere hope that the CCP will abide by the same manner of judging things.'

We submitted an extensive programme for normalizing Chinese-Soviet relations at both the party and the state level. This programme included proposals on implementing bilateral meetings of delegations of the CPSU and the CCP on the highest level, on the mutual discontinuation of polemics, concrete proposals on extending Chinese-Soviet trade and scientific, technical and cultural co-operation, and on co-ordinating the foreign-policy activities of the CPR and USSR.

Our efforts, however, both failed to meet with understanding and met with obstinate resistance from the Chinese leaders. The CCP Central Committee completely ignored the proposal on a bilateral meeting on the highest level. The CCP leadership failed to accede to an expansion of economic, technical and cultural co-operation and even took additional steps to further curtail such co-operation. In April 1965, the CPR government officially renounced co-operation with the USSR in constructing a number of industrial projects stipulated in the Chinese-Soviet 1961 agreement.

In early July, the CPR left the joint Institute for Nuclear Research. The CPR government rejected the Soviet proposal on co-operation of the CPR with other socialist countries in the work for the exploration and exploitation of outer space.

All this showed that the CCP leadership had embarked on a further deterioration of relations between the CPR and the USSR. The Chinese leadership states more and more frequently that the CCP is waging a political struggle against the Soviet

Union. Contrary to common sense they present it as a struggle 'of the state of the proletariat against the state of the bourgeoisie'.

The anti-Soviet course has now become an inseparable part of the entire ideological work of the CCP, both within and outside the country.

The Chinese people are made to believe that the Soviet Union is one of their chief enemies. Meetings are being conducted at Chinese offices and enterprises at which every participant is obliged to come up with some criticism of the Soviet Union. The organization of anti-Soviet rallies has become a system. On 6 March 1965, an anti-Soviet demonstration was even organized in front of the USSR Embassy.

The Chinese leadership increasingly intensifies subversive activities against the Soviet state and social order. The Peking radio beams articles and magazines to the USSR in an attempt to pit various strata of the Soviet people against one another, to obstruct friendship among the peoples of the USSR and to undermine their confidence in the party and in Soviet activists. This is being done to such an extent that direct appeals are being made to engage in political action against the CPSU Central Committee and the Soviet Union.

The CPR leadership propagates ever more obstinately the thesis of potential military clashes between China and the Soviet Union. On 29 September 1965, Chen Yi (foreign minister) . . . spoke utterly falsely of a possible 'co-ordination' of Soviet actions in the north of China with the aggressive war of the United States against the CPR. . . .

The newspaper, *Jen-min Jih-pao*, of 30 September published an article . . . containing such slanderous statements as that the 'revisionists' wanted to split Sinkiang from China seeking 'again to embark on the old road of Russian Tsarism'.

The slanderous character of these speeches is obvious. But it is important to note something else: the idea is obstinately suggested to the Chinese people that it is necessary to prepare for a military conflict with the USSR.

The CPSU Central Committee has already informed the fraternal parties that the Chinese side is provoking border conflicts. Such conflicts have again increased in recent months. . . .

The attitude of the CPR leadership towards the struggle o the DRV and all Vietnamese people against the United States aggression is currently causing great damage to the joint cause of the countries of socialism and the world-wide liberation movement.

The Soviet Union delivers large amounts of weapons to the DRV, including rocket installations, anti-aircraft artillery, airplanes, tanks, coastal guns, warships and other items. In 1965 alone, weapons and other war material worth about 500 million roubles were placed at the disposal of the DRV. The DRV is receiving support in the training of pilots, rocket personnel, tank drivers, artillerymen and so on. Our military aid is being rendered to the extent the Vietnamese leadership itself thinks necessary. The Soviet Union grants extensive military and other supplies to the National Liberation Front of South Vietnam.

The CPSU has proposed to the Chinese leaders more than once that joint actions (of all socialist countries) to support Vietnam be organized. But the Chinese leadership opposed such action by the socialist states. In connection with the expansion of the United States aggression against the DRV, our Party has proposed twice that the representatives of the three parties—the Vietnam Workers Party, the CPSU and the CCP—meet at the highest level to achieve agreement on co-ordinated action for aid for the DRV. These proposals which were received by the Politburo of the Central Committee of the Vietnam Workers Party with approval, were not accepted by the Chinese leaders.

At the same time, the CCP leadership hindered the implementation of the agreement of the government of the USSR with the government of the DRV on an immediate increase in military aid for the DRV. The CCP leaders did not permit Soviet transport planes with weapons to fly over CPR territory.

Then, Chinese personalities also placed obstacles in the way of the transportation of war material to Vietnam by rail. Thus, at their request, an additional shipment of military equipment, including anti-aircraft artillery, which is needed so urgently to protect the Vietnamese cities and villages against the United States air pirates, was recently delivered to the Vietnamese comrades. The Chinese authorities refused for a long time to relay the freight, under the pretence that the papers for its transit had not yet been filled out and they did not know 'whether Vietnam needs this war material'.

By stating openly that they do not desire joint action with the USSR and the other socialist countries, by emphasizing the differences of views with the Soviet Union, and by hindering its aid to the DRV, the Chinese leaders basically encourage the United States aggressors in their war acts against Vietnam.

From all this it became clear that the Chinese leaders need a lengthy Vietnam war to maintain international tensions, to represent China as a 'besieged fortress'. There is every reason to assert that this is one of the goals of the policy of the Chinese leadership in the Vietnam question to originate a military conflict between the USSR and the United States. They want a clash of the USSR with the United States so that they may, as they say themselves, 'sit on the mountain and watch the fight of the tigers'. . . .

The nationalist big-power policy of the Chinese leaders has led to the fact that the CPR recently has suffered a number of serious setbacks on the international scene. The actions of the CCP leaders has led to a spreading of mistrust of the CPR, even in countries which until very recently were regarded as its friends. This became especially clear on the African continent and in a number of Asian countries.

The facts show that the CCP leaders today are directing their foreign political activity not so much against the imperialist states but against the Soviet Union and the socialist world system as a whole. The subdivision of the world into two contrasting systems, the socialist and the capitalist, has disappeared from the materials of the Chinese press. . . .

The Chinese leaders have established factional groups in approximately thirty countries. The front line of the struggle of these groups is directed exclusively against the Marxist-Leninist parties and against the general line of the communist world movement. By supporting these groups and promoting their disruptive activity, the Chinese leaders openly interfere with the internal affairs of other communist parties.

They regard the splitting of the fraternal parties as a 'fully legal affair' and even declare to the whole world that they have not yet sufficiently supported the disruptive groups and that they are therefore planning 'to increase work in this field'. . . .

The meaning of their ideas on questions concerning war, peace and revolution has become completely clear. The course toward socialist revolution, which the working class, rallying the people's masses around itself, accomplishes, has been replaced with a course toward a world war. These ideas were most completely explained in the recent article by Lin Piao, deputy chairman of the CCP, published in September 1965. . . . Lin Piao contends that world revolution is nothing but a 'people's war' of the countries of Asia, Africa and Latin America—of the 'world village' against the states of North America and western Europe—the 'world city'. . . .

The efforts of the CCP leaders to force all parties of the non-socialist countries to accept the goal of an immediate revolution independent of actual conditions in effect means to try to force upon the communist movement putschist, conspiratory tactics. These tactics, however, offer the imperialist bourgeoisie the opportunity to bleed the revolutionary communist and workers' movement, to expose the leadership and the activists of a number of communist parties to destruction.

The CCP leadership completely ignores the great diversity of the conditions in the countries of Asia, Africa and Latin America. It addresses all nations of these countries with the appeal for armed revolt.

DOCUMENT 64. EXTRACTS FROM AN EDITORIAL IN *Kommunist*, NO. 5, 1969, ON THE EXTENSION OF THE ANTI-SOVIET ACTIVITY OF CHINA

Political contacts and economic ties between the People's Republic of China and leading powers of the capitalist world have expanded recently. This would cause no anxiety to the friends of the Chinese people if such actions were not subordinated by the Mao group to the struggle against the socialist countries and if they did not endanger the interests of the working people of China.

Among the practical steps taken by the Mao group on this plane, the proposal of the PRC to the USA in November 1968 expressing its readiness to sign an agreement on the five principles of peaceful co-existence is of major importance. Peking's proposal for Sino-American talks in Warsaw to be resumed last February was assessed in Washington as reflecting a 'serious change in China's foreign policy' and the desire of the Chinese leadership to make a deal. A change in the date of the meeting by the Maoists in no way indicates a change in their intentions and their desire that Nixon's election promise of 'reducing America's obligations' be carried out in the first place in Asia. They count on American imperialism directing its aggressive aspirations towards Europe.

The more active struggle of the Maoists against the socialist countries and their flirtation with the capitalist states receive ever more clearly expressed support in the west. Certain US circles have already proposed the removal of the embargo, the clearing of the road for American-Chinese trade, the establishment of 'close ties' between the USA and China and the use of China (in Asia) and the FRG (in Europe) to create a vice to 'restrain' the socialist countries.

The Maoists are attempting to achieve a *rapprochement* with Japan on a pan-Asian and even racial basis. Mao Tse-tung and his group openly support the territorial claims of the Japanese revenge-seekers with regard to the Soviet Union and express their readiness to sign a separate Sino-Japanese peace treaty. Japan now occupies first place in the trade of the PRC.

In Europe, China is actively developing ties with the Federal Republic of Germany, which today occupies second place in China's trade with the capitalist countries. Relations between China and West Germany have already gone beyond the framework of ordinary trade transactions. Secret political contacts exist between Bonn and Peking. The realization of China's nuclear missile programme was to a considerable degree made possible as a result of technical assistance from the FRG in important electronic instruments and the direct participation of West German specialists. The FRG press writes about the 'colossal interest shown by German heavy industry in trade with China', and says that 'the Federal Republic and Red China could undoubtedly have closer interests'.

It is significant that immediately after the November statement of the Chinese foreign ministry on Sino-American relations, Willy Brandt, the West German foreign minister, made it known that Bonn intended to take steps for the further expansion of ties with China. Franz Josef Strauss, one of the leaders of the reactionary forces, declared that their plans for strengthening their position in the struggle against the status quo in Europe were linked with Mao's policy. Events confirm the conclusion drawn earlier on the coincidence of the positions of the Maoists and the ruling circles in the FRG on such questions as the struggle against the socialist camp, a hostile attitude towards the GDR, the desire to get access to nuclear weapons, the aggravation of tension in Europe and a revision of state borders.

The more active European policy followed by Peking, the manoeuvres in the sphere of Sino-American relations, and the activities of the Maoists in Asia—all this shows that these foreign policy actions are based on hegemonistic aims and on readiness to use any and all forces in the political struggle against the USSR and other fraternal countries. According to some reports, the Maoists are now looking for contacts with NATO, expressing their 'understanding' as regards the latest aggressive preparations of this bloc directed against the Warsaw Treaty countries.

The pattern of China's foreign economic ties has radically changed over the past few years. On the initiative of Peking, China's trade with the socialist countries fell by almost two-thirds from 1961 to 1967, with their share in China's foreign trade dropping from 64 per cent to 23 per cent. During the same period the volume of China's trade with the developed capitalist countries increased threefold. China accepts credits, technical aid and assistance in training personnel from them. The capitalist countries, seeking further to set China against the socialist countries, have considerably relaxed trade restrictions with the PRC.

While expanding economic ties and searching for political contacts with the capitalist countries, the Mao Tse-tung group, in practice, is keeping aloof from the anti-imperialist struggle, leaving aside its hackneyed anti-American statements which no one takes seriously now. The new features in China's foreign policy are of a dangerous nature for the cause of the revolution and socialism; they confirm the readiness of the Mao group to establish contacts with any forces in order to struggle against the countries of socialism and to make complete use for these purposes of the opportunity for a *rapprochement* with the imperialist states.

The Maoists have recently exerted new efforts to strengthen their influence in the countries of the 'Third World'.

The Peking leaders are compelled to take into account that attempts to spread revolutionary chaos everywhere and the methods of crude blackmail and pressure have resulted in a deterioration of relations, and even in a number of the developing countries in Africa and Asia officially breaking off relations with China. Following the events in Indonesia, China's influence was also lost or undermined in such countries as Burma, Nepal, Cambodia, Ghana, Tunisia, Kenya, Burundi, the Central African Republic, Dahomey and others.

The PRC is stepping up its foreign-policy activities in a number of Asian countries. At the same time, Maoist diplomacy subordinates its manoeuvres to hegemonistic plans. In order to intensify its influence Maoist China strives to play on the contradictions between Asian countries, to incite acute internal conflicts within these countries, and plays on the racial community of Asian peoples, promising assistance to some of them and blackmailing others with nuclear weapons. Posing as a champion of the interests of the Asian peoples, the Mao group actually is unconcerned about their fate. By carrying out a programme of nuclear armament, Peking shows complete disregard for the fact that, as a result of the Chinese nuclear tests in the atmosphere, the population of a number of Asian countries is being subjected to a direct threat of radio-active poisoning. Peking today is making its tactics more flexible and is concentrating its efforts—economic assistance and political pressure—on individual countries, seeing them as bridgeheads for spreading its influence and Maoist conceptions. This is the case in Asia with Laos, Cambodia, Burma, Yemen and Pakistan, and in Africa with Guinea, Tanzania, the Congo (Brazzaville) and Zambia.

The Mao group is using its influence on Third World countries to discredit and undermine the influence of the socialist states. In particular, by advancing the idea of setting up a special Afro-Asian community which would counter the socialist countries, the Mao Tse-tung group discards the class approach to international relations. The attempts of the Maoists to weaken the ties between the developing and the socialist countries are fraught with the danger of holding up not only the economic progress of the young states, but also the process of their political liberation. As experience shows, Peking's line towards the Third World clears the road for the forces of reaction and neo-colonialism and for military bureaucratic regimes. The Chinese policy in Indonesia, Ghana and other countries was one of the causes leading to anti-democratic *coups* and the overthrow of governments that pursued an anti-imperialist policy.

Objectively, the Maoists cause the greatest harm to those parties and groups which follow their policy. At the same time as pursuing their hegemonistic aims, Mao Tse-tung and his group do not stop at encouraging such actions which lead to the destruction of entire communist parties, as was the case in Indonesia. They incite physical violence against those representatives of progressive forces who attempt to free themselves of their influence. In this respect the case of the Communist Party of Burma, which Peking egged on in 1968 to wage a 'cultural revolution', is characteristic. This took the form of a bloody massacre of communists who were not in agreement with the Mao Tse-tung policy. As a result, the leadership of the Communist Party suffered greater losses than during the twenty years of guerilla warfare.

The policy conducted by the Maoists in the Third World of stirring up conflicts and of encouraging extremist, nationalist circles has been clearly manifested in the Arab countries, where the Mao Tse-tung group is attempting to strengthen its influence on Palestinian organizations which come out against a political settlement of the Middle East conflict. Several centres on the territory of the PRC are engaged in providing military and political training for rebels from the developing countries; incidentally, they are being trained not so much for waging struggle against colonialism as for carrying out Peking's special aims in the Third World.

China is modifying its methods of penetrating into the developing countries, striving to undermine the latter's ties with the socialist countries, to transform them into its own sphere of influence and to make the developing countries a tool in conducting their policy. Thus, the fight of imperialism and of reaction against the forces struggling for national and social liberation is being helped. . . .

The past period was marked by the fiasco of the plans of the Mao group to expand and deepen the split in the world communist movement. The Peking leaders failed to win over a single communist party or to achieve any growth in the influence of pro-Chinese groupings among the masses.

On the contrary, some of the parties which shared the views of the Chinese leadership in the past are ever more critically examining the political line which the Mao Tse-tung group is attempting to force upon them. Differences of principle have arisen between the Communist Party of Japan and the present Peking leadership. A deep split is observed in the parallel Communist Party of India which came into being under Chinese influence. Its leadership is coming out against many of the political directions advanced by Peking, as a result of which a new pro-Chinese faction has split away.

Many of the pro-Peking groupings are experiencing a crisis. The group headed by J. Grippa in Belgium which, since 1964, underwent six splits, has disintegrated. The Maoists over a long period gave this group the role of an 'international centre' for subversive activities against the communist movement. A split has also taken place in the leadership of the recently organized pro-Chinese 'Communist Party' of Italy. Dissatisfaction with Peking's crude dictation is maturing in a number of pro-Maoist groups; a period of sobering up is to be observed as a result of the fiascos of the Maoist conceptions and the decline in the international prestige of the PRC. Interest in Chinese publications has fallen sharply. The loud tones of these publications, their importunate lauding the Mao cult of the individual, the pseudo-revolutionary slogans which in the past were regarded as an expression of 'new revolutionary thought'—all this ever more frequently evokes sneers, protest and sharp condemnation today. . . .

In a number of countries, in particular in Japan, Argentina, Norway and Denmark, the policy adopted is to achieve a *rapprochement* with the so-called people's socialist parties and in other countries with ultra-left organizations; in some places the Maoists are to an ever greater degree linking up with Trotskyites. The elimination of differences between pro-Chinese and Trotskyite elements is most clearly seen in a number of Latin American countries. Maoist propaganda takes over the slogans of 'left' movements in the west, seeking to present the 'cultural revolution' in China as the realization of the ideals of the left forces in practice—the egalitarian trend, the mass movement of the lower strata against the ruling bureaucracy, the mass drawing of the youth into real political life, the 'emancipation of the individual', etc.

Peking closely follows the stormy development of youth and student actions in western Europe. This, in particular, is seen in the rapid and noisy reaction of Maoist propaganda to the 1968 May to June events in France. Recent facts have shown that the student movement, in which anarchist, Trotskyite and other ultra-left sentiments are spread to a considerable degree, can be used by the Maoists as a favourable media for spreading their influence. It is no accident that at the height of the student actions in France the total numerical strength of the pro-Chinese groups more than doubled. Peking in every way plays on the revolutionary impatience of youth. Chinese propaganda to an ever greater degree concentrates its efforts on proving the thesis that the communist parties have—allegedly —lost their vanguard role. Peking and its followers also devote great attention to organizational matters, counting on setting up pro-Chinese alliances. In Albania a conference of pro-Peking youth from a number of European countries has already been held. It took a decision to hold a youth festival in Tirana in 1969.

The Peking leadership is also resorting to new tactics as regards international democratic organizations (the World Federation of Trade Unions, the World Democratic Youth Federation, the World Council of Peace and others). Their main purport, which is becoming ever more obvious, is a new attempt to strike a blow at these organizations 'from below', by strengthening the splitting activities of its agents in the national trade union, youth, women's and other organizations.

*

The Soviets were on the defensive as far as the territorial issue between them and the Chinese was concerned. The Soviet Far East was colonized under the Tsars and much of it remains thinly populated. Moreover Mao's interview with the Japanese socialists included an attack on Soviet imperialism in other parts of the world, too. The Soviet Union, as a multi-national state, tended to over-react to such criticism.

For some years the long frontier between the two powers had witnessed frontier 'incidents'. The skirmish on Damansky Island on the Ussuri River in 1969 was the most serious border incident involving the two powers. It is perhaps for this reason that it was given the widest publicity by the Soviets and the Chinese.

The Soviets were very much at a disadvantage and Khrushchev's proposal for an agreement to renounce the use of force in settling frontier disputes was the natural reaction of a satiated world power, seeking to keep undisturbed that which it had seized in the past by military force. Khrushchev's letter was followed by a resolution in the General Assembly.

DOCUMENT 65. EXTRACT FROM A *Pravda* EDITORIAL OF 2 SEPTEMBER 1964, DEALING WITH MAO TSE-TUNG'S TALK TO A GROUP OF JAPANESE SOCIALISTS (NOVOSTI PRESS AGENCY BOOKLET, MOSCOW, 1964)

Mao Tse-tung began his talk with statements about the so-called intermediate zone. This theory had come into being as early as 1946. In its original form it boiled down to the following: the Chinese leaders divided the whole world into three parts or zones. The first—American imperialism, the United States; the second—the Soviet Union and other socialist countries; the third zone, as it were lying between them (hence 'intermediate')—mainly the countries of Asia, Africa and Latin America.

Now Mao Tse-tung is introducing a correction into this 'theory'. Slanderously declaring that the USSR 'entered into a conspiracy with the United States to struggle for world domination', he actually combines the two main zones into one. This scheme leaves him with two zones: the 'Soviet-American' and the so-called 'intermediate' zone, which actually includes China as well. In this way the division of the world into two opposing social systems, recognized by all Marxists, disappears.

According to the Chinese theoreticians, the intermediate zone represents revolution and progress. As for the Soviet Union and the United States, they, according to this theory, 'entered into a conspiracy' in order to struggle for world domination. Hence the conclusion is drawn about the necessity for a struggle by the peoples of the intermediate zone against American imperialism and, at the same time, against the Soviet Union. Such is the main purpose of the theoretical exercises of the Chinese leadership.

To say that the theory of the intermediate zone has nothing in common with Marxism is to say very little. This is not merely an un-Marxist, but a militant anti-Marxist, anti-Leninist conception.

The basic principle of Marxism-Leninism consists in a class approach to all the phenomena of the life of society and in assessing all these phenomena from the standpoint of the proletariat, the most progressive class. Precisely such an approach underlies the analysis of our epoch given by the communist and workers' parties of the world in the declaration and the statement of the Moscow meetings. The world of today is not divided into geographical zones but into opposing social systems—the socialist and the capitalist systems. Revolutionary transition from capitalism to socialism constitutes the basic content of our epoch: all the revolutionary forces of our time—the world system of socialism, the working-class movement in the capitalist countries and the national liberation movement—merge in a single front and jointly oust imperialism, achieving more and more successes in the struggle for the cause of peace, democracy and socialism.

Yet this class approach does not satisfy the Peking theoreticians. They brush it aside completely. Their 'intermediate zones' include on an equal footing both countries fighting against imperialism and for their national independence, and imperialist states; both the working class, the working masses of the capitalist countries, and the ruling bourgeoisie. In other words, 'horses and people are all mixed up', as the poet has said, and thus Chairman Mao mixes together in an intermediate zone the exploiters and the exploited, the oppressors and the oppressed.

In the talk it was stated: 'All the peoples of Asia, Africa and Latin America come out against imperialism. Europe, Canada and other countries also come out against imperialism.' Mark this—not the working people of Europe and Canada, but the whole of Canada, including the capitalist monopolies, the reactionary bourgeois parties, the French 'ultras', the Bonn revenge-seekers and the like. All these, it turns out, are fighters against imperialism, and the revolutionary movement has no alternative but to welcome into its ranks Messrs Krupp, Thyssen and Rothschild and, it may be, even General Franco himself.

In accordance with the theory of the intermediate zone, the course of events in the world is not determined by the struggle of some powers and geographical regions against others. This theory actually ignores the nature of the social system of this or that country. Not only does it merely ignore the class approach but it replaces it by an ultra-nationalistic approach prompted by the aims of the great-power policy of the CCP leaders.

Guided by such an approach, the Chinese leaders are playing their dangerous political game. Since they regard the socialist camp as an obstacle standing in the way of the realization of their hegemonistic schemes with regard to the national liberation movement, they are trying to cut off this movement from the world system of socialism. That is why they construct the first intermediate zone out of the countries of Asia, Africa and Latin America, including China. Since the Chinese leaders are looking for rich economic partners and potential allies in the international arena among the developed capitalist countries, they include nearly the whole capitalist world in an intermediate zone and issue it with credentials as a 'fighter against imperialism'.

Besides this, Chairman Mao now and then issues personal credentials to those imperialist countries with which Peking is flirting with particular enthusiasm. It was only yesterday that Chinese propagandists were referring to General de Gaulle as a 'fascist and a bandit'. But it was sufficient for him to hint at the possibility of a *rapprochement* with Peking and the General became one of the most active fighters against American imperialism. This is not enough. The Chinese leaders clearly hint in a number of pronouncements that 'France may restore her influence in Asia'.

Examples of this kind are also found in the talk which is published today. Japan is a developed country, Mao Tse-tung says, and 'she may help us in many respects. In the political respect we must also support each other'.

This invitation to co-operate is immediately backed up by credentials issued, not to the country as a whole, but to its ruling class. 'Japanese monopoly capital belongs to the second intermediate zone,' Mao Tse-tung says. 'Even this capital is displeased with the United States and some of its representatives openly come out against the United States. Although the monopoly capital of Japan is now dependent on the USA, time will pass and it will throw off the American yoke.' Thus it follows that it will be, not the Japanese people, not the working class who will throw off the yoke of their own and foreign oppressors, as the progressive representatives of the Japanese working peoples say, but monopoly capital which will throw off the yoke of its American counterpart.

Thus, French and Japanese monopoly capital are classed with the anti-imperialists. And what will happen if tomorrow the United States monopolies find it advantageous for themselves to revise their policy of not recognizing the People's Republic of China and offer it economic co-operation? Will they, too, be issued with credentials as 'fighters against imperialism'? Will it then be necessary to include the United States in the 'intermediate zone' as well?

We must be grateful to Chairman Mao Tse-tung: no one has exposed the real aims of the Chinese leadership better than he has. The theory of the intermediate zone is a hopeless, futile attempt to provide some 'ideological basis' for an openly nationalistic policy.

Of course, there are contradictions between the imperialists of the United States and Japan, as well as between France and other capitalist countries, and a struggle is being waged for markets and spheres of capital investment. The revolutionary forces are making use of these contradictions. But to use contradictions in the imperialist camp in the interests of the common struggle for the cause of peace and social progress is one thing, and to flirt with the class enemy and form blocs with that enemy is something entirely different.

Yet the Chinese leaders, who call themselves internationalists, are actually ready to come to an agreement with anybody for the sake of the struggle against friends and allies of People's China—the Soviet Union and other socialist countries.

Mao Tse-tung described the struggle waged by the leadership of the CCP against the Soviet Union and other socialist countries as a 'paper war' and added that such a war did nobody any harm since no one was killed in it. This, in the first place, contains a recognition of the fact that the Chinese leaders regard their polemics with the CPSU and other fraternal parties as a 'kind of war'. In the second place, it clearly reveals the supercilious attitude of the leaders of the CCP towards the interests of the unity of the world communist and liberation movement.

The communists of the whole world are expressing their deep concern over the situation that has taken shape in the international communist movement through the fault of the Chinese leaders. The harm which those leaders have done to the cause of the peoples' struggle for peace, national independence and social progress is obvious to everyone. And here is Mao Tse-tung declaring: 'There's no reason to worry. This is a war without anybody being killed in it, without any casualties!'

No, we cannot agree with the Chinese leaders' assessment of their own actions. Their struggle against the CPSU, against the world communist movement, against the USSR and other countries of socialism is not a 'paper war'. As regards its fierceness and its scale and methods, it does not differ from the cold war of imperialism against the socialist countries.

Mao Tse-tung's pronouncements on the territorial question clearly show how far the Chinese leaders have gone in the 'cold war' against the Soviet Union. He is not simply claiming this or that part of Soviet territory but is presenting his claims as part of some 'general territorial question'.

We are faced with an openly expansionist programme with far-reaching pretensions.

This programme did not appear today or yesterday. In 1954 a textbook on modern history was put out in the People's Republic of China with a map of China showing her as she was, in the opinion of the authors, before the First Opium War. In China this map included Burma, Vietnam, Korea, Thailand, Malaya, Nepal, Bhutan and Sikkim; in the north the border ran along the Stanovoi mountain range, cutting the Maritime Territory from the USSR; in the west a part of Kirghizia, Tajikistan and Kazakhstan (up to Lake Balkhash) was also included in China. Sakhalin, too, was shown as Chinese territory. If one is to believe the textbook, all these lands and countries were 'state territory of China' and were taken away from her.

At that time it seemed that the publication of such a textbook was a result of laxity or the provocative activities of nationalistic elements. Yet subsequent events refuted that conjecture. Maps showing various parts of the Soviet Union and other countries neighbouring on China as Chinese territory continued to be published in the People's Republic of China.

Chinese representatives have recently begun to mention, with increasing frequency, hundreds of thousands of square kilometres of Soviet territory which allegedly belong 'by right' to China.

A recent issue of the Peking magazine *Lishi Yanchu* (No. 4, 1964) alleged that Russia had 'seized vast lands to the north of the River Heilung and to the east of the River Ussuri. . . . Russia annexed at various times the vast lands in Sinkiang and in the area of the north-east'.

Now Mao Tse-tung has declared in his talk: 'About a hundred years ago the area to the east of Baikal became the territory of Russia and from then on Vladivostok, Khabarovsk, Kamchatka and other points have been the territory of the Soviet Union. We have not yet called for an account on this score!'

By what right, however, are the Chinese leaders claiming lands that did not belong to China? They refer to the fact that many hundreds of years ago Chinese troops came to these areas and that the Chinese emperor collected tribute from the local people. Indeed, were it not for the fact that such a serious question is involved, 'historical arguments' of this kind could only be described as childish.

The history of mankind is full of examples of the emergence and the fall of states, the resettlement of peoples during which the frontiers between states changed more than once. By resorting to the method of 'historical references' in the question of frontiers one can prove anything. For instance, one can prove that England is French territory, because she was once the possession of a Duke of Normandy. One can prove, on the contrary, that France is an English possession because, in her day, during the Hundred Years' War, she was almost completely conquered by the English. With the help of such arguments one can also prove that the frontiers of the People's Republic of China pass only along the line of the Great Wall of China, which is less than 100 kilometres from Peking. Indeed, China's frontier did once pass there and the wall itself is evidence of this.

Yet even if the references to 'historical rights' are taken seriously, it will emerge that in this case they do not correspond in any way to the facts. As is known, in the middle of the seventeenth century China's possessions reached only to the Hsingan mountain range, that is to say, considerably to the south of the River Amur. The territories to the north of Hsingan were inhabited by local indigenous tribes (Evenks, Dauers, etc.), who were subjected from time to time to raids by the Manchus and paid tribute to them. There was no indigenous Manchu and Chinese population in the Amur valley. The process of defining the actual frontiers took place with the development of the northern half of the Amur basin by Russia and of the southern part by China. More than 100 years ago this state of the frontier was fixed in the Aigun and Peking treaties.

No one is arguing: the Tsarist government carried out a predatory policy, just as the Chinese emperors themselves did to the extent of their abilities.

At various times someone was stronger and got the upper hand over the others. This resulted in a certain change in the settlement of the peoples. Yet the common people did not think about any territorial gains. They worked on the land they had to live on, watering it with their sweat. One can only be amazed that there are persons who are questioning the right of workers and peasants to the land on which they have been living and working from ancient times, merely on the grounds that once upon a time one emperor defeated another and then himself suffered defeat.

Do those who question the fact that a territory of more than one-and-a-half million square kilometres belongs to the Soviet Union, think how these claims will be taken by Soviet people who have been living and working on this land for several generations and consider it to be their homeland, the land of their forefathers?

That is why we say that the present frontier developed

historically and was fixed by life itself, and the treaties on the frontier are a basis which cannot be disregarded.

The CPSU headed the struggle of the working class and the working masses of Russia against Tsarism and utterly defeated it. It is well known that in the very first years of its existence the Soviet government liquidated all the unequal treaties with China. Continuing the Leninist policy, the Soviet government gave up the naval base at Port Arthur and handed over, free of charge, to the government of the People's Republic of China all its rights in the joint management of the Chinese-Chanchung railway with all the property belonging to the railway. Lenin angrily condemned the seizure of Port Arthur by the Tsarist government and the infiltration of Manchuria. Yet it was none other than Lenin who said: 'Vladivostok is far away, but this city is ours.'

The Soviet Union is an absolutely new state formation which emerged as a result of the voluntary unification of Soviet republics created on the ruins of the Tsarist empire. And whereas the frontiers of Tsarist Russia were determined by the policy of imperialist predators, the frontiers of the Soviet Union were formed as a result of a voluntary declaration of the will of the peoples on the basis of the principle of the free self-determination of nations. The peoples who have joined the Soviet Union will never allow anyone to encroach upon their right to decide their destiny themselves.

In his talk Mao Tse-tung bemoans the fate of Mongolia which, so he says, was put by the Soviet Union 'under . . . its rule'. This can only arouse indignation. Everybody knows that the Mongolian People's Republic has been a sovereign socialist state for more than forty years now and enjoys all the rights of an independent country.

Why did Mao Tse-tung have to make such obviously wild statements? The point is that the existence of an independent Mongolian state which maintains friendly relations with the USSR and other socialist countries, does not suit the Chinese leaders. They would like to deprive Mongolia of her independence and make her a Chinese province. The leaders of the People's Republic of China made an offer to Nikita Khrushchev and other Soviet comrades to 'reach agreement' on this during their visit to Peking in 1954.

Nikita Khrushchev naturally refused to discuss this question and told the Chinese leaders that the destiny of the Mongolian people was determined, not in Peking and not in Moscow, but in Ulan Bator, and that the question of Mongolia's statehood could be settled only by the country's working people themselves and by nobody else.

As has already been pointed out above, the Chinese leaders are trying to raise territorial claims to the level of some general principle. Yet this involves the mainstays of international relations. What would happen if all states were to follow the Peking recipe and start presenting claims and counter-claims to one another for a revision of historically formed frontiers? There is no difficulty in answering this question. This road would mean an inevitable worsening of international tensions and would be fraught with military conflicts, with all the consequences ensuing therefrom.

DOCUMENT 66. SOVIET STATEMENT OF 29 MARCH 1969 DEALING WITH THE ARMED CLASH WITH THE CHINESE ON THE USSURI RIVER (*Pravda*, 29 MARCH 1969)

Armed border incidents provoked by the Chinese side have taken place recently on the River Ussuri in the area of Damansky Island. The Chinese authorities did not have and could not have any justification for the organization of such incidents, clashes and bloodshed.

These events can cause rejoicing only to those who would like by any means to dig a gulf of hostility between the Soviet Union and the Chinese People's Republic. They have nothing in common with the fundamental interest of the Soviet and Chinese peoples.

The circumstances of the armed attacks on Soviet frontier guards on the River Ussuri are well known. These were premeditated and pre-planned acts.

On the morning of 2 March an observation post detected a violation of the Soviet border near Damansky Island by about thirty Chinese soldiers. A group of Soviet frontier guards, led by an officer, approached the violators with the intention, as had been the case on previous occasions, of issuing a protest and demanding that they leave Soviet territory.

The Chinese soldiers let the Soviet frontier guards approach them to a distance of a few metres and then suddenly, without any warning, opened point-blank fire at them.

At the same time artillery, mortar and small arms fire was opened at another group of Soviet frontier guards who were near the Soviet bank from an ambush on Damansky Island, where Chinese soldiers had earlier taken up positions under cover of darkness, and from the Chinese bank.

The Soviet frontier guards accepted battle and with the help of a neighbouring frontier post expelled the violators from Soviet territory. As a result of this treacherous attack there were killed and wounded on both sides.

Despite the Soviet government's warning and call to refrain from such provocations, on 14 to 15 March the Chinese side undertook new attempts in the same area to make an armed incursion into the territory of the Soviet Union.

Supported by artillery and mortar fire, units of the Chinese regular army attacked Soviet frontier troops protecting Damansky Island. The attack was resolutely beaten off and the violators thrown out of Soviet territory. This provocation by the Chinese side resulted in further casualties.

In their statement, the Chinese authorities are now trying to escape responsibility for the armed clashes. They contend that it was not the Chinese, but Soviet frontier guards, who violated the state border and they claim that this island does not belong to the Soviet Union.

The Chinese side does not deny that its military personnel acted in accordance with a prepared plan but, resorting to a false statement, it tries to present the use of arms by the Chinese violators as a 'forced measure'.

It follows from the Chinese statements that the question of Damansky Island is only a part of some territorial problem, allegedly inherited from the past, which has yet to be solved and which is connected with the re-carving of state frontiers.

Moreover, the Chinese government refuses to take into consideration the treaties that exist between China and the USSR, ignores the long-standing practice of Soviet-Chinese inter-state relations and distorts history to suit its territorial claims.

All this, as we see, stems from the fundamental change which has taken place in recent years in the policy of the government of the People's Republic of China towards the Soviet Union and the Soviet people.

As is known, Chinese official propaganda questions the present borders of China's neighbouring states, where a historical community of the peoples populating them has long taken shape. The claims to neighbouring territories are made on the pretext that they were once the subjects of dispute between some feudal chiefs, emperors and Tsars, or that Chinese conquerors or merchants once set foot there.

The armed provocations of the Chinese authorities on the River Ussuri in the area of Damansky Island are, therefore, not accidental. These actions, as well as the engineering of general tension on the Soviet-Chinese frontiers, are doing great harm to the cause of socialism and peace, to the common front of the anti-imperialist struggle and to friendship between the Soviet and Chinese peoples.

The Soviet government, guided by an earnest desire to ensure lasting peace and security and maintain friendship and co-operation with the Chinese people, believes that it is necessary to take practical steps without delay to normalize the situation on the Soviet-Chinese frontier.

It urges the government of the People's Republic of China to refrain from any actions on the frontier that may cause complications and urges the Chinese government to solve any differences that may arise in a calm atmosphere and through negotiations.

The Soviet government also proposes that Soviet and Chinese official representatives resume as soon as possible the consultations that were started in Peking in 1964.

The Soviet government is firmly convinced that in the final count the vital interests of the Soviet and Chinese peoples will make it possible to remove and overcome difficulties in Soviet-Chinese relations.

The Soviet government has stated, and considers it necessary to repeat, that it resolutely rejects any encroachments by anyone on Soviet territory and that any attempts to talk to the Soviet Union and the Soviet people in the language of weapons will be firmly repulsed.

The Soviet people unanimously support the Leninist foreign policy of the Communist Party of the Soviet Union and the government of the USSR and all measures to ensure the inviolability and security of the sacred frontiers of our socialist motherland.

DOCUMENT 67. EXTRACT FROM KHRUSHCHEV'S MESSAGE TO THE GOVERNMENTS OF ALL COUNTRIES CALLING FOR AN AGREEMENT TO RENOUNCE THE USE OF FORCE IN SETTLING TERRITORIAL AND FRONTIER DISPUTES, 31 DECEMBER 1963 (*SN*, 6 JANUARY 1964)

I think that you will agree with me that if we try to pick out the questions which most often give rise to dangerous friction between states in different parts of the world, these will undoubtedly be territorial disputes, problems concerning the frontiers between states, reciprocal or one-sided claims by states to one another's territory. Here are the factors which lead us to this problem. All this is taken from life, and one cannot but ponder over it, I think.

The question of boundaries or, to be more specific, of territorial claims and disputes, is not a new one, of course. It has existed practically throughout the entire history of mankind, and not infrequently has caused sharp conflicts between states and mutual mistrust and enmity among the peoples. The seizure of foreign territories was the invariable concomitant of the wars of conquest waged by many rulers in ancient times, in the Middle Ages and in the course of modern history. And what about the many colonial wars? Invariably their main aim, too, was to seize other peoples' territories, to enslave other peoples. No one can deny this now, no matter how the colonialists, in their day, covered up their sinister deeds by talk about a 'civilizing mission'.

In our century, too, the territorial claims of states have caused a number of armed conflicts. The desire to seize foreign territories played a great part in the two world wars which were engendered by imperialism. Tens of millions of lives were sacrificed to the Moloch of war. The strivings of those who in the Kaiser's Germany, on the one hand, and in the countries of the Entente, on the other, hatched plans for carving up the map of Europe and other parts of the world once again in their own favour, gave impetus to events which resulted in the First World War. The claims of Hitler's Germany and its allies in aggression to *Lebensraum* at the expense of other nations paved the way to the Second World War.

But while it is true that territorial claims have in many cases led to wars and armed conflicts, it is also equally true that wars as means of settling territorial disputes have always been very costly for the peoples. No sooner had one state seized by armed force territory from another state, than the latter began to prepare a new war in order to regain the lost territory. After that the cycle repeated itself. Suffice it to recall, for instance, how Alsace and Lorraine changed hands and how rivers of blood were shed at each change. After each war for territories, the territorial disputes between states proved to be, perhaps even more, and not less, acute than before the war.

Many of these territorial disputes were inherited by our generation, too. Now the number of such disputes and reciprocal claims has increased still more. One of the reasons for this is that many young sovereign states which recently won their national independence, have inherited from the colonial regimes a large number of artificially embroiled frontier problems. A glance at the political map of the world today will show scores, if not hundreds, of areas which are disputed by various states.

Of course, territorial claims and disputes between states differ in character. There are some that are associated with the completion of the liberation of this or that people from colonial oppression or foreign occupation.

It is well known that by no means all the young national states managed, immediately after they had become independent, to liberate from the power of the colonialists all the territories that are theirs by right.

Taiwan is a case in point. From time immemorial this island has been an integral part of the Chinese state. The unlawful occupation of Taiwan by American troops should be terminated. The island is an inalienable part of the People's Republic of China and would long since have been reunited with it but for outside interference by another state. . . .

All this, of course, also applies to the territories of the peoples who have not yet achieved national independence and whose status is still colonial. One cannot accept the casuistry of the colonialists who still retain colonies and claim that these colonial territories are component parts of the metropolitan country. There should be no ambiguity about that: the right of all colonial peoples to liberation, to freedom and independence, proclaimed in the United Nations Declaration on Granting Independence to Colonial Countries and Peoples, cannot be called into question by anyone. . . .

There is one more problem, that of the unification of Germany, Korea and Vietnam, which is associated to a certain extent with the territorial question. Each of these countries has been divided in the post-war period into two states with different social systems. The desire of the peoples of these countries for unification should be treated, of course, with understanding and respect.

It goes without saying, however, that the question of re-unification should be settled by the peoples of these countries and their governments themselves, without any interference or pressure from outside and. certainly, without foreign military intervention—occupation, as is actually the case, for instance, in South Korea and South Vietnam.

No force should be used in settling this question and the peoples of these countries should be given the opportunity to solve the problems of unification by peaceful means. All other states should contribute to this.

This, however, is not the question we are examining here. The question before us is how to deal with territorial disputes and claims which arise over the actually existing and well-established frontiers of states. . . .

I do not know what words I should choose, but it is my wish to express with the utmost clarity the idea that there are not, nor can there be, territorial disputes in our time between states already formed, or unresolved frontier questions, of such a kind that it is permissible to use armed force in order to settle them. No, this cannot be allowed to happen, and we must do everything possible to rule out the possibility of events developing in such a way.

It may be asked, and I expect this question has already come to your mind: 'Is the Soviet Union proposing that all the territorial issues between states should be deleted with one stroke and that all attempts to settle them should be abandoned, just as if these issues did not exist at all?' No, that is not the point. We realize that some countries have weighty reasons for their claims. In all the current frontier disputes between states the sides must, of course, study the question thoroughly in order to settle these issues. We are entirely in favour of this. The only thing we are against is military methods of settling territorial disputes. That is what we should agree on—precisely on this.

As for the peaceful means of settling territorial disputes, experience proves that they are feasible.

Even the existence of different social systems and forms of state power in the world of today need not be an obstacle to the peaceful solution of territorial problems, provided, of course, that this is sincerely desired by both sides. Life itself shows that whenever states firmly abide by the principles of peaceful co-existence and display goodwill, restraint and due regard for each other's interests, they are quite capable of extricating themselves from the maze of historical, national, geographical and other factors and finding a satisfactory solution.

It is also important to stress that while the military road, that is to say, the use of force, by no means leads to the ending of territorial conflicts, but rather deepens and aggravates them, the peaceful road, on the contrary, eliminates such conflicts and to a considerable extent removes the very source of the dispute, because more opportunities for a solution are provided by a level-headed examination of issues than in a case in which the sides in dispute are ready to start a shooting war against each other.

Everything, including the tremendous changes which have recently taken place in the world and which shed new light on many international problems, the territorial problem among others, goes to show that at the present time we have a situation in which it is possible to set and accomplish in a practical way the task of ruling out from international life the use of force in territorial disputes between states.

The possibility of a radical turn in the solution of these questions by peaceful means is also facilitated by the increasing recognition of the ideas of the peaceful co-existence of states with different social systems. The idea of peaceful co-existence, which lies at the root of our Leninist foreign policy, found expression in the decisions of the historic Bandung Conference, in the Charter of the Organization of African Unity, and in many other international documents. More and more governments in the world are coming firmly to the conclusion that in the nuclear age war can no longer be a means of settling international disputes, and that peaceful co-existence is the only foundation on which the relations between states can and should be built.

Nor can one fail to see that the present extremely rapid development of science and technology, which opens up tremendous prospects for increasing industrial and agricultural production in all territories, exposes still further the falsity of the arguments of those who are in the habit of referring to over-population or the insufficient economic effectiveness of their own territory in order to justify their territorial claims.

The peaceful settlement of territorial disputes is also favoured by the fact that in the practice of international relations there already exists a store of improved methods of peacefully settling outstanding issues: direct negotiations between the states concerned, the use of good offices, requests for assistance from international organizations, etc. Although, in my opinion, the United Nations in its present form is far from being an ideal instrument of peaceful co-operation between states, even this organization, given an impartial approach, can make a positive contribution to the cause of the peaceful settlement of territorial and frontier issues.

Taking all this into consideration, the Soviet government, guided by the interests of strengthening peace and preventing war, is submitting the following proposal for the consideration of the governments of all states: that an international agreement (or treaty) be concluded on the renunciation by states of the use of force for settling territorial disputes or questions of frontiers. In our opinion, such an agreement should include the following principal propositions:

1 A solemn undertaking by the states parties to the agreement not to resort to force to alter the existing state frontiers.
2 Recognition that the territory of states should not, even temporarily, be the object of any invasion, attack, military occupation or any other forcible measures directly or indirectly undertaken by other states for whatsoever political, economic, strategic, frontier, or any other considerations.

3 A firm declaration that neither differences in social or political systems, nor denial of recognition or the absence of diplomatic relations, nor any other pretexts can serve as justification for the violation by one state of the territorial integrity of another.

4 An undertaking to settle all territorial disputes exclusively by peaceful means, such as negotiations, mediation, conciliatory procedure, and also other peaceful means at the choice of the parties concerned in accordance with the United Nations Charter.

Needless to say, such an international agreement should cover all territorial disputes concerning the existing frontiers between states.

The proposed agreement would be a confirmation, specification and development of the principles of the United Nations Charter concerning the relations between states on territorial matters, and an expression of goodwill and of the determination of states firmly to abide by these principles.

The Soviet government is profoundly convinced that the assumption by the states of a commitment to settle territorial disputes exclusively by peaceful means will introduce more order in international affairs. The conclusion of an international agreement by states renouncing the use of force for the settlement of territorial disputes, would, like a fresh breeze, dispel many of the things in international life which are artificially exaggerated and which create obstacles to the easing of tension in the world and to the consolidation of peace. It would bring about a new and considerable improvement in the international climate and would create a good basis for greater trust between states.

It can be said with confidence that in the new situation which would be created by the conclusion of an agreement on the renunciation by states of the use of force for the solution of territorial questions, it would be much easier to find a solution to other basic international problems, too. This refers primarily and above all to the problem of disarmament.

Indeed, the desire of some states to resort to force against other states in order to settle frontier disputes in their favour has always been, and continues to be, one of the main factors stimulating the arms race. Territorial disputes between states are a nutrient medium for militarism, as well as for fomenting the passions which are so willingly exploited by those who regard an unbridled arms race as a source of profit. In conditions in which states will no longer have worries about their frontiers and in which any plans for changing those frontiers by force will be banned by international law, many of the motives by which states have been guided in increasing their armed forces, are bound to disappear.

This will expose still more the insolvency of those who either hesitate to agree to disarmament or, trying to conceal their unwillingness to reach agreement on this question, point to difficulties arising from the present situation in view of unsettled territorial disputes. The great powers must set an example in disarmament.

It is also clear that opportunities for large-scale peaceful international co-operation will immeasurably increase in conditions in which states will have no grounds for mutual suspicions with regard to frontiers. A powerful impetus will be given to the development of trade and transport communications, cultural exchanges and scientific contacts for the good of the peoples.

(f) THE INVASION OF CZECHOSLOVAKIA

Before resorting to force communists use arguments to influence those who have erred. During the first half of 1968 the Czechoslovaks on the one side and their brothers-in-arms on the other were locked in a war of words. In order to give their voice greater weight the Soviets called on their allies. A discussion took place with the Czechoslovaks in March 1968 and when this did not cause a change in Czech policy they were summoned to Warsaw. They refused to come. So the powers assembled in Warsaw addressed a letter to them. On each occasion the Rumanians were absent. The letter was not effective. The Czechoslovaks were invited to the Soviet Union. Again they refused to go, fearing that they might not return. Finally a bizarre meeting took place between the Politburos of the Czechoslovak and Soviet communist parties in a railway carriage on Czechoslovak soil in the tiny frontier station of Čierna nad Tisou. The talks, it seemed, were successful. A few days later an agreement was signed between all the Warsaw Pact countries in appropriate ceremonies in the Slovak capital Bratislava. It seemed all had been settled. Two-and-a-half weeks later the armies of the Bratislava signatories occupied Czechoslovakia.

The Warsaw Letter was partly an answer to the manifesto known as 'Two Thousand Words to Workers, Farmers, Scientists, Artists and Everyone', written by the writer Ludvik Vaculik. It gave much offence to the Soviets.

DOCUMENT 68. THE WARSAW LETTER; EXTRACT FROM THE LETTER ADDRESSED TO THE CZECHOSLOVAK COMMUNIST PARTY BY THE COMMUNIST PARTIES OF THE WARSAW PACT COUNTRIES, 15 JULY 1968 (*Pravda*, 19 JULY 1968)

The development of events in your country evokes deep anxiety in us. It is our profound conviction that the offensive of the reactionary forces, backed by imperialism, against your party and the foundations of the social system in the Czechoslovak Socialist Republic threatens to push your country off the road of socialism and that it is consequently jeopardizing the interests of the whole socialist system.

We expressed these apprehensions at the meeting in Dresden and in the course of bilateral meetings, as well as in letters which our parties sent in the recent period to the Praesidium of the Central Committee of the Communist Party of Czechoslovakia.

Recently we made to the Praesidium of the Central Committee of the Communist Party of Czechoslovakia the offer to hold a new joint meeting on 14 July this year so as to exchange information and opinions on the state of affairs in our countries, including the development of events in Czechoslovakia. Unfortunately, the Praesidium of the Central Committee of the CPCS did not take part in this meeting and did not use the opportunity for a collective, comradely discussion on the situation that has developed. That is why we have considered it necessary to make known to you in this letter, with complete sincerity and frankness, the view which we hold in common.

We want you to understand us properly and to make a correct assessment of our intentions.

We neither have had, nor do we have, the intention of interfering in such matters as are strictly the internal business of your party and your state, or of violating the principles of respect, independence and equality in the relations among communist parties and socialist countries.

We are not approaching you as representatives of yesterday who would like to interfere in the correction of mistakes and short-comings, including breaches of socialist legality which took place.

We are not interfering in the methods of planning and management of Czechoslovakia's socialist national economy or in actions taken by you with the aim of improving the structure of the economy and developing socialist democracy.

We shall welcome the settlement of relations between Czechs and Slovaks on healthy foundations of friendly co-operation within the framework of the Czechoslovak Socialist Republic.

At the same time we cannot agree to have hostile forces push your country away from the road of socialism and create a danger of Czechoslovakia being severed from the socialist com-munity. This is something more than your own concern. It is the common concern of all the communist and workers' parties and states united by alliance, co-operation and friendship. It is the common concern of our countries, which have joined in the Warsaw Treaty, to safeguard their independence and peace and security in Europe, and to place an insurmountable barrier against the intrigues of the imperialist forces, against aggression and revanchism.

At the sacrifice of tremendous losses the peoples of our countries achieved victory over Hitlerian fascism and won freedom and independence and the opportunity to follow the path of progress and socialism. The frontiers of the socialist world have moved to the centre of Europe, to the Elbe and the Bohemian Forest. And we shall never agree to these historic gains of socialism and the independence and security of our peoples being placed in jeopardy. We shall never agree to imperialism, using peaceful or non-peaceful methods, making a breach from within or from outside in the socialist system and changing the correlation of forces in Europe in favour of imperialism.

The strength and firmness of our alliances depend on the internal strength of the socialist system in each of our fraternal countries and on the Marxist-Leninist policy of our parties, which play the leading role in the political and social life of their nations and states. Undermining the leading role of the communist party leads to the liquidation of socialist democracy and of the socialist system. The foundations of our alliance and safety of the community of our countries are thereby imperilled.

You are aware of the understanding with which the fraternal parties treated the decisions of the January plenary meeting of the Central Committee of the CPCS, as they believed that your party, firmly controlling the levers of power, would direct the entire process in the interests of socialism and not allow anti-communist reaction to exploit this for its own purposes. We shared the conviction that you would cherish like your own eye the Leninist principle of democratic centralism as your most treasured possession. Disregard of any aspect of this principle—democracy or centralism—inevitably serves to weaken the party and its guiding role by transforming the party either into a bureaucratic organization or into a debating society. We discussed all these matters time and time again at the meetings we had and we received from you assurances that you were aware of all the dangers and were fully determined to repulse them.

Unfortunately events have taken another course.

Taking advantage of the weakening of the party leadership of the country and demagogically abusing the slogan of 'democratization', the forces of reaction triggered off a campaign against the Communist Party of Czechoslovakia and its honest and devoted cadres, clearly seeking to abolish the party's leading role, to subvert the socialist system and to place Czechoslovakia in opposition to the other socialist countries.

The political organizations and clubs that have emerged recently, outside the framework of the National Front, have become, in effect, headquarters of the forces of reaction. The social democrats are persistently striving to establish their own party, are organizing underground committees and are seeking to divide the working-class movement in Czechoslovakia and to take over the leadership of the country in order to carry out a bourgeois restoration. Anti-socialist and revisionist forces have seized the press, radio and television, making of them a rostrum for attacking the communist party, disorienting the working class and all working people, spewing forth unbridled anti-socialist demagogy and undermining the friendly relations between the Czechoslovak Socialist Republic and other socialist countries. Certain mass information media are conducting a systematic campaign of real moral terrorism against people who are opposing the forces of reaction or are expressing anxiety over the trend of developments.

In spite of the decisions of the May plenary meeting of the Central Committee of the CPCS, which drew attention to the threat emanating from right-wing and anti-communist forces as the main danger, the increasing attacks that reaction has mounted have not met with any rebuff. This is precisely why reaction has been able to address publicly the entire country and to print its political platform under the title of 'Two Thousand Words', which contains an outright call for struggle against the communist party and constitutional authority and for strikes and disorders. This call constitutes a serious danger to the party, the National Front and the socialist state, and is an attempt to introduce anarchy. In essence, this statement is the organizational and political platform of counter-revolution. The claims made by its writers to the effect that they are not seeking to overthrow the socialist system, to operate without the communists or to break alliances with the socialist countries, should not deceive anyone. That is empty talk, the purpose of which is to legalize the platform of counter-revolution and hoodwink the vigilance of the party, the working class and all working people.

Far from being repudiated, this platform, which has been so widely circulated at a crucially important moment on the eve of the extraordinary congress of the CPCS, has, on the contrary, found open supporters, in the party rank and file and leadership, who are backing up the anti-socialist calls. . . . A situation has thus arisen which is absolutely unacceptable for a socialist country.

It is in this atmosphere that attacks are also being made on the socialist foreign policy of the CSR and on the alliance and friendship with socialist countries. Voices are heard demanding a revision of our common co-ordinated policy in relation to the

FRG in spite of the fact that the West German government invariably pursues a policy that is hostile to the interests of our countries' security. Overtures by the authorities and revenge-seekers of the FRG are meeting with a response among leading circles in your country.

The whole course of events in your country in recent months shows that the forces of counter-revolution, supported by imperialist centres, have developed a broad offensive against the socialist system without encountering due resistance from the party and the people's power. There is no doubt that the centres of international imperialist reaction are also involved in these events in Czechoslovakia and are doing everything in their power to inflame and worsen the situation, inspiring anti-socialist forces to act along these lines. The bourgeois press, under the pretext of praising 'democratization' and 'liberalization' in the CSR, is waging a campaign of incitement against the fraternal socialist countries. The ruling circles of the FRG are especially active, attempting to make use of the events in Czechoslovakia in order to sow discord among the socialist countries, isolate the GDR and carry out their revenge-seeking schemes.

Don't you see these dangers, comrades? Is it possible, in such conditions, to remain passive, to confine yourselves to mere declarations and assurances of loyalty to the cause of socialism and to your commitments as allies? Don't you see that counter-revolution is wresting from you one position after another and that the party is losing control over the course of events and is retreating still further under pressure from anti-communist forces?

Is it not for the purpose of sowing distrust and enmity towards the Soviet Union and other socialist countries that the press, radio and television of your country have unleashed a campaign in connection with the staff exercises of the armed forces of the Warsaw Treaty Organization? Matters have gone so far that the joint staff exercises of our troops, with the participation of a number of units of the Soviet Army, as is customary for military co-operation, are being used for the purpose of groundless accusations to the effect that the sovereignty of the Czechoslovak Socialist Republic is being violated. And this is taking place in Czechoslovakia, whose people hold sacred the memory of the Soviet soldiers who gave their lives for the freedom and sovereignty of that country. At the same time, near the western frontiers of your country, exercises of military forces of the aggressive NATO bloc are being carried out, with the army of revenge-seeking West Germany taking part. Yet not a single word is being said about that.

Those who inspire this unfriendly campaign evidently want to confuse the minds of the Czechoslovak people, to disorient them and undermine the plain truth that Czechoslovakia can retain her independence and sovereignty only as a socialist country and as a member of the socialist community. And only the enemies of socialism can today gamble with the slogan of 'defending the sovereignty' of the CSR from the socialist countries, from those countries with whom alliance and fraternal co-operation create a most reliable foundation for the independence and free development of each of our peoples.

We are convinced that a situation has arisen in which the threat to the foundations of socialism in Czechoslovakia jeopardizes the common vital interests of other socialist countries. The peoples of our states would never forgive us for being indifferent and careless in the face of such a danger.

We live at a time when peace and the security and freedom of the peoples more than ever demand the unity of the forces of socialism. International tension is not easing. American imperialism has not given up its policy of force and of open intervention against the peoples fighting for freedom. It is continuing its criminal war in Vietnam; it supports the Israeli aggressors in the Middle East and hinders a peaceful settlement of that conflict. The arms race has not been slowed down. The Federal Republic of Germany, where the neo-fascist forces are growing, is attacking the *status quo*, demanding a revision of frontiers; it does not want to give up its aspirations, either of seizing the GDR or of getting access to nuclear weapons; it opposes the disarmament proposals. In Europe, where tremendous means of mass destruction have been accumulated, peace and the security of the peoples are being maintained above all thanks to the strength, unity and peaceful policy of the socialist states. All of us are responsible for this strength and unity of the socialist countries and for the fate of peace.

Our countries are linked with one another by treaties and

agreements. These important mutual obligations of states and peoples are based on the common aspiration to defend socialism and ensure the collective security of the socialist countries. Historic responsibility rests with our parties and peoples for ensuring that the revolutionary gains are not lost.

Each of our parties is responsible not only to its own working class and its people, but also to the international working class and the world communist movement, and it cannot escape the obligations ensuing from this. We must therefore come out in solidarity and be united in defending the gains of socialism, our security and the international positions of the whole of the socialist community. That is why we believe that it is not only your task but also ours to administer a decisive rebuff to the anti-communist forces and to make decisive efforts to preserve the socialist system in Czechoslovakia.

The cause of defending the power of the working class and all working people and the socialist gains in Czechoslovakia demands:

a resolute and bold offensive against the right-wing and anti-socialist forces, and mobilization of all the means of defence created by the socialist state;

the stopping of the activity of all political organizations coming out against socialism;

control by the party of the mass information media—the press, radio and television—and the use of these in the interests of the working class, all working people and socialism;

the closing of the ranks of the party itself on the principled basis of Marxism-Leninism and unswerving observance of the principle of democratic centralism, and a struggle against those who, by their activity, are helping the hostile forces.

We are aware that forces exist in Czechoslovakia which are capable of defending the socialist system and inflicting defeat on the anti-socialist elements. The working class, the working peasantry, the progressive intelligentsia—the overwhelming majority of the working people of the Republic—are ready to do everything necessary for the sake of further developing the socialist society. The task today is to provide these healthy forces with a clear-cut prospect, to stir them to action, to mobilize their energy for the struggle against the forces of counter-revolution in order to safeguard and consolidate socialism in Czechoslovakia.

In the face of the danger of counter-revolution and in response to the appeal of the Communist Party, the voice of the working class should ring out with all its strength. The working class, together with the working peasantry, exerted the greatest effort for the sake of the triumph of the socialist revolution. It is precisely they who most of all cherish the safeguarding of the gains of socialism.

We express the conviction that the Communist Party of Czechoslovakia, conscious of its responsibility, will take the necessary steps to block the path of reaction. In this struggle you can count on the solidarity and all-round assistance of the fraternal socialist countries.

DOCUMENT 69. THE BRATISLAVA COMMUNIQUÉ (*Rudé Právo*, 4 AUGUST 1968)

Statement of representatives of the communist parties of Czechoslovakia, Bulgaria, Hungary, Poland, the German Democratic Republic and the Soviet Union on 4 August 1968.

The fraternal parties have become convinced on the basis of historical experience that it is possible to advance firmly along the path of socialism and communism only by following strictly and consistently the general laws governing the construction of a socialist society and primarily by strengthening the guiding role of the working class and its vanguard—the communist parties. In so doing, every fraternal party, while creatively solving the problems of further socialist development, takes into consideration specific national features and conditions.

Unshakable fidelity to Marxism-Leninism, indoctrination of the popular masses in the spirit of the ideas of socialism and proletarian internationalism, and a merciless struggle against bourgeois ideology and all anti-socialist forces, constitute the guarantee of success in strengthening the positions of socialism and repulsing the intrigues of imperialism.

The fraternal parties firmly and resolutely counterpose their inviolable solidarity and high level of vigilance to all attempts by imperialism and all other anti-communist forces to weaken the guiding role of the working class and the communist parties. They will never allow anyone to drive a wedge between the socialist states or to undermine the foundations of the socialist system. Fraternal friendship and solidarity in this direction are in the vital interests of all peoples and constitute a reliable basis for solving the social-economic and political tasks on which our countries' communist parties are working.

The fraternal parties consider it their duty to show constant concern for enlarging the political activity of the working class, the peasantry, the intelligentsia and all working people; for achieving all-round progress for the socialist social system; for developing further socialist democracy; and perfecting the style and methods of party and state work on principles of democratic centralism.

*

The Soviet invasion of Czechoslovakia was a case of naked aggression. But even the Soviets felt that they needed some excuse. Following the example of Hungary in 1956 they claimed that they had been invited by some Czechoslovak state and party leaders. They did not state who these were. They did, however, arrest and abduct to Moscow the Czechoslovak party leader, Dubček, and the prime minister, Černik. It was only after they were unable to establish a new government that they were forced to restore them to their positions in Prague.

DOCUMENT 70. SOVIET STATEMENT ANNOUNCING THE INVASION, 21 AUGUST 1968 (*Pravda*, 22 AUGUST 1968)

Tass is authorized to state that party and government leaders of the Czechoslovak Socialist Republic have asked the Soviet Union and other allied states to render the fraternal Czecho-slovak people urgent assistance, including assistance with armed forces.

This request was brought about by the threat which has arisen to the socialist system in Czechoslovakia and to the state-hood established by the constitution, a threat emanating from the counter-revolutionary forces which have entered into col-lusion with foreign forces hostile to socialism.

The events in Czechoslovakia and around her have repeatedly been the subject of exchanges of views between leaders of fraternal socialist countries, including the leaders of Czechoslovakia. These countries are unanimous that the support, consolidation and defence of the peoples' socialist gains is a common internationalist duty of all the socialist states. This common stand of theirs was solemnly proclaimed in the Bratislava statement.

The further aggravation of the situation in Czechoslovakia affects the vital interests of the Soviet Union and other socialist states and the security interests of the states of the socialist community. The threat to the socialist system in Czechoslovakia at the same time constitutes a threat to the foundations of peace in Europe.

The Soviet government and the governments of the allied countries—the People's Republic of Bulgaria, the Hungarian People's Republic, the German Democratic Republic and the Polish People's Republic—proceeding from the principles of unbreakable friendship and co-operation and in accordance with the existing contractual commitments, have decided to meet the above-mentioned request to render the necessary help to the fraternal Czechoslovak people.

This decision is fully in accord with the right of states to individual and collective self-defence envisaged in the treaties of alliance concluded between the fraternal socialist countries. This decision is also in line with the vital interests of our countries in safeguarding peace in Europe against the forces of militarism, aggression and revanche, which have more than once plunged the peoples of Europe into war.

Soviet armed units, together with armed units of the above-mentioned allied countries, entered the territory of Czechoslovakia on 21 August. They will be immediately withdrawn from the Czechoslovak Socialist Republic as soon as the threat that exists to the gains of socialism in Czechoslovakia and the threat to the security of the socialist commonwealth countries is eliminated and the lawful authorities find that the further presence of these armed units is no longer necessary there.

The actions which are being taken are not directed against any state and in no measure infringe the state interests of anybody. They serve the purpose of peace and have been prompted by concern for its consolidation. The fraternal countries firmly and resolutely counterpose their unbreakable solidarity to any threat from outside. Nobody will ever be allowed to wrest a single link from the commonwealth of socialist states.

*

The invasion had also to be justified ideologically. The two extracts quoted here are important theoretical statements on the ideological unity of the socialist commonwealth. They are known in the west as the Brezhnev doctrine. The idea is by no means new but it has never before been so explicitly stated. One may argue that the liberal phase of polycentrism is now dead and that the Soviets seek to draw closer the bonds of empire. They have not been unsuccessful. Needless to say, other socialist countries, Rumania and Yugoslavia, felt themselves very much threatened by this doctrine.

DOCUMENT 71. EXTRACTS FROM A *Pravda* ARTICLE, 26 SEPTEMBER 1968, BY S. KOVALEV, 'SOVEREIGNTY AND THE INTERNATIONALIST OBLIGATIONS OF SOCIALIST COUNTRIES' (*CDSP*, xx, 39, 16 OCTOBER 1968, PP. 10–12)

In connection with the events in Czechoslovakia the question of the relationship and interconnection between the socialist countries' national interests and their internationalist obligations has assumed particular urgency and sharpness. The measures taken jointly by the Soviet Union and other socialist countries to defend the socialist gains of the Czechoslovak people are of enormous significance for strengthening the socialist commonwealth, which is the main achievement of the international working class. . . .

There is no doubt that the peoples of the socialist countries and the communist parties have and must have freedom to determine their country's path of development. However, any decision of theirs must damage neither socialism in their own country, nor the fundamental interests of other socialist countries nor the world-wide workers' movement, which is waging a struggle for socialism. This means that every communist party is responsible not only to its own people but also to all the socialist countries and to the entire communist movement. Whoever forgets this in placing sole emphasis on the autonomy and independence of communist parties lapses into one-sidedness, shirking his internationalist obligations. . . .

Each communist party is free in applying the principles of Marxism-Leninism and socialism in its own country, but it cannot deviate from these principles (if, of course, it remains a communist party). In concrete terms this means primarily that every communist party cannot fail to take into account in its activities such a decisive fact of our time as the struggle between the two antithetical social systems—capitalism and socialism. This struggle is an objective fact that does not depend on the will of the people and is conditioned by the division of the world into two antithetical social systems. . . .

It should be stressed that even if a socialist country seeks to take an 'extra-bloc' position, it in fact retains its national independence thanks precisely to the power of the socialist commonwealth—and primarily to its chief force, the Soviet Union—and the might of its armed forces. The weakening of any link in the world socialist system has a direct effect on all the socialist countries, which cannot be indifferent to this. Thus, the anti-socialist forces in Czechoslovakia were in essence using talk about the right to self-determination to cover up demands for so-called neutrality and the CSR's withdrawal from the socialist commonwealth. But implementation of such 'self-determination', i.e. Czechoslovakia's separation from the socialist commonwealth, would run counter to Czechoslovakia's fundamental interests and would harm the other socialist countries. Such 'self-determination', as a result of which NATO troops might approach Soviet borders and the commonwealth of European socialist countries might be dismembered, in fact infringes on the vital interests of these countries' peoples, and fundamentally contradicts the right of these peoples to socialist self-determination. The Soviet Union and other socialist states, in fulfilling their internationalist duty to the fraternal peoples of Czechoslovakia and defending their own socialist gains, had to act and did act in resolute opposition to the anti-socialist forces in Czechoslovakia.

Comrade W. Gomulka, first secretary of the central committee of the Polish United Workers' Party, used a metaphor to illustrate this point:

To those friends and comrades of ours from other countries who believe they are defending the just cause of socialism and the sovereignty of peoples by denouncing and protesting the introduction of our troops in Czechoslovakia, we reply: If the enemy plants dynamite under our house, under the commonwealth of socialist states, our patriotic national and internationalist duty is to prevent this by using any means that are necessary.

People who 'disapprove' of the actions taken by the allied socialist countries ignore the decisive fact that these countries are defending the interests of world-wide socialism and the world-wide revolutionary movement. The socialist system exists in concrete form in individual countries that have their own well-defined state boundaries and develops with regard for the specific attributes of each such country. And no one interferes with concrete measures to perfect the socialist system in various socialist countries. But matters change radically when a danger to socialism itself arises in a country. World socialism and a social system is the common achievement of the working people of all countries, it is indivisible, and its defence is the common cause of all communists and all progressive people on earth, first and foremost the working people of the socialist countries. . . .

What the right-wing, anti-socialist forces were seeking to achieve in Czechoslovakia in recent months was not a matter of developing socialism in an original way or of applying the principles of Marxism-Leninism to specific conditions in that country, but was an encroachment on the foundations of socialism and the fundamental principles of Marxism-Leninism. This is the 'nuance' that is still incomprehensible to people who trusted in the hypocritical cant of the anti-socialist and revisionist elements. Under the guise of 'democratization' these elements were shattering the socialist state step by step; they sought to demoralize the communist party and dull the minds of the masses; they were gradually preparing for a counter-revolutionary coup and at the same time were not being properly rebuffed inside the country.

The communists of the fraternal countries naturally could not allow the socialist states to remain idle in the name of abstract sovereignty while the country was endangered by anti-socialist degeneration.

The five allied socialist countries' actions in Czechoslovakia are consonant with the fundamental interests of the Czechoslovak people themselves. Obviously it is precisely socialism that, by liberating a nation from the fetters of an exploitative system, ensures the solution of fundamental problems of national development in any country that takes a socialist path. And by encroaching on the foundations of socialism, the counter-revolutionary elements in Czechoslovakia were thereby undermining the basis of the country's independence and sovereignty.

The formal observance of freedom of self-determination in the specific situation that had taken shape in Czechoslovakia would signify freedom of 'self-determination' not for the people's masses and the working people, but for their enemies. The anti-socialist path, the 'neutrality' to which the Czechoslovak people were being prodded, would lead the CSR straight into the jaws of the West German revanchists and would lead to the loss of its national independence. World imperialism, for its part, was trying to export counter-revolution to Czechoslovakia by supporting the anti-socialist forces there.

The assistance given to the working people of the CSR by the other socialist countries, which prevented the export of counter-revolution from the outside, is in fact a struggle for the Czechoslovak Socialist Republic's sovereignty against those who would like to deprive it of this sovereignty by delivering the country to the imperialists.

Over a long period of time and with utmost restraint and patience, the fraternal communist parties of the socialist countries took political measures to help the Czechoslovak people to halt the anti-socialist forces' offensive in Czechoslovakia. And only after exhausting all such measures did they undertake to bring in armed forces.

The allied socialist countries' soldiers who are in Czechoslovakia are proving in deeds that they have no task other than to defend the socialist gains in that country. They are not interfering in the country's internal affairs, and they are waging a struggle not in words but in deeds for the principles of self-determination of Czechoslovakia's peoples, for their inalienable right to decide their destiny themselves after profound and careful consideration, without intimidation by counter-revolu-tionaries, without revisionist and nationalist demagoguery.

Those who speak of the 'illegality' of the allied socialist countries' actions in Czechoslovakia forget that in a class society there is and can be no such thing as a non-class law. Laws and norms of law are subordinated to the laws of the class struggle and the laws of social development. These laws are clearly formulated in the documents jointly adopted by the communist and workers' parties.

The class approach to the matter cannot be discarded in the name of legalistic considerations. Whoever does so and forfeits the only correct, class-oriented criterion for evaluating legal norms, begins to measure events with the yardsticks of bourgeois law. Such an approach to the question of sovereignty means, for example, that the world's progressive forces could not oppose the revival of neo-Nazism in the FRG, the butcheries of Franco and Salazar or the reactionary outrages of the 'black colonels' in Greece, since these are the 'internal affairs' of 'sovereign states.'

DOCUMENT 72. EXTRACT FROM A *Pravda* ARTICLE OF 11 SEPTEMBER 1968 BY S. KOVALEV, 'COUNTER-REVOLUTION—PEACEFUL AND NON-PEACEFUL'

On seeing the collapse of their plans, the reactionaries in the imperialist camp are raging with fury, engulfing the masses of the people in seas of slander and misinformation. It is not just that they are covering up their tracks. They still hope to succeed in maintaining in the minds of millions of people confusion and a failure to grasp the real essence of the events in Czecho-slovakia. In this they are relying first of all on the fact that quite a lot of people in the world have not yet managed to assess these events correctly. Many of those people approved, at the time, of the Soviet Union's actions in helping the working people of Hungary to suppress a counter-revolutionary revolt, but now express their failure to understand the resolute measures taken by the five socialist countries.

Quite apart from everything else, this is explained by the fact that these persons have failed to arrive at a thorough understanding of a new historical phenomenon—so-called 'quiet' or 'peaceful' counter-revolution.

Indeed, everybody has become accustomed to picturing counter-revolution in the form of armed revolt and direct military attacks on revolutionary parties, governments, etc. Starting with the suppression of the uprising of the Paris workers in June 1848 and of the Paris Commune in 1871 and ending with the suppression of the German and Hungarian revolutions after the First World War and of Republican Spain in the period from 1936 to 1939, and also events of a later period, reaction acted against the people by means of open armed violence.

Big changes, however, had to take place, and did take place, in the tactics of anti-socialist forces in the new stage of historical development in which socialism has become a world system, while the strength of imperialism has been seriously undermined.

Reaction has begun to use (in the first stages) forms of 'quiet' or 'peaceful' struggle against socialism. This has been confirmed, in particular, by the course of developments in Czechoslovakia, where anti-socialist forces, camouflaging their counter-revolutionary plans, declared that they were coming out, not against socialism as such, but against 'bad' socialism and for 'good' socialism. It transpired, however, that according to their interpretation, 'bad' socialism was the real, true socialism won by the working people, while 'good' socialism was right-wing reformist 'democratic socialism', signifying a turn towards the bourgeois system.

They exaggerate in every way the errors committed in building a new society and do this solely for the purpose of claiming that those errors and distortions were allegedly the essence of 'old-style' socialism.

The anti-socialist elements in Czechoslovakia, in order to blunt the vigilance of the working people, did not at first openly demand the liquidation of the socialist state, of the leading role of the communist party and of the socialist economy. They likewise paid lip-service to the alliance with socialist countries. They were 'only' against 'bureaucratic conservatives' in the state and party apparatus and against the 'dictatorship' of a single party; they were only for the 'improvement' of the economy and for the 'normalization' of relations with socialist countries. On closer inspection it becomes clear that all this was a cover for an onslaught on the very foundation of the power of the working people—their socialist state—and that, concealed behind these and similar slogans, was the desire to disorganize the communist party, to remove it from the leadership of society and to press for the transition to a market economy, i.e. a capitalist economy, and for a break with the socialist commonwealth. Just as a revolution cannot be accomplished without smashing the reactionary state machine and replacing it by a new one, so counter-revolution has set itself a similar aim—that of smashing the socialist state apparatus and replacing it by its own apparatus. In the beginning this is attempted by peaceful means, replacing cadres loyal to socialism by advocates of so-called 'liberalization'. Thus, the plan for a 'quiet' counter-revolution consists in 'not making much noise' to begin with, in acting gradually, avoiding open attacks on the socialist gains and at the same time slandering, falsifying, corrupting and undermining everything. It was thus intended to prepare for the 'peaceful' degeneration of the socialist system into the capitalist one.

Relatively peaceful means of struggle were, however, reserved by reaction only for the 'first stage'. As has already been shown by the Hungarian events of 1956 and, in particular, by the events in Czechoslovakia, counter-revolution is far from relying only on 'peaceful means'. While carrying out its subversive work, it also makes active preparations for armed struggle against the socialist system. This is proved by the underground activities of the counter-revolution in Czechoslovakia, which had prepared in advance weapons, radio stations, printing presses, stocks of paper for counter-revolutionary publications, organized armed groups, etc.

In the 'second stage' the masks are thrown off. 'Men of action', whose task is to carry through the counter-revolutionary coup to its conclusion, are called to the leadership. They issue a direct call for armed struggle and begin it wherever possible. The slogan of 'neutrality', that is to say, tearing the socialist country away from the socialist commonwealth as a whole, is put forward . . . As the events in Czechoslovakia have shown, external reactionary forces were also to support the internal counter-revolution.

The tactics of 'peaceful' counter-revolution (in the initial stage) are very cunning ones, because their aim is to deceive the masses inside the country by talk about the need for 'improving' socialism, allegedly in the interests of the people, and to deceive gullible people in foreign countries.

It must be said that in view of certain conditions, it was not without success that these tactics were employed in Czechoslovakia. Considerable masses of the population inside the country let themselves be deceived by demagogic bourgeois-nationalist slogans.

Quite a number of people, including communists in fraternal parties, did not understand the new methods of counter-revolution either; they believed the statements about the 'democratization' of socialism and did not analyse the real activities of those who, while using as a cover talk about 'improving' the socialist system, were trying to destroy that system.

Since in the 'first stage' of the counter-revolution in Czechoslovakia there were no killings of communists and no gallows—and people usually associate these with the deeds of reaction—many people were surprised and asked what danger there could be to socialism. Yet it was precisely on delusions of that kind that the anti-socialist elements were counting.

If we are to share the views of 'those who do not understand', it transpires that first we should have waited for the shooting and hanging of communists and only then should we have gone to the assistance of the champions of socialism.

But to have waited until counter-revolution had aimed its sub-machine guns at communists and all who cherish the cause of socialism would have been a criminal and fatal policy for revolutionaries to pursue.

*

The Soviet-Czechoslovak treaty of 6 May completed the humiliation of the Czechoslovaks. Like victims of Stalinist show trials the Czechoslovaks were forced to reel off a catalogue of sins and to thank the Soviets for invading them. The treaty itself formally incorporates the Brezhnev doctrine. It grants the Soviets the right to intervene in Czechoslovakia by military force whenever it considers socialism to be threatened. The treaty is much more extensive in scope than its predecessor the treaty of 1943, renewed for a further twenty years in 1963. Czechoslovakia is now forced to come to the aid of the Soviet Union not only against Germany and her allies but also against 'any state or group of states' that the Soviets might designate. Czechoslovak troops could find themselves fighting the Chinese. It was at the April 1969 plenary meetings of the Czechoslovak Communist Party that Husák replaced Dubček.

DOCUMENT 73. EXTRACT FROM THE COMMUNIQUÉ ON THE VISIT OF A SOVIET DELEGATION TO CZECHOSLOVAKIA, DURING WHICH A NEW FRIENDSHIP TREATY WAS SIGNED BETWEEN THE TWO COUNTRIES, 6 MAY 1970 (*Rudé Právo*, 8 MAY 1970)

During the Soviet delegation's visit, the Czechoslovak people showed once again that feelings of sincere friendship and respect for the Soviet people and their Communist Party live on in the hearts and minds of the Czechs and Slovaks. The working people of Czechoslovakia are profoundly grateful to the Soviet Union for the liberation and for its great assistance in the restoration of Czechoslovakian national economy and in socialist construction. Czechoslovak working people are convinced that the friendship and alliance with the Soviet Union, which were sealed by the blood that the two peoples shed in the struggle against Hitler fascism, became the firm guarantee of the security and peaceful development of the Czechoslovak state after its liberation and an important factor for its economic and political stability.

The Czechoslovak side attached high value to the fraternal internationalist assistance of the Soviet Union and other socialist countries in 1968, which frustrated the attempts at a counter-revolutionary coup in Czechoslovakia. This assistance saved the Czechoslovak Socialist Republic from bloodshed and from a disastrous development that threatened the cause of socialism and the security of the peoples in Europe and throughout the world.

Since the April 1969 plenary meeting of the Central Committee of the Communist Party of Czechoslovakia took a course aimed a consolidating the Marxist-Leninist character of the party and the positions of socialism in the CSR, all kinds of extraneous matter that had accumulated in Soviet-Czechoslovak relations because of the subversive activity of the right-wing and counter-revolutionary forces have been successfully removed. All the conditions now exist for extending comradely co-operation and strengthening the ideological and militant unity of the two countries on the basis of Marxism-Leninism and proletarian internationalism.

This has been reflected in the signing of the new Soviet-Czechoslovak Treaty of Friendship, Co-operation and Mutual Assistance. The party and government delegations attach a high value to the importance of this Treaty. While duly developing the traditions of the Treaty of Alliance of 1943, the new Treaty takes full account of the changes in international life that have taken place during the past quarter of a century and reflects the growing strength of the positions of socialism in the world and the raised level of Soviet-Czechoslovak co-operation. The nature of this Treaty is in keeping with the new type of relations that has taken shape between the socialist states.

Both delegations pointed out with satisfaction that the new Treaty reflected the efforts of both countries to strengthen the unity and solidarity of the socialist commonwealth and made a big contribution to promoting peace, security and co-operation among all European states. The Treaty confirms the allegiance of the Soviet Union and Czechoslovakia to the principle expressed in the Bratislava statement of 3 August 1968, under which the support, strengthening and protection of the socialist gains that were won at the cost of the heroic efforts and selfless work of every people is the joint internationalist duty of all socialist countries.

During the talks there was a thorough exchange of views on questions of bilateral inter-party and inter-state relations and also on a wide range of international problems of mutual interest.

The Czechoslovak comrades informed the Soviet delegation on the specific measures that are being implemented by the party and state bodies, on the basis of the decisions of the most recent plenary meetings of the Central Committee of the Communist Party of Czechoslovakia, to consolidate the political situation, to stabilize the national economy and to ensure the overall consolidation of the situation in the party and the country.

The Party and government delegation of the CSR stressed the importance of principle in the exchange of party membership cards in the Communist Party of Czechoslovakia. Through the exchange of the party membership cards the Party must purge itself of right-wing opportunist elements, passive members and careerists and restore in full its Marxist-Leninist character, in order to raise the level of its fighting spirit and consolidate its leading role in all fields of social and political life. This line of the Communist Party of Czechoslovakia is being received with understanding and support by the broad masses of the Czechoslovak people, who regard the strengthening of the Party as the main guarantee of the socialist development of their country. . . .

The two parties pointed out that since the visit to the Soviet Union of the Czechoslovak party and government delegation in October 1969, relations between the USSR and the CSR had further gained in strength. Political, trade, economic, scientific and technical co-operation are developing between the Soviet Union and Czechoslovakia, which is in line with the vital interests of the peoples of both countries and serves the cause of peace and socialism. The Soviet Union and Czechoslovakia attach great importance to the further development of all-round co-operation within the framework of the Warsaw Treaty and the Council for Mutual Economic Assistance. They will continue in every way to promote the strengthening of the joint defence potential of the socialist commonwealth, will strengthen the co-ordination of activity by the socialist countries on the international scene and will raise the level of efficiency of their co-operation in the economic, scientific and technical fields.

Considerable attention was paid during the talks to questions of foreign policy. Both sides unanimously pointed out that the USSR and the CSR attached the utmost importance in their foreign policy to ensuring the unity of the socialist countries, proceeding on the basis of the irrefutable fact that the socialist commonwealth is the decisive revolutionary force of our times. The joint actions of the socialist countries are an important factor in rallying the international communist movement and all the anti-imperialist forces.

PART III

The Soviet Union and the Third World

(a) THE END OF COLONIALISM

At the 20th Party Congress in 1956 Khrushchev replaced Stalin's bi-polar theory concept of the world as divided into two antagonistic camps by one in which these two camps sought to influence a 'zone of peace', that is, the newly independent states of Asia and Africa. This new policy was immediately successful.

DOCUMENT 74. EXTRACT FROM AN ARTICLE ON COLONIALISM BY V. SEMYONOV IN *Kommunist*, NO. 18, DECEMBER 1956 (*CDSP*, IX, 10, 17 APRIL 1957, PP. 3–7)

Events in the east are developing with sweeping force and hold the attention of the whole world. Only ten or fifteen years ago most of the Asian countries were either colonies or semi-colonies. Now independent states have arisen there. The entire colonial system in Asia is on the way out. . . .

Altogether, since the end of the Second World War, more than 1,300 million people have been liberated from a colonial or semi-colonial regime and have embarked on the path of national independence. About 160 million persons live in countries which still have colonial status.

Everything testifies to the tremendous scope of the process of disintegration of the colonial system of imperialism, to the fact that the liberation movement of the peoples of the east is being joined by more and more tens and hundreds of millions of people. This struggle is taking place in entirely new historical conditions, altogether different from what they were in the past, amid the transformation of socialism into a world system of states and amid the further deepening of the general crisis of capitalism. . . .

Twenty-three new countries have arisen on the territory of the former colonies in the east in the course of the disintegration of the colonial system. Most of those countries are now members of the United Nations. In the main they can be divided into three groups, according to the degree of state and national independence which they have achieved.

The first group embraces the countries which have won complete liberation in the post-war period not only from colonial bondage but also from social enslavement, and which have taken the road to building socialism. These include the great Chinese People's Republic, the Korean People's Democratic Republic and the Democratic Republic of Vietnam. . . .

The victory of the Chinese people radically changed the political situation throughout Asia; it made it much easier for India, Burma, Indonesia, Ceylon and other south-east Asian countries to consolidate their independence and contributed to the further advance of the liberation movement in all the colonial and dependent countries. The successful development of the Chinese People's Republic has greatly accelerated the disintegration of the colonial system of imperialism.

The second group of new states in the east consists of those in which the people have won state independence. Having broken away from imperialism they achieved the withdrawal of foreign troops from their territory and international recognition of their sovereignty, and freed themselves from participation in military blocs with the colonial powers. Among these countries which vary greatly in their level of social and economic development are India, Indonesia, Egypt, Syria, Burma and many others. . . .

True, the imperialists still retain very strong positions in the economy of these countries and preserve definite contacts with part of the intelligentsia, officials and comprador bourgeoisie who play the role of forces of 'internal colonialism'. Open or concealed resistance by the imperialists and their agents to measures aimed at decisively breaking with the old ways is still strong in many of these countries even after their proclamation of independence. . . .

Sukarno, outstanding leader of the Indonesian liberation movement, described national independence as the 'golden bridge' to freedom and to transformation of social relations in the colonial countries. He has justly pointed out that merely by taking political power into their hands and becoming independent, the peoples of the colonial countries obtain the 'opportunity to break entirely with capitalism and imperialism'. . . .

As the experience of many eastern countries shows, the winning of political independence creates the prerequisites also for a mass peasant movement for land, and for the workers' struggle for social changes. The winning of state political independence is a revolution in the life of formerly colonial peoples. Unfortunately this is not clear to all. Take, for example, the fact that foreign capital still exerts very great influence on the economy of many countries in the east which have won political independence. From this some Soviet Orientalists have drawn the incorrect conclusion that after gaining independence these countries remain, in point of fact, colonial in status. The adherents of this incorrect view confuse two different questions —the question of political liberation and self-determination of the peoples of formerly colonial countries, and the question of achievement of economic independence by countries of the east which have only recently cast off the colonial yoke. . . .

To assert that the winning of state independence by the countries of the east in the conditions of imperialism does not substantially change their status is theoretically wrong and politically harmful. The error of such a view lies chiefly in underestimation of the forces and possibilities of the national liberation movement and national revolutions in the east. The winning of state independence by the countries of the east after centuries of colonial oppression evoked such mass patriotic enthusiasm that the colonialists, notwithstanding their economic and military superiority, have been forced to retreat and yield position after position in a stubborn struggle with the peoples of the east.

In our times, when a world system of socialist states exists and the colonial system is disintegrating, imperialism is far from being as powerful and as stable as it was in the past. Unquestionably, it still retains very substantial positions in the countries of the east, it still holds many of them in economic bondage. But it is also clear that, having won political liberation, the peoples of the east have gained important positions for realizing their irrepressible striving towards sovereignty and independence in all spheres of their life, including the economic.

The appearance in the political arena of the new countries of the east substantially changes the general balance of forces and strengthens the peace front. . . . The new countries of the east are acting more and more vigorously in the United Nations in the defence of peace and the sovereign rights of peoples fighting for national independence.

In the third group of newly formed countries in the east can be included, for example, the Philippines, South Korea and Iraq. Although they have obtained formal state independence, many of the countries in this group are still tightly linked to the big imperialist, colonial powers, not only by the ties of economic dependence but by unequal treaties, which, contrary to the principles of the United Nations, seriously—although in varying degree—restrict the independence and sovereignty of these new countries. . . .

The 20th Party Congress pointed out that the theses of the Sixth Congress of the Comintern on the colonial question had committed mistakes in judging the role of the national bourgeoisie in the liberation struggle of the peoples of the colonies and semi-colonies. The theses affirmed that, as the mass liberation movement of the people of the colonial countries develops, the national bourgeoisie of these countries deserts to the camp of the adversaries of the national democratic revolution and becomes an openly counter-revolutionary force. Events have not confirmed this conclusion. The example of China has clearly shown and proved the possibility—given a correct policy by the communist party—of co-operation of the working class even with the national bourgeoisie, and not only during the period of the national democratic revolution, but also in the period of building socialism.

The experience of India, Indonesia, Egypt and other countries has shown likewise that, together with broad masses of the working classes and intelligentsia, a large part of the national bourgeoisie (except the comprador bourgeoisie) the clergy and even certain landowning circles are drawn into the national liberation movement in the east. In many countries one form or another of coalition of the patriotic forces has arisen, with the goal of strengthening the independence of the country and combating the colonialists.

In view of the fact that religious belief is widespread and

closely linked with the prevailing relations in the east, progressive national movements in many countries of the east take on the specific form of religious nationalism. For this reason the activity and the national-political platform of religious sects, reformation trends and religious leaders deserve special attention and study. What is more, in Indonesia the Moslem religion has long been and to a certain degree still is the ideological banner of the masses in opposing the colonialists. Al Azkhar University in Cairo, the famous Moslem university, now plays a prominent role in the struggle of the Arab and other Moslem peoples against colonialism. At the same time, undoubtedly, in many places the clergy continue to play an extremely reactionary political role, acting as a support of the foreign colonialists. However, the facts cited above testify to the incorrectness of indiscriminate condemnation and the need to make a concrete study of the specific situation in the east.

There was a time in our literature on the east when a nihilistic appraisal of Gandhi, the outstanding leader of the Indian liberation movement, was common. Our party has criticized this mistaken view, which was based partly on insufficient knowledge of India and of Gandhi, and even more on a dogmatic, sectarian and therefore non-Marxist approach to social life in the East. . . .

While not concealing his communist views and certainly not taking the standpoint of 'non-violence' or 'self-purification' or denying the importance of class struggle, the Marxist studying the life and work of Gandhi cannot but see that his chief qualities were those of a fighter for the liberation of India—qualities, it should be said, that were in many ways characteristic of the liberation movement in India of those days. Gandhi's distinguishing features were tireless and self-sacrificing struggle against colonialism, racism and national inequality, an instinctive attraction to socialism, which, of course, he understood in his own way, the desire to merge his life with the life of the common people—the poor peasants and the workers—and to improve their lot. Gandhi called upon the intelligentsia to use Indian languages (not English), summoned the people to civil disobedience to the British colonial administration, urged religious tolerance, unity of Hindus and Moslems, and denounced the caste system.

Undoubtedly Gandhi's life and work held much that was tragic, inconsistent and contradictory. He himself often admitted his inconsistency, and it was often noted by his immediate associates. But to fail to see the links between all this and the specific historical development of India, to concentrate solely on the things which sharply divide us from Gandhi, would be tantamount to abandoning scientific investigation at the point where it really should begin, to underestimating the national liberation movement in the east as an ally of the progressive trends in the west.

Typical of many countries of the east nowadays is the widespread anti-capitalist sentiment among the people and the intelligentsia. It is manifested in the resolutions of such mass political parties as the Indian National Congress and in the speeches and writings of prominent leaders in Burma, Indonesia and elsewhere. This fact and many more testify that, in embarking on the path of national regeneration and development, the working masses in many of the countries of the east have no desire to retrace the painful path of capitalist development, which is linked with poverty, starvation, wars and merciless exploitation of the working class and peasantry. Of course, in many cases the anti-capitalist phraseology of some political leaders is explained by the fact that socialism has become 'fashionable', or it is even invoked deliberately to deceive the working people. However, many supporters of progress in the countries of the east are sincerely seeking a way that would enable their countries to avoid the tortures of capitalism and, by-passing the capitalist stage of development or the stage of highly developed capitalism, to shift quickly to socialism.

Lenin pointed out that, given the existence of socialist countries with a high level of economic development, the backward peoples of the east would be able to find new forms and ways of converting to socialism without going through the capitalist stage. In many countries of the east we now see searches for this way of development. Naturally, the progressive forces of the world sympathize with this. In accord with the new historical conditions, with the existence of a world system of socialist countries, the attitude of Marxists to the socialist strivings of a Narodnik type and varieties of Utopian socialism, which are widespread in the east, cannot but change. In our day these tendencies are often symptoms of the break-up of the capitalist system and for specific circles can be a form of approach and transition to progressive conclusions.

It must not be forgotten that socialism in our times has ceased to be only the scientific theory or doctrine of this or that party or social class. Socialism has been translated into life, has been tested in the fire of the greatest liberating revolutions and wars, has been tested by the struggle of hundreds of millions, above all in the Union of Soviet Socialist Republics, where capitalist and all other forms of exploitation of man by man have long been abolished and where there are no longer any exploiting classes. Both the Chinese People's Republic and other states which have taken the road of socialist development have accumulated a wealth of experience which can be freely utilized by the peoples of the east. This experience testifies in particular to the complete substantiation of the scientific conclusions of Marxist-Leninist theory concerning the need for assuring the leading role in building socialism to the working class, for a close alliance between the workers and the working peasantry—an alliance which is the main force in the struggle to build the new society—and concerning the need for merciless crushing of the resistance of the exploiting forces, which stop at nothing in their endeavour to preserve their domination over the peoples and to prevent the dawn of the bright day of socialism. The experience gained also testifies that socialism cannot be built with the hands of any group of reformers, no matter how wise they be, that socialism is the result of the conscious work of the masses—the workers, peasants, intelligentsia and of all who are ready to consecrate their efforts and knowledge to building the new society.

The experience of China shows that development of the countries of the east toward socialism is fully possible within the framework of a coalition of political parties standing for socialism. Of course, peaceful development does not at all preclude, but, on the contrary, presupposes class struggle, the struggle of the supporters of social progress against the reactionary and exploiting forces seeking to go back to agreement with imperialism and to frustrate the movement of the peoples for a better future.

As for the countries in the pre-capitalist stage of development, the possibility of their advance to socialism, by-passing the stage of capitalism with the support of the developed socialist countries, has been demonstrated both theoretically and practically in the experience of a number of countries and peoples. Undoubtedly here, too, life may give rise to future forms of transition to socialism.

In any case, the question of the ways of development of the eastern countries will be decided not in the tranquillity of the sanctum, not by the logical deductions of the learned, but in the course of life itself, in the process of the struggle among the various social forces.

Irrespective of this or that trend of development in the countries of the east, their fight for political and economic independence, for their sovereign rights, is objectively an anti-imperialist fight and shakes the big imperialist powers' domination in international relations within the capitalist camp and strengthens the positions of the peace supporters throughout the world. . . .

The disintegration of the colonial system of imperialism would be impossible in the conditions of domination by a single and all-embracing system of imperialism. Before the October revolution of 1917 the colonial peoples tried tens and hundreds of times to throw off the yoke of the colonialists and become masters in their own countries, but all their uprisings—for example, the anti-imperialist uprising in China at the beginning of the twentieth century—all the rebellions of the oppressed peoples, were brutally crushed by punitive expeditions, at times with the participation of several or even all the big colonial powers.

The victory of the great October socialist revolution, which overthrew the rule of the landlords and capitalists in one of the biggest imperialist countries, Russia, delivered a crushing blow to the colonial system of imperialism and marked the beginning of its *crisis*. Under the influence of the October revolution, and as the general crisis of capitalism, as a system, deepened, the liberation movement in the east, spearheaded against colonialism and imperialism, grew into a powerful, all-embracing and invincible movement of the peoples.

The Leninist policy of the Soviet state and its moral and political support for the countries of the east, irrespective of their internal structure, in their struggle for national independence exerted a profound influence on the peoples of these countries. They saw in the Soviet Union a great country, able honestly and sincerely to respect their rights and interests, ready to support their national liberation movement sincerely, without seeking any gains for itself and even making definite sacrifices for the sake of strengthening friendship. . . .

The rise and consolidation of an economically powerful world system of socialist states, headed by the Soviet Union and the Chinese People's Republic, have fundamentally changed the objective situation of the countries of the east fighting against colonialism. In the past, when imperialism was an all-embracing world system, the colonial and dependent countries could not break away from dependence on the financial capital of the imperialist powers—the domination of financial capital could not be eliminated by any changes in the sphere of political democracy. 'The colonies,' pointed out Lenin, 'have no capital or hardly any capital *of their own*, and under the conditions of financial capital they can obtain it only by submitting to political subordination.'

But the capitalist system is no longer the only system; the former monopoly of big capital has been broken. The socialist states are helping the former colonies of the east with ever-increasing, disinterested economic and cultural support and aid, based on equality and mutual benefit. In their foreign policy the socialist countries, as is known, adhere to the Leninist principle of non-interference in the internal affairs of other states. . . .

*

Soviet support for the underdeveloped nations meant also a revision of the Soviet attitude to the United Nations because the attachment of these nations to the UN could not be doubted. In the period from the beginning of the Korean war to the death of Stalin, Soviet activity in the UN was minimal. From 1953 onwards UN members were startled by sudden Soviet activity and participation in various UN agencies. In 1960 Khrushchev appeared in person in the General Assembly. Although his resolution to put an end to colonialism immediately was not accepted by the General Assembly, an overwhelming majority voted for a resolution worded more mildly than the Soviet one. The session of the General Assembly which Khrushchev attended was spectacular in that many of the world's leaders turned up too. The session was also remarkable for Khrushchev's boorish behaviour. While Harold Macmillan was addressing the delegates Khrushchev took off his shoe and banged it loudly on the desk.

DOCUMENT 75. EXTRACT FROM KHRUSHCHEV'S SPEECH IN THE GENERAL ASSEMBLY, 23 SEPTEMBER 1960 (FIFTEENTH GENERAL ASSEMBLY SESSION, 869TH PLENARY MEETING)

Anybody who ascends this rostrum and looks round this hall must, I think, appreciate what an eminent and responsible gathering he is addressing.

This should be the most responsible meeting of State representatives in the world. It is not for nothing that it is known as the General Assembly of the United Nations. I need not go into the meaning of that title at this juncture; I would merely like to stress these two words—United Nations. Many nations are represented in this hall, and these nations should be united not only by the walls of this building but by the highest common interests of mankind.

The representatives of almost 100 states have met here today to consider major international problems. The representatives of new Members of the United Nations will soon be with us; then the walls of this hall will, so to speak, recede to accommodate a still greater number of lands and countries. We should all wholeheartedly welcome this development, because we are anxious that all States in the world should be represented in the United Nations.

Naturally, our thoughts are now focused on the matters which most trouble and disturb mankind. Perhaps it is precisely here in this Assembly that the world is seen in all its diversity and, of course, in all its contradictions. It has fallen to our lot to live in the stormiest and yet the most splendid period in the history of mankind; future generations will envy us.

Many of the things some people considered, not so long ago, to be immovable and eternal, have outlived their time and have ceased to exist. A new, more progressive and more equitable order has become established. Our epoch has brought swift changes in the way of life of human societies, an unprecedented growth in our power over the forces of nature and an unparalleled advance towards a more progressive social order. Yet although we live in the twentieth century, traces of past centuries and, indeed, remnants of barbarism, are still in evidence. However, one of the important features, indeed the salient feature, of this epoch is the awakening of formerly backward, downtrodden and oppressed peoples.

Our century is the century of the struggle for freedom, the century in which nations are liberating themselves from foreign domination. The peoples desire a worthwhile life and are fighting to secure it.

Victory has already been won in many countries and lands. But we cannot rest on our laurels, for we know that tens of millions of human beings are still languishing in colonial slavery and are suffering grave hardships.

They are doing so in a period which we call one of great and promising scientific discoveries. With his brain and hands, man has created space ships which circle the earth. He is already able to send men far beyond the limits of our planet. We have split the atom and are penetrating the mysteries of protein structure. We travel on and above the earth at astounding speed; the extent of our knowledge is a source of amazement even to ourselves.

It might seem that all was well with the world. Yet can it be said that the world is well ordered in every respect, or that it is free from poverty and deprivation? We should again reflect on the fact that, according to United Nations statistics, hundreds of millions of men and women on different continents drag out an existence at starvation or near-starvation level. Our world is not free from fear for the future; it realizes the dangers of the division into military alliances and of the continuously accelerating nuclear arms race. The great achievements of man's genius may be used either for man's benefit or to his detriment. This is the difficult choice confronting us. . . .

Our time is characterized by the emancipation and national rebirth of peoples who for centuries were kept apart by the colonialists from the mainstream of human development, a process which is taking place before all our eyes. In a mere fifteen years, about 1,500 million people, or half the population of the earth, have cast off the shackles of colonialist oppression. Dozens of new national States have arisen from the ruins of the old colonial empires.

A new period has begun in the history of mankind, in which peoples of Asia, Africa, and Latin America have begun to take an active part in determining the destiny of the whole world, side by side with the peoples of Europe and North America. Unless this unalterable fact is recognized, there can be no realistic foreign policy in harmony with the needs of the times and corresponding to the peace-loving aspirations of the peoples.

Is the solution of major international problems really conceivable today without the participation of the People's Republic of China? Is it possible to solve these problems without the participation of India, Indonesia, Burma, Ceylon, the United Arab Republic, Iraq, Ghana, Guinea and the other States? If anyone has this idea, let him try to disregard the opinion and the votes of the representatives of the Asian, African, and Latin American States here in the United Nations. It is true that the appearance of the new Asian and African States in the United Nations is giving rise to apprehension in certain Western countries. More than that, people are beginning to discuss ways of limiting the further influx of newly-emerging States into the United Nations.

As regards the Soviet Union, I can say frankly that we are glad to see a great number of new States making their appearance in the United Nations. We have always opposed and we shall continue to oppose any curtailment of the rights of peoples who have won their national independence. We share with these States the desire to preserve and strengthen peace, to create on our planet conditions for the peaceful co-existence and co-operation of countries regardless of their political and social structure, in accordance with the peaceful principles proclaimed at the Conference of African and Asian States at Bandung. The facts show that the liberation of nations and peoples under colonial domination leads to an improvement in international relations, an increase in international co-operation and the reinforcement of world peace.

The peoples of the new States have convincingly shown, not only that they are capable of dispensing with the control and tutelage of the colonial Powers, and can govern themselves, but also that they are actively forging a new life and that they administer and manage their resources, their countries' wealth, incomparably more skilfully and prudently than the colonial authorities.

Early this year I had the opportunity of visiting India, Indonesia, Burma and Afghanistan. I must say that I was very deeply impressed by their great achievements in raising the level of their national economies and culture. We saw large new construction projects in these countries—dams, roads, and new universities and institutes.

Would the picture be the same in the colonies? There neither is nor could be anything of the kind there. In the colonies arbitrary rule by foreigners prevails. The peoples of the colonial countries are not only deprived of the right to independence and self-government; in addition, their national and human feelings and their self-respect are scorned and outraged at every turn. Through ruthless exploitation and robbery, the foreign monopolists wring everything of value from the colonies, plundering their wealth like barbarians.

As a result of colonialist control, the colonial economies have remained extremely backward and the working people lead a miserable existence. It is precisely in the colonies that you will find the longest working day, together with the lowest national income, the lowest wages, the highest illiteracy rate, the shortest life expectancy and the highest mortality rate among the population.

I need not elaborate here on the miserable plight of the more than 100 million people who still languish in colonial bondage and who are deprived of all their rights. The archives of the United Nations contain more than enough reports from various United Nations bodies, more than enough petitions and complaints, revealing the situation of the populations of those countries and territories where, under various guises, the colonial system of government is still preserved. These documents are an indictment of the shameful colonial system. What is going on in these countries and regions justly arouses the anger and indignation of all right-thinking individuals on earth. But the days of untroubled domination by the alien oppressors are drawing to a close, even in the colonies they still retain.

Although the old order may persist in the colonies, the people there are changing. They are growing increasingly conscious of their position and are firmly refusing to bear the colonial yoke. And when the peoples rise to fight for their freedom, for a better life, then no force in the world can stop this mighty movement.

Look at what is happening now in the colonies. Africa is seething and bubbling like a volcano. For some six years now the Algerian people have been waging a heroic and selfless struggle for their national liberation. The peoples of Kenya, Tanganyika, Uganda, Ruanda-Urundi, Angola, Mozambique, Northern Rhodesia, Sierra Leone, South West Africa, Zanzibar and also West Irian, Puerto Rico and many other colonies are fighting an increasingly stubborn battle for their rights.

It should be clear to everyone that there is no means and no force which can halt this struggle of the peoples for their liberation, for it is a great historic process, one of ever-growing and invincible power. It may be possible to prolong the dominion of one State over another for a year or two, but just as in the past the bourgeois order of things came to replace feudalism and as, now, socialism is replacing capitalism, so colonial slavery is giving place to freedom. Such are the rules of human development, and only adventurers can believe that mountains of corpses and millions of victims will delay the advent of a radiant future.

We must have done with colonialism, for it brings misfortunes and suffering not only to the peoples of the enslaved countries—misfortunes and suffering, tears and deprivation are the lot of the peoples of the metropolitan countries too. Who can say that the mothers of France, whose children are dying on the fields of Algeria, are less unfortunate than the Algerian mothers who are burying their sons in their own land?

Today, when the blood of the colonial peoples is flowing, we cannot turn away, we cannot close our eyes to this bloodshed and pretend that peace reigns. What kind of a peace is it when cruel wars are raging—unequal wars, too, in terms of the conditions under which the opposing sides are fighting. The troops of the colonial Powers are armed to the teeth with all the most modern means of mass destruction. In the hands of the peoples battling heroically for their freedom are nothing but obsolete and primitive weapons. But however destructive the wars waged by the colonialists, victory will be on the side of the peoples fighting for their freedom.

There are some countries which, despite great sympathy and fellow-feeling for the oppressed peoples in their struggle, nevertheless have misgivings about spoiling their relations with the colonial Powers; they do not, therefore, raise their voices against these destructive wars but keep peace with the colonialists. Others are colonialists themselves and from them nothing can be expected. The allies of the colonial Powers in aggressive military blocs support the colonialist policy, with all its evil concomitants. But the overwhelming majority of mankind has long since passed final judgement on the colonial system.

The Soviet Union, faithful to the policy of peace and support for the struggle of oppressed peoples for their national independence, the policy proclaimed by Vladimir Ilyich Lenin, founder of the Soviet State, calls upon the United Nations to raise its voice in defence of the just liberation of the colonies and to take immediate steps towards the complete abolition of the colonial system of government.

The need for the complete and final abolition of the colonial system in all its forms and manifestations is demonstrated by the entire course of the history of the world in recent decades. This system is doomed and its end is simply a matter of time. To all intents and purposes the only question now is whether the colonial system can be buried quietly or whether its burial will be accompanied by risky ventures on the part of the adherents of colonialism, resorting to extreme measures. Events in the Congo are a fresh reminder of the dangers that exist.

It is the duty of the United Nations, which is called upon to promote the strengthening of the peace and security of the peoples, to do all in its power to prevent fresh outbreaks of military conflict in Asia, Africa, and Latin America as a result of friction between the colonial Powers and the peoples fighting for their freedom and independence. It is hardly necessary to point out that the great Powers may be drawn into the orbit of any such conflict and then, inevitably, a war which has begun by being local would develop into a general war, a world war. It is not enough, however, merely to defend ourselves against the intrigues of the colonialists, to survive one international crisis after another. It is necessary permanently to protect mankind against these intrigues, to safeguard the world from colonialists' military adventures. It is necessary to put an end to colonialism once and for all, to throw it on to the dust-heap of history.

Who if not the United Nations should speak out in favour of the abolition of the colonial system of government seeing that, according to the Charter, it is the organization's duty to reaffirm faith in human rights, in the dignity and worth of the human person, in the equal rights of nations large and small. How is it possible to develop friendly relations among nations based on respect for the principle of equal rights and self-determination of peoples, which is the purpose of the United Nations, and at the same time to tolerate a situation in which, as a result of the predatory policy of the Powers that are strong militarily and economically, many Asian and African peoples cannot win their right to determine their own struggle against the oppressors? How is it possible to 'achieve international co-operation in solving international problems of an economic, social, cultural or humanitarian character, and in promoting and encouraging respect for human rights and for fundamental freedoms for all without distinction as to race, sex, language, or religion'—you have probably noticed that I am quoting from paragraph 3 of Article I, of the United Nations Charter, entitled 'Purposes and Principles'—and at the same time to close our eyes to so shameful a feature of present-day society as the colonial system?

It is time for us to undertake the final assault on colonialism just as, a century or a century and a half ago, civilized mankind took the offensive against the slave trade and slave ownership, and put an end to them, thus throwing the door wide open for both the political and the economic development of society.

The Soviet Government believes that the time has come to pose the question of the full and final abolition of the colonial system of government in all its forms and varieties in order to make an end of this infamy, this barbarism, this savagery.

Not everyone here—and I realized this when I was preparing my statement—not everyone here will welcome these proposals because representatives of colonial Powers are sitting here side by side with people who are free. These representatives are hardly likely to welcome our freedom-inspired proposals!

Firmly adhering to the principle that the United Nations should be a centre for harmonizing the actions of nations in the attainment of the common ends proclaimed in the Charter, the Soviet Government submits for the consideration of the General Assembly at this session a draft declaration on the grant of independence to colonial countries and peoples, solemnly proclaiming the following demands:

1. All colonial countries and Trust and Non-Self-Governing Territories must be granted forthwith complete independence and freedom to build their own national States in accordance with the freely-expressed will and desire of their peoples. The colonial system and colonial administration in all these forms must be completely abolished in order to afford the peoples of the territories concerned an opportunity to determine their own destiny and form of government.

2. Similarly, strongholds of colonialism in the form of possessions and leased areas in the territory of other States must be eliminated.

3. The Governments of all countries are urged to observe strictly and steadfastly the provisions of the United Nations Charter and of this Declaration concerning the equality and respect for the sovereign rights and territorial integrity of all states without exception, allowing no manifestations of colonialism or any special rights or advantages for some States to the detriment of other States.

Convinced that the complete abolition of the colonial system of government will be a fine and genuinely humanitarian act, and a major advance along the path of civilization and progress, we fervently appeal to all States represented in the United Nations to support the provisions of this Declaration.

The draft declaration prepared by the Soviet Government and submitted for your consideration sets out in detail the considerations which prompted us to bring this matter before the General Assembly. We would ask that this draft declaration should be distributed as an official document of the United Nations General Assembly.

I should like to make the following further points in my statement in the general debate.

The adoption by the United Nations of measures for the final abolition of the colonial system would not only create favourable conditions for localizing and eliminating the threat of war which now exists in areas where a military conflict is in progress between the colonialists and the peoples fighting for their independence; it would also, in many instances, rescue the possibilities of the outbreak of further military conflicts between the States in these parts of the world. The peoples of the countries now suffering from the humiliations bred by foreign domination would gain a clear and immediate prospect of peaceful liberation from the foreign yoke and States clinging to their colonial possessions would be responsible before the United Nations and before the world for the fulfilment of the provisions of the proposed Declaration. This prospect will, of course, only become a reality if the colonial Powers do not evade compliance with United Nations decisions.

We must also remember the great changes the abolition of the colonial system of government would bring about in the lives of the peoples of the enslaved countries. It would be not merely a victory for elementary human justice and international law, which the United Nations is in duty bound to strive for, not in theory but in fact; it would also bring to the peoples who are backward after so many centuries of oppression the benefits of modern science, technology, culture and social progress.

It would be difficult to exaggerate the vast significance which the abolition of the colonial system would have for the entire world. Everyone knows that the economies of the colonies and the Trust Territories are at present subordinated to the mercenary interests of foreign monopolies, and the industrialization of these countries is being deliberately impeded. Imagine that the situation has changed and that these countries and territories, having become independent, are in a position to make ample use of their rich natural resources and to proceed with their industrialization, and that a better life has begun for their peoples. This would lead to a tremendous growth in the capacity of the world market which would no doubt have a beneficial effect, not only on the economic development of the countries of the east but also on the economies of the industrially-developed countries of the west. 190. A positive role in overcoming the age-old backwardness of the countries that are being liberated would be played by economic and technical assistance through the United Nations on a bilateral basis. Of course, this will require considerable funds. Where can they be obtained without overburdening the population of the industrially developed countries? Once again from this rostrum I draw your attention to the source which could be provided by disarmament. The allocation of only one-tenth of the funds which the great Powers are now spending for military purposes would increase the amount of assistance to underdeveloped countries by $10,000 million a year. Yet the cost of constructing all the units of one of the world's largest power systems, in the Inga region of the Congo by which a tremendous area in Africa could be made to blossom, is estimated at $5,000 million.

It is also pertinent to recall that it is the moral duty of the States which possessed colonies in the past to return to the liberated peoples of those countries at least a part of the riches taken from them through cruel exploitation of the people and the plundering of their natural resources. . . .

If, instead of plundering and exploiting, the metropolitan states had really been guided by the interests of the colonial peoples, if they had really given them the assistance of which they like to talk, the peoples of the colonies and the metropolitan countries would have developed uniformly instead of presenting such striking differences in the development of their national economy, culture and prosperity. How can one speak of co-operation, when the level of living in the Western countries is not even comparable to that in the colonies? That is not co-operation, but the domination of one group by the other, a situation in which the latter utilize the labour and wealth of the former, exploit and plunder them and pump their national resources into the metropolitan countries. The colonial peoples have but one road of escape from want and arbitrary rule—the liquidation of the colonial system of government.

The supporters of the colonial system are frightening the populations of the metropolitan countries by asserting that the abolition of the system will inevitably be followed by a drastic deterioration in the mode of life of the people of the industrialized countries. These assertions are clearly groundless.

In the first place, they betray their authors, who involuntarily admit that the metropolitan countries are continuing to plunder the colonies and dependent countries from which they derive fabulous profits. That is indeed a fact, but it is equally true that the super-profits go not to the metropolitan peoples at large but, mainly, into the pockets of the monopolists. It is not the peoples of the metropolitan countries but the millionaires and billionaires who cling to the colonial system.

In the second place, the course of development of many countries that have attained their national independence shows convincingly that with the rapid growth of their national economy, their home markets expand beyond comparison, and they can consume imcomparably greater quantities of industrial goods from the more highly developed countries, while, at the same time, because of the growth of their own productive forces, they are able to supply more of the raw materials and the various products and goods needed by the economies of the industrialized countries. This is a more progressive and sensible system of relations among countries, that increases the prosperity of the peoples both in the erstwhile economically backward colonial and dependent countries and in the more highly developed ones.

The entire march of events and the course of economic and political development pass the inexorable judgement of history on the obsolete and shameful colonial system.

We cannot, of course, expect that our proposals for the liquidation of the colonial system, consistent though they are with mankind's vital interests, will meet with sympathy on the part of those who are still clinging to the colonial order of things. I can hear in advance the criticism of those who defend the colonial system. But to those accustomed to build their prosperity at the expense of the oppressed peoples of the colonies we say this: Think, look carefully at what is happening around you. If not today, then soon, very soon, will come the final collapse of the colonial order, and if you do not get out of the way in time, you will be swept away just the same. The life of the doomed colonial system of government cannot be lengthened either by plots or even by force of arms. Such efforts will merely intensify and embitter the struggle of the peoples against this utterly decayed system.

But the number of supporters of the colonial system, even in the colonial Powers themselves, is steadily dwindling and, in the final analysis, they will not have the last word. For this reason, we are appealing to the good sense and the foresight of the peoples of the Western countries, to their Governments and representatives at this Assembly of the United Nations: let us agree on steps to liquidate the colonial system of government and so speed up this natural historical process; let us do everything to ensure that the peoples of the colonial and dependent countries attain equality of rights and become able to decide their own fate.

We welcome the sacred struggle of the colonial peoples for their liberation. If the colonial Powers, instead of heeding the voice of reason, persist in their old colonialist policy of keeping the colonial countries in subjection, the peoples which stand for the liquidation of the colonial regimes will have to give all possible help to those fighting for their independence against the colonialists and against colonial slavery. Moral, material and other assistance must be given so that the sacred and just struggle of the peoples for their independence can be brought to its conclusion.

The Soviet Union, for its part, has been giving assistance to economically underdeveloped countries and will continue to do so in ever-increasing volume. We are genuinely helping the peoples of these countries to establish their independent economies and to develop their own industry, which is the mainstay of true independence and of increasing prosperity for the people.

Peoples which oppress others cannot be free. Every free people must help those who are still oppressed to gain their freedom and independence.

Allow me to express the hope that the present session of the General Assembly will be an historic landmark on the road to the complete and final elimination of colonial systems on our planet. This would be an act of great historic importance, in keeping with the aspirations of all peoples struggling to secure national independence for progressive mankind as a whole.

DOCUMENT 76. EXTRACT FROM THE STATEMENT Of EIGHTY-ONE COMMUNIST PARTIES MEETING IN MOSCOW, NOVEMBER 1960 (*New Times*, NO. 50, 1960)

In the present situation, favourable domestic and international conditions arise in many countries for the establishment of an independent national democracy, that is, a state which consistently upholds its political and economic independence, fights against imperialism and its military blocs, against military bases on its territory; a state which fights against new forms of colonialism and the penetration of imperialist capital; a state which rejects dictatorial and despotic methods of government; a state in which people are ensured broad democratic rights and freedoms (freedom of speech, press, assembly, demonstrations, establishment of political parties and social organizations), the opportunity to work for the enactment of an agrarian reform and other domestic and social changes, and for participation in shaping government policy. The formation and consolidation of national democracies enables the countries concerned to make rapid social progress and play an active part in the people's struggle for peace against the aggressive policies of the imperialist camp, for the complete abolition of colonial oppression.

DOCUMENT 77. EXTRACT FROM BREZHNEV'S REPORT TO THE 23RD CONGRESS OF THE CPSU, 29 MARCH 1966 (23RD CONGRESS OF THE COMMUNIST PARTY OF THE SOVIET UNION, NOVOSTI PRESS AGENCY, MOSCOW, 1966, PP. 37–40)

The CPSU informs the congress with satisfaction that in the past few years our relations with the overwhelming majority of the independent countries of Asia and Africa have developed successfully. There has been a considerable extension of trade, economic and cultural co-operation between the USSR and these countries. Nearly 600 industrial, agricultural and other projects are being built in Asian and African countries with the aid of our design organizations with the participation of Soviet building specialists. Soviet geological surveying teams are working in many of these countries in jungles and sun-scorched deserts, helping the young countries to explore their mineral resources and make them serve their national economy.

More than 100 educational and medical institutions as well as research centres have been built or are under construction in these countries with Soviet assistance. The number of students from Asian, African and Latin American countries studying at Soviet institutions of higher learning and technical schools has almost doubled in the past five years. The number of Soviet teachers, doctors and other specialists in the cultural field now working in twenty-eight Asian and African countries has increased fourfold. In these countries Soviet people are working selflessly, conscientiously, without sparing themselves. They are contributing greatly towards strengthening friendship between our countries. The proletarian internationalism of the Soviet people is manifested in all this.

Our Party and government are also rendering all possible support to the newly-free countries in the international arena as well. The USSR actively opposes imperialist interference in the internal affairs of the young national states. It opposes the attempts of the neo-colonialists to provoke conflicts between the independent countries with the object of exhausting their strength in internecine struggle. In many vital international issues we are successfully co-operating with the independent countries of Asia, Africa and Latin America. We shall continue to promote this co-operation in the interests of progress and peace.

Comrades, an important development of the past few years has been the emergence of a number of newly-free countries on the road of progressive social development. Experience has thereby confirmed the conclusion drawn by the 1960 Moscow meeting of communist and workers' parties, and recorded in its statement: the masses 'are beginning to see that the best way to abolish age-old backwardness and improve their living standard is that of non-capitalist development. Only in this way can the peoples free themselves from exploitation, poverty and hunger.'

Major social reforms have been carried out in such countries as the United Arab Republic, Algeria, Mali, Guinea, the Congo (Brazzaville) and Burma. Foreign monopolies are being driven out. Feudal estates are being confiscated and capitalist enterprises nationalized. The state sector in the economy is being enlarged, industrialization implemented and broad social legislation adopted in the interests of the people. It goes without saying that the form and scale of these processes differ in the different countries. The revolutionary creative work of the peoples who have proclaimed socialism as their objective is introducing features of its own into the forms of the movement towards social progress.

We have established close, friendly relations with the young countries steering a course towards socialism. Naturally, the further these countries move towards the objective they have chosen the more versatile, profound and stable our relations with them will become. The relations between the CPSU and the revolutionary democratic parties of these countries are likewise developing.

The achievements scored by the newly-free countries that have taken the road of social progress is evoking the special hatred of the imperialists, who are spinning a web of conspiracies against them. Recent developments show that the reactionary forces have become more active, particularly in the African continent. Imperialist plots have been exposed and thwarted in a number of African countries. In face of the intrigues and plots of the imperialists and the conspiracies of the agents bribed by them, the liberated peoples are doing the only correct thing, they are resolutely repelling the enemies of freedom and progress and displaying increasing vigilance. The communist party and the entire Soviet people indignantly condemn the criminal policy of plots and subversion against independent countries.

Special mention must be made of the courageous liberation struggle of the peoples of Latin America.

Only recently the USA regarded Latin America as a reliable bastion. Today in every country in that continent the people are waging a struggle against US imperialism and its accomplices—the local military, feudal lords and bourgeoisie, who are linked up with foreign monopolies. This struggle is headed by the working class and the communist parties.

An important factor of our day is the consolidation of the unity of the Asian, African and Latin American peoples in the struggle against imperialism. The Afro-Asian solidarity movement, the movement for the unity of the Arab peoples and for the unity of the peoples of Africa, and the solidarity movement of the peoples of the three continents are in line with the vital interests of these peoples and we actively and ardently support them.

Comrades, the Communist Party of the Soviet Union regards as its internationalist duty continuous all-round support of the peoples' struggle for final liberation from colonial and neo-colonial oppression.

Our party and the Soviet state will continue to:

render the utmost support to the peoples fighting for their liberation and work for the immediate granting of independence to all colonial countries and peoples;

promote all-sided co-operation with countries that have won national independence and help them to develop their economy, train national cadres and oppose neo-colonialism; strengthen the fraternal links of the CPSU with the Communist Parties and revolutionary democratic organisations in Asian, African and Latin American countries.

The successes of the national liberation movement are inseparably bound up with the successes of world socialism and the international working class. The firm and unbreakable alliance of these great revolutionary forces is the guarantee of the final triumph of the cause of national and social liberation.

(b) THE MIDDLE EAST

Nasser nationalized the Suez Canal on 26 July 1956. The Soviets expressed their support for this action. When the Anglo-French attack on Egypt began it seems that the Soviet jet bombers handed over to Egypt were quickly flown out of the country and so were a large number of Russian and Czechoslovak military instructors and advisers, presumably to prevent them falling into the hands of the invaders. Instead Khrushchev talked about sending 'volunteers' to fight for Egypt. On 5 November, in a note handed to the British ambassador in Moscow, it was intimated that rockets might be used against Britain and France. However, on the same day, in Bulganin's letter to Eisenhower, it was stated that the two powers should act together to curb aggression. The American government rejected the Soviet proposal and warned that rocket attacks on Britain and France would be followed by retaliation against the Soviet Union.

It must be remembered that at this time Soviet forces were fighting in Hungary.

DOCUMENT 78. STATEMENT OF THE SOVIET GOVERNMENT ON ARMED AGGRESSION AGAINST EGYPT, 31 OCTOBER 1956 (*New Times*, NO. 45)

Egypt is the victim of aggression. Her territory has been invaded by Israeli forces and there is an imminent threat of a landing of British and French troops.

On the night of 29 October, Israeli forces crossed the Egyptian border and opened armed hostilities, advancing across the Sinai Peninsula towards the Suez Canal.

These actions of the Israeli government constitute armed aggression and are a flagrant violation of the United Nations Charter. The facts clearly show that the invasion was designed to be used by the western powers, in the first place by Britain and France, as a pretext to move their forces into the territory of Arab states and, in particular, into the Suez Canal zone. The western powers cite in justification of their aggressive actions the colonialist declaration made by the United States, Britain and France in 1950, which was unanimously repudiated by all the Arab states. In acting as an instrument of the imperialist circles that are seeking to restore the oppressive colonial regime in the east, the Israeli government has flung down the gauntlet to all the Arab peoples, to all the peoples of the east who are struggling against colonialism. Israel's extremist ruling circles have embarked on a course that is criminal and dangerous, primarily to Israel herself, to her future.

On 30 October, following on Israel's armed attack, the British and French governments presented an ultimatum to Egypt, demanding that she place at the disposal of their forces key positions in Egyptian territory—at Suez, Port Said and Ismalia—ostensibly for the purpose of preventing hostilities between Israel and Egypt. Despite the fact that the government of Egypt, acting in defence of her sovereignty and territorial integrity, declined this demand, Britain and France have dispatched forces for a landing on Egyptian territory. The British and French governments have thus adopted the course of armed intervention against Egypt, grossly flouting her legitimate rights as a sovereign state.

These actions of the British and French governments are inconsistent with the principles and purposes of the United Nations, are a flagrant violation of the obligations solemnly undertaken by the member states of the Organization, and constitute aggression against the state of Egypt.

The government of the Soviet Union emphatically condemns the aggressive actions of the British, French and Israeli governments. The freedom-loving nations of the world entertain the warmest sympathy for the just struggle of the Egyptian people to uphold their national independence.

The Soviet government considers that the UN Security Council must move to preserve peace and tranquillity in the Near and Middle East by taking immediate measures to secure the cessation of the aggressive actions of Britain, France and Israel against Egypt and the immediate withdrawal of the invading forces from her territory.

The Soviet government considers that the entire responsibility for the dangerous consequences that may follow from these aggressive actions against Egypt will rest upon the governments which have embarked on the course of violating peace and security, on the course of aggression.

DOCUMENT 79. THREE LETTERS OF BULGANIN TO SIR ANTHONY EDEN, PRESIDENT EISENHOWER, AND MR DAVID BEN-GURION, 5 NOVEMBER 1956 (*SN*, 6 NOVEMBER 1956)

Bulganin's message to Sir Anthony Eden

The Soviet government considers it necessary to draw your attention to the fact that the aggressive war engineered by Britain and France against the Egyptian state, in which Israel played the role of an instigator, is fraught with very dangerous consequences for universal peace.

The special emergency session of the General Assembly has adopted a decision on the immediate ending of hostilities and the withdrawal of foreign troops from Egyptian territory. Disregarding this, Britain, France and Israel are intensifying military operations, are continuing the barbarous bombing of Egyptian towns and villages, have landed troops on Egyptian territory, are reducing her inhabited localities to ruins and are killing civilians.

Thus, the government of Britain, together with the governments of France and Israel, has embarked upon unprovoked aggression against Egypt.

The motives cited by the British government in justifying the attack on Egypt are absolutely fallacious. First of all, the British government stated that it was intervening in the conflict between Israel and Egypt in order to prevent the Suez Canal from becoming a zone of military operations. Following the British and French intervention, the Suez Canal area has become a zone of military operations and navigation through the canal has been disrupted, which harms the interests of nations using the canal.

Attempts to justify the aggression by reference to the interest of Britain and France in freedom of navigation through the Suez Canal are also fallacious. We understand your special interest in the canal. This, however, does not entitle you to conduct military operations against the Egyptian people. At the same time, the governments of Britain and France cannot assume the role of judges in the question of the means of securing freedom of navigation through the Suez Canal, since many other states that are denouncing the aggressive actions of Britain and France and demanding the maintenance of peace and tranquillity in the Near and Middle East, have no less interest in it. Furthermore, it is well known that freedom of navigation through the Suez Canal was fully ensured by Egypt.

The Suez Canal issue was only a pretext for British and French aggression, which has other and far-reaching aims. It cannot be concealed that in actual fact an aggressive predatory war is now unfolding against the Arab peoples with the object of destroying the national independence of the states of the Near and Middle East and of re-establishing the regime of colonial slavery rejected by the peoples.

There is no justification for the fact that the armed forces of Britain and France, two great powers that are permanent members of the Security Council, have attacked a country which only recently acquired its national independence and which does not possess adequate means for self-defence.

In what situation would Britain find herself if she were attacked by stronger states, possessing all types of modern destructive weapons? And such countries could, at the present time, refrain from sending naval or air forces to the shores of Britain and use other means—for instance, rocket weapons. Were rocket weapons used against Britain and France, you would, most probably, call this a barbarous action. But how does the inhuman attack launched by the armed forces of Britain and France against a practically defenceless Egypt differ from this?

With deep anxiety over the developments in the Near and Middle East, and guided by the interests of the maintenance of universal peace, we think that the government of Britain should listen to the voice of reason and put an end to the war in Egypt. We call upon you, upon Parliament, upon the Labour Party, the trade unions, upon the whole of the British people: put an end to the armed aggression; stop the bloodshed. The war in Egypt can spread to other countries and turn into a Third World War.

The Soviet government has already addressed the United Nations and the president of the United States of America with the proposal to resort, jointly with other United Nations member-states, to the use of naval and air forces in order to end the war in Egypt and to curb aggression. We are fully determined to crush the aggressors by the use of force and to restore peace in the East.

We hope that at this critical moment you will show due common sense and draw the appropriate conclusions.

Bulganin's message to President Eisenhower

At this anxious and crucial moment for the cause of universal peace, I appeal to you on behalf of the Soviet government.

A week has already gone by since the armed forces of Britain, France and Israel, who is obedient to the will of outside forces, attacked Egypt without any grounds for this, bringing with them death and destruction. British and French aircraft are inhumanly bombing Egyptian aerodromes, ports, installations, towns and inhabited localities. British and French troops have landed on Egyptian territory. Great riches created by the efforts of the Egyptian people are being destroyed by the fire of the occupation forces, and the human losses are increasing day by day.

Before the eyes of the whole world, a war of aggression is developing against Egypt, against the Arab peoples, whose only guilt consists in the fact that they are defending their freedom and independence.

The situation in Egypt calls for immediate and most decisive actions on the part of the United Nations. If such actions are not taken, the United Nations will lose its prestige in the eyes of all mankind and will collapse.

The Soviet Union and the United States of America are both permanent members of the Security Council and great powers possessing all modern types of weapons, including atomic and hydrogen weapons. We bear a special responsibility for stopping the war and restoring peace and tranquillity in the area of the Near and Middle East.

We are convinced that if the government of the USSR and the United States firmly declare their determination to ensure peace, and come out against aggression, then aggression will be ended and there will be no war.

Mr President, in these ominous hours when the loftiest moral principles, the foundations and aims of the United Nations are being put to the test, the Soviet government proposes to the government of the United States of America the establishment of close co-operation in order to curb aggression and end further bloodshed.

The United States possesses a strong navy in the Mediterranean zone. The Soviet Union also possesses a strong navy and powerful aviation.

The joint and immediate use of these means by the United States of America and the Soviet Union, on a decision of the United Nations, would be a reliable guarantee for ending aggression against the Egyptian people, against the countries of the Arab East.

The Soviet government appeals to the government of the United States of America for the pooling of their efforts in the United Nations for the adoption of resolute measures to curb aggression.

The Soviet government has already submitted appropriate proposals to the Security Council and the special emergency session of the General Assembly.

Such joint steps by the United States and the Soviet Union

do not threaten the interests of Britain and France. The masses of the people of Britain and France do not want war, and they, like our people, want to preserve peace. Many other countries besides Britain and France are also interested in immediate pacification and restoration of the normal functioning of the Suez Canal, which has been interrupted by the hostilities. The aggression against Egypt has not by any means been committed for the sake of freedom of navigation through the Suez Canal, which had been ensured. This predatory war was unleashed in order to restore the colonial regimes in the east that had been overthrown by the peoples. If this war is not curbed, it is fraught with the danger of, and can develop into, a Third World War.

If the Soviet Union and the United States of America support the victim of aggression, other countries that are members of the United Nations will join us in our endeavours. This will greatly enhance the United Nations' prestige, and peace will be restored and strengthened.

The Soviet government is ready to enter into immediate negotiations with the government of the United States concerning the practical implementation of the aforementioned proposals, so that effective actions for peace could be taken within the next few hours.

At this grave moment in history when the fate of the whole of the Arab East and, at the same time, the fate of peace are being decided, I await your favourable reply.

Bulganin's message to Mr David Ben-Gurion

The Soviet government has already expressed its resolute condemnation of the armed aggression against Egypt by Israel, as well as by Britain and France, which was a direct and open violation of the Charter and principles of the United Nations.

The overwhelming majority of the countries of the world have also denounced, at the special emergency session of the General Assembly, the act of aggression perpetrated against the Egyptian state and have called upon the governments of Israel, Britain and France to cease military operations immediately and to withdraw the invading forces from Egyptian territory.

All peace-loving mankind is indignantly condemning the

criminal actions of the aggressors who have encroached upon the territorial integrity, sovereignty and independence of the Egyptian state.

Disregarding this, the government of Israel, acting as an instrument of outside imperialist forces, is continuing the reckless adventure, challenging all the peoples of the east who are fighting against colonialism for their freedom and independence, and all the peace-loving peoples of the world.

Such actions by the government of Israel graphically show the worth of all the false assurances about Israel's love for peace and her desire for peaceful co-existence with the neighbouring Arab states. With these assurances the Israeli government has in fact only tried to blunt the vigilance of the other peoples while preparing a traitorous attack against her neighbours.

Fulfilling the will of others, acting on instructions from abroad, the Israeli government is criminally and irresponsibly playing with the fate of peace, with the fate of its own people. It is sowing a hatred for the state of Israel among the peoples of the east such as cannot but make itself felt with regard to the future of Israel and which put in jeopardy the very existence of Israel as a state.

The Soviet government, vitally interested in the maintenance of peace and the safeguarding of tranquillity in the Near and Middle East, is at the present time taking measures in order to put an end to the war and curb the aggressors.

We expect that the government of Israel will change its mind, while there is still time, and discontinue its military operations against Egypt. We call upon you, upon Parliament, upon the working people of the state of Israel, upon all the people of Israel: put an end to the aggression, stop the bloodshed, and withdraw your troops from Egyptian territory.

Taking into account the situation that has arisen, the Soviet government has decided to instruct its ambassador in Tel Aviv to depart from Israel and leave immediately for Moscow.

We hope that the government of Israel will properly understand and assess this warning of ours.

*

Soviet relations with Egypt did not deteriorate after the fall of Khrushchev. At the same time it must be remembered that they have never run smoothly. Still, by 1966 they were probably closer than in Khrushchev's day. The Aswan Dam was being built by Soviet engineers and with Soviet money and the Egyptian army was equipped with Soviet weapons. Internally Nasser was building a society which Soviet writers were now referring to as 'socialist'. Kosygin, on his visit, brought along with him the commander-in-chief of the Soviet navy. The build-up by the Soviets of a fleet in the eastern Mediterranean would have a number of beneficial results. It would encourage the Egyptians and the Syrians. It would act as a deterrent to Israel. Soviet ships could also sail down the Suez Canal and so change the balance of power in the Indian Ocean. Thirteen months after Kosygin's visit the Suez Canal was closed as a result of the Arab-Israeli war of June 1967.

DOCUMENT 80. EXTRACT FROM A SPEECH OF KOSYGIN IN THE EGYPTIAN PARLIAMENT, 17 MAY 1966 (*Pravda*, 18 MAY 1966)

The great October socialist revolution gave a powerful impetus to the national liberation movement of all the peoples interested in abolishing the imperialist system of enslavement and exploitation, and provided favourable conditions for their struggle. The [Egyptian] revolution of 23 July 1952 was a vivid stage in this struggle and had great importance for the peoples of the East.

While the United Arab Republic was accomplishing the tasks of national construction along the road of progress, friendly relations between our countries developed and ever grew in strength.

The proclamation by the United Arab Republic that its national aim is the building of socialism brings our countries still more closely together. We attach high value to the significance of the Charter of National Actions—this important programme document drafted under the guidance of Gamal Abdel Nasser, your president and chairman of the Arab Socialist Union. The ideals of socialism are, of course, close and dear to the peoples of the Soviet Union who have built the first socialist society in the world. Common interests in the struggle for social progress are thus added to the community of our interests in the struggle for the independence of the peoples. All this creates firm foundation for co-operation and joint actions by our countries in the ranks of the progressive revolutionary forces of our time.

We fully understand the great importance for your people of a number of major economic and social reforms which have been carried out in the United Arab Republic. They have substantially altered the structure of your society. If we add to this the considerable successes scored in the spheres of education, public health, social services and cultural construction, we can see how much has been accomplished in these years. The results of the fulfilment of the United Arab Republic's First Five-Year Plan also testify to this.

The great changes which have taken place in your country are clearly to be seen here, too, in the session hall of the National Assembly. Parliament met here before 1952, too, but it was a Parliament of pashas and magnates, who were far remote from the people and their interests. The National Assembly of the UAR today is the most representative Parliament the country has had throughout its entire history. Representatives of the Egyptian people are now at work in this building.

The advance of the United Arab Republic along the road of progress calls for a big effort to overcome the difficulties that arise. The Soviet people fully understand these difficulties. We ourselves had to rise from age-old backwardness to steep steps, and we know very well how difficult it is. The older generation of Soviet people remember how difficult it was, especially at first, when we had to leave conventional ways which had taken shape in the course of centuries, and had to pave the road to the new and protect our achievements against external and internal enemies. We know from personal experience that industrialization and agrarian reforms require great exertions by the whole people, but the Soviet people have always overcome the obstacles that arose in their way and, under the leadership of the communist party, have turned their country into a leading industrial power which today accounts for almost a fifth of the world's industrial output. . . .

The government of the UAR, headed by President Gamal Abdel Nasser, has already for fourteen years carried out an independent foreign policy, a policy of the defence of national interests and of social progress and of peace. All these years have seen the growth of its international prestige and the strengthening of its authority.

Your republic is in the van of the anti-imperialist struggle of the peoples of the Near East and Africa. It helped the Algerian people materially and militarily during their eight-year war for liberation. It supports the national liberation movements in Oman, Aden, Southern Arabia and other countries.

We in the Soviet Union are fully aware of the great work which is being done by President Nasser and the government of the UAR to strengthen the unity of the Arab peoples. The pooling of efforts by such countries as the UAR, Algeria, Syria, Iraq and others would be of great importance for strengthening the common anti-imperialist front. It is with great respect also that we regard the activities of the UAR in rallying the countries of Africa together, since these activities are in accord with the efforts of the peoples of all the African countries to unite in joint struggle for the final abolition of all kinds of foreign domination and oppression.

The great efforts your country is exerting in rendering assistance to the fraternal people of the Yemen Arab Republic and in protecting them from encroachments by outside forces are also well known. The Soviet Union supports the position of the United Arab Republic on the Yemeni question. We also welcome the desire of the leaders of your government to find ways of settling the situation in the Yemen which would guarantee its independent and democratic development.

Your country is also playing an important role in the struggle of the Arab peoples for a solution of the problem of Palestine. We understand the great interest of the Arabs in this problem and we are in favour of a settlement on a just basis. The Soviet Union, as hitherto, sympathizes with the struggle for the restoration of the legitimate, inalienable rights of the Palestinian refugees.

The United Arab Republic, and President Nasser personally, are playing an important part, too, in the movement of non-aligned countries which has already spread far beyond the boundaries of the Near East and Africa. Such influential states as the United Arab Republic in Africa, India in Asia and many other liberated countries are standing firm on the position of non-alignment. This movement constitutes a big force in the struggle against colonialism and imperialism and contributes to the safeguarding of security and peace and the strengthening of co-operation between states.

There is, therefore, every reason to say that Cairo today is one of the recognized centres of international policy and, moreover, of a policy which helps the cause of peace and freedom.

The establishment and strengthening of co-operation between your country and the Soviet Union is a most important factor which has a great influence on the whole course of development in the Near East. Our friendly co-operation reinforces the trends towards progress and liberation in this area, and beyond it, and helps to strengthen peace.

The identity of the positions of the USSR and the UAR has been repeatedly demonstrated in our joint practical steps and our common actions.

Speaking here in the National Assembly after his return from his visit to the Soviet Union last year, President Gamal Abdel Nasser said that the Soviet people were not isolating their progress from the cause of world progress, and were thereby doing a great service to the cause of national liberation. We are grateful for these words, which reflect the essence of our policy of internationalism and fraternal co-operation with all peace loving and freedom-loving peoples. The 23rd Congress of the Communist Party of the Soviet Union, recently held in Moscow, in its decisions confirmed the unchanging nature of the policy of strengthening co-operation with the liberated countries to the utmost.

In the United Arab Republic we see a state with which we are linked by deep and permanent interests, a state which is in the stage of transition from capitalism to socialism. Today from the rostrum of this distinguished assembly, I should like to emphasize that the Soviet Union proceeds and will proceed with the utmost further development of friendship and co-operation with the United Arab Republic. This is our unchangeable course.

It is with satisfaction that we note the expansion of contacts between the United Arab Republic and the socialist countries, our friends and allies. The expansion of contacts between your country and Bulgaria, Hungary, the GDR, Poland, Czechoslovakia and Yugoslavia, is a positive feature in international affairs. Expressing the sentiments of the Soviet people, I should like to emphasize that your people have good and reliable friends who watch their struggle with deep sympathy.

We regard the efforts of the government of the United Arab Republic to ensure the security of its country and strengthen its defences with complete understanding. You know that the necessary co-operation in this sphere has been established between our countries and that it will continue to grow and develop.

As economic co-operation between the Soviet Union and the United Arab Republic continues to expand, it is increasingly outgrowing the framework of the usual formal relations between states. The joint work of the Soviet and Arab workers and specialists at the Aswan Dam project, for example, is not merely the implementation of economic agreements, but a demonstration of our peoples' solidarity in face of the forces of imperialism which are trying to prevent the national economies of young states from growing in strength. This is natural and logical, in view of the solid foundation of our friendly relations.

Co-operation between the Soviet Union and the United Arab Republic is also manifested in full with regard to major international problems which are not of regional, but of universal importance.

This applies above all to the question of general and complete disarmament, all the problems associated with the prevention of thermo-nuclear war, including the question of the non-proliferation of nuclear weapons, the task of relaxing international tension and the need for the peaceful settlement of disputes between states.

The Soviet Union together with the UAR, wants the earliest possible conclusion of a treaty on the non-proliferation of nuclear weapons, a treaty which will be truly effective and dependable. We cannot afford the slightest carelessness in this question which affects the vital interests of the Soviet Union, its friends and allies. If the latter-day revenge-seekers and militarists were to obtain access to weapons of mass destruction, it would have the gravest consequences for peace and the security of the peoples. The problem of the non-proliferation of nuclear weapons also has a direct bearing on safeguarding the security of your country and all the Arab states, since forces are to be found in the Near East, too, which are thinking of possessing such weapons.

The government of your republic also makes its useful contribution to the cause of ending the nuclear arms race. We fully support the UAR proposal for banning underground nuclear-weapon tests.

*

In June 1967 the Arabs suffered their most crushing defeat at the hands of the Israelis in spite of the fact that their armed forces were equipped with Soviet weapons and in spite of the fact that many of their officers had been trained in eastern-bloc countries. The Arab defeat was a blow to Soviet prestige. In spite of large Soviet naval units in the area the Soviets did not interfere in the fighting, though they might have done so had the Israelis marched on Cairo and Damascus. Instead Israeli actions were vigorously condemned.

It will be noted that the statement was signed by the Yugo-slavs but not by the Rumanians. The friendship of Tito and Nasser had been close for years and to Tito a non-aligned Egypt was an important link in the bloc of non-aligned states. By 1967 this bloc had, in fact, disintegrated, but this did not prevent Tito issuing a strong anti-Israeli statement as early as 5 June. Indeed Yugoslavia was perhaps the most pro-Arab and the most anti-Israeli of all the socialist states, and the very rapid and complete rearmament of the Egyptian army is perhaps due to Tito's pleadings with the Russians.

The Rumanian Party leader, Ceausescu, attended the meeting in Moscow but refused to sign the statement. Rumania was also the only socialist country not to break off diplomatic relations with Israel.

Anti-Zionism has always been an element of communism and anti-Semitism certainly flourished in the last years of Stalin's life and since. Traditionally the Soviet Union dislikes the existence in its midst of a large population which has emotional ties with the outside. Over two million Jews live in the Soviet Union. This suspicion of the Jews was inevitably strengthened by the ever heavier commitment of the Soviet Union to the Arab cause. In the case of Poland the June 1967 events led directly to the drive against the pitifully small Jewish population there.

DOCUMENT 81. EXTRACT FROM THE STATEMENT OF THE COMMUNIST PARTIES AND GOVERNMENTS OF BULGARIA, HUNGARY, THE GERMAN DEMOCRATIC REPUBLIC, POLAND, CZECHOSLOVAKIA, THE SOVIET UNION AND YUGOSLAVIA ON THE SITUATION IN THE MIDDLE EAST, 9 JUNE 1967 (*Pravda*, 10 JUNE 1967)

[The parties and governments] studied the situation that has taken shape in the Near East as a result of Israel's aggression, which is the outcome of a conspiracy against the Arab countries by certain imperialist forces, above all the United States. The participants in the meeting exchanged views on measures required to cut short the aggression and to avert its consequences which would be dangerous to the cause of universal peace.

The participants in the meeting deem it necessary to draw conclusions from the fact that Israel did not comply with the decision of the Security Council and did not stop military actions against the Arab states. The Israeli occupation of the territory of the Arab states would be used to restore a foreign colonial regime.

On 9 June, despite the cease-fire statement by the government of Syria, Israeli troops started a new offensive on Syria's border, subjecting Syrian towns to barbaric bombing.

Struggling against imperialism for their freedom and independence, for the integrity of their territories, for the inalienable sovereign right to decide for themselves all questions of their domestic life and foreign policy, the peoples of the Arab countries are upholding a just cause. The peoples of the socialist countries are completely on their side.

The peoples of the UAR and several other Arab countries have scored historic victories in recent years in the winning of national independence and freedom. Important social transformations in the interests of the working masses were carried out.

We express confidence that these gains will be preserved, that progressive regimes will be consolidated despite the difficulties in the way of the Arab peoples.

At a difficult hour for the states of the Arab East, the socialist countries declare that they are in full and complete solidarity with their just struggle and will render them aid in repelling aggression and defending their national independence and territorial integrity.

The states participating in this meeting demand that Israel stop immediately military actions against the neighbouring Arab countries and withdraw all its troops from the territories behind the truce line.

It is the duty of the United Nations Organization to condemn the aggressor. If the Security Council does not take the proper measures, grave responsibility will rest with those states which failed to fulfil their duty as members of the Security Council.

Resolute concerted action by all peace-loving and progressive forces, by all those who treasure the cause of freedom and independence of peoples, is necessary today as never before.

If the government of Israel does not stop the aggression and withdraw its troops behind the truce line the socialist states which signed this statement will do everything necessary to help the peoples of the Arab countries administer a resolute rebuff to the aggressor, to protect their lawful rights, to extinguish the hotbed of war in the Near East and restore peace in that area.

The just struggle of the Arab peoples will triumph.

(c) THE UNITED NATIONS

The Congo became independent in 1960 but soon sank into anarchy and confusion. The Belgian intervention, the attempted secession of Katanga, an area rich in copper in which European capital was heavily involved, and the involvement of large United Nations peace-keeping forces there, gave the Soviets an opportunity to fish in troubled waters. Lumumba, the premier, in conflict with the president, Kasavubu, was an obvious candidate for Soviet support and after his murder, so was his successor, Gizenga. Lumumba became quite a symbol for the Soviets and after his death a university was opened in Moscow for African students which bore his name.

Khrushchev had for some time been toying with the idea of

turning the office of secretary general into a three-man secretariat representing the socialist, the neutralist and the capitalist states. He went to the United Nations himself to put forward his plan which received no support from the neutrals to whom it was intended to appeal. After Hammarskjöld's death the Soviets dropped their plan and gave their vote to U Thant.

DOCUMENT 82. EXTRACT FROM A LETTER OF KHRUSHCHEV TO NEHRU, 22 FEBRUARY 1961 (*SN*, 28 FEBRUARY 1961)

I am addressing this message to you to set forth the views of the Soviet government in connection with the atrocious slaughter of an outstanding leader of the national liberation movement of Africa, the head of the government of the Republic of the Congo, Patrice Lumumba, and his comrades. . . .

I shall not conceal the fact that as I write these remarks it is only with a great deal of effort that I am able to keep down the anger which I felt on receiving the news of the murder of Patrice Lumumba, and my feelings of loathing towards his executioners. Yet no matter how difficult it is to restrain one's feelings over this heinous crime which so sharply affects the conscience of every honest man, it is the duty of statesmen to be guided above all by the logic of reason, by the interests of their peoples and the interests of ensuring peace. Time erases the scars inflicted by suffering, but political problems remain and they must be solved.

It is our belief that today the necessity has arisen, not only to give fresh thought to the way in which the friends of the Congo can help the Congolese people in their just fight for their independence, but also to consider the wider issues affecting the United Nations as a whole and its future. . . .

The slaughter of prime minister Lumumba and his comrades has exposed, for all the world to see, the disgusting role played in the Congolese events by United Nations secretary-general Hammarskjöld. The brutal murder of the outstanding leaders of the Congo Republic tragically demonstrated how inadmissible is the situation in which a stooge of the imperialists and colonialists heads the United Nations executive machinery.

It was none other than Hammarskjöld who abetted the

seizure of prime minister Lumumba by bandits who had been handed their weapons by Belgium and other colonial states. Having entered into collusion with the colonialists, Hammarskjöld used his position as secretary-general in order to delay in every possible way the implementation of measures to protect the legitimate government and parliament of the Congo. Is it not significant that during his visit to the Congo Hammarskjöld negotiated with all and sundry, kowtowed to the puppets of the colonialists such as Kasavubu, Tshombe and others, but did not even want to meet Patrice Lumumba, the legitimate prime minister of the country, at whose request the troops of certain United Nations member states were sent to the Congo?

And when Patrice Lumumba and other statesmen were subjected to torture by the mercenary hangmen and it was obvious to the whole world that a vile assassination was being prepared, the United Nations secretary-general washed his hands of the whole affair and adopted a hypocritical pose of 'non-interference'.

The crudely staged farce of the 'escape' of Lumumba was directly linked with the perfidious actions of Hammarskjöld with regard to the independent Republic of the Congo and its leaders. To put it bluntly, it was in essence Hammarskjöld who murdered Lumumba.

Whoever held the knife or revolver was, after all, not the only murderer; the chief assassin was the one who handed him the weapon. Such are the facts, woeful and shocking as they are. And these facts have compelled the Soviet government to draw the conclusion that Hammarskjöld's entire line in the Congo has been, from beginning to end, one of base treachery with regard to the interests of the Congolese people and abuse of the principles of the United Nations and the elementary standards of decency and honour. Such an individual has no right to hold a leading post in the United Nations. We cannot reconcile ourselves to this villainy which has been perpetrated with the connivance of the United Nations. We cannot reconcile ourselves to the fact that the United Nations secretary-general is a man who has sullied himself by a foul murder.

In order to prevent the 'Cold War' from becoming more and more intense, in order to prevent a 'Hot War', the United Nations structure must be reorganized. Whether it be

Hammarskjöld or anyone else, the United Nations machinery will, in the present state of affairs, in any event be headed by a stooge of the colonial and imperialist powers who will protect their interests. The United Nations can become a truly international body only if such abuses are ruled out altogether.

Our position on this question was plainly set forth as long ago as last September by the USSR delegation to the 15th session of the United Nations General Assembly, when we introduced the proposal on the reorganization of the United Nations structure so that there might be no single-handed authority of the secretary-general, which today reflects the interests of the colonial and imperialist powers. We proposed at that time that there should be in the United Nations, not one, but three secretaries, each of whom would represent one of the three main groups of states that have now taken shape in the world—the states that are members of the military blocs of the western powers, the socialist states, and the neutral countries.

With such a structure each group would have equal possibilities of influencing the nature of the decisions taken by the United Nations and these decisions would not be directed against the interests of any one of these three groups of countries making up the United Nations. Not the narrow interests of this or that grouping, but the common interests of all the United Nations members, the interests of peace and co-operation among all states, irrespective of their social and political systems, would then determine the United Nations' activities and it would really be an organization of united nations as it should be, but as is not the case today under the present structure which does not correspond to the actual affairs existing in the world.

We are by no means seeking any special privileges in the United Nations for the socialist countries in relation to any other groups of states. It should be borne in mind that the relative influence of this or that group of countries in the United Nations is not something permanent—it changes with the passage of time. And even if the present structure is preserved, with the imperialist and colonial powers actually dominant in the United Nations and pursuing their policy through an obedient Hammarskjöld, the time may indeed come when the decisive influence—and an influence encompassing the secretary-general—will belong to another group of states, for instance, the socialist states. This, however, is not our desire. All we are striving for is that all groups of states should have truly equal opportunities in the United Nations and should not impose their will upon one another but should co-operate on an equal footing in the interests of strengthening peace.

Today, however, the situation is such that owing to its present structure, one group of states dominates the United Nations, a group which, incidentally, is the smallest in numbers and population, but one which, through the executive bodies of the United Nations, is pursuing its aggressive colonialist policy. In short, the imperialist powers are today seeking to exploit the United Nations both against the socialist countries and against those states which have freed themselves from colonial dependence and taken the road of a neutralist policy.

This line is, of course, doomed to failure. And even if anyone should succeed in railroading a decision imbued with this spirit through the United Nations, such decisions cannot have any validity and could never correspond to the tasks put before the United Nations at its creation, the tasks of easing international tensions and preventing military conflicts.

Conclusion

A question arises: has Soviet foreign policy been successful?
But how does one measure success? Has the power of the
Soviet Union increased? Is the Soviet Union militarily safer
now than it was in 1953? As the building of communism
is a primary aim of Soviet foreign policy can it be said that real
advances have been made on this road? Has the world communist movement become stronger during this period? Have
more countries come under communist rule and have communist parties in non-socialist countries become stronger or
weaker? All these are pertinent questions.

In an inquiry of this kind one must differentiate the aims of
the Soviet Union as one of the world's great powers and seek
to measure success on this basis. One must also be aware of the
fact that the Soviet Union aims to spread world communism
and that this aim can be incompatible with the aim of strengthening the Soviet Union. In some sense this is an unrealistic way
of putting this question. A Soviet communist would not differentiate between the aims of communists and the aims of the
Soviet Union. Yet such an attempt must be made. It might
also be added that up to the death of Stalin a non-Soviet
communist would take the preservation of communism in the
Soviet Union as an all-important objective. Conversely the
preservation of communist rule in other communist states is an
equally important objective. Thus it was stated at the Budapest
conference of communist parties in February and March 1968
that the strengthening of communism in one state helps all the
others. Conversely its weakening harms all the others. It was
on this basis that the Warsaw Pact countries acted in Czechoslovakia in August 1968. Or again Tito, although well aware
of the abuses which had existed in Hungary under Rakosi, and
well realizing the hostility that Rakosi had shown him over a

period of years, was not, however, prepared to see the liquidation of communist rule in Hungary.

The whole question is further complicated by the divergent aims of communist states. In theory, differences are recognized and permitted. And such differences can be solved by mutual discussion. Under Stalin, no such discussion could take place. Behind a screen of voluntary agreement it was Moscow's word which counted and other parties had to accept Moscow's dictates. If they were unwilling to do so they were in effect expelled from the communist system and branded as traitors, spies, wreckers, fascists, lackeys of the imperialists and other choice epithets of the communist vocabulary.

Under Stalin's successors such discipline was no longer possible. Khrushchev was certainly willing to accept a measure of disagreement on tactical questions. Rather naïvely he believed that Moscow had the power and the prestige to impose such control. But, of course, things went wrong. Tito was pleased to re-establish contacts with the Soviet Union but he would not allow Yugoslavia to become reintegrated in the bloc. Hence the reconciliation of 1955 was followed by a second—though more gentle—disagreement in 1957 and 1958, and a rather sharper but short-lived disagreement after the invasion of Czechoslovakia. It will be noted that each of these conflicts followed Soviet military intervention.

Communist unity was permanently shattered by the quarrel with China. It seems unlikely that such a conflict could have been avoided. Yet the form it took, the speed with which it unfolded, were not inevitable and were very largely due to the particularly Marxist interpretation of internal and international events shared by both the leaders of China and those of the Soviet Union. The problem was always the same. World communist strategy was to be decided, at least in broad outline, in Moscow. The Chinese, though they accepted this, took it upon themselves to remind the Russians of their revolutionary duty. They could do this because they were guided by Marxism-Leninism like the Russians, and maintained, as did Protestants in the Reformation, that the correct interpretation of the sacred writings of Marxism-Leninism was a guide to action: hence the highly intellectual and very learned disquisitions of both parties about the meaning of Marxism-Leninism and the history of socialism, interspersed, of course, with violent abuse. Alternatively, the strategy of world communism could be decided by agreement and discussion. In theory this is what the Comintern was supposed to do after the October revolution. In practice, with the failure of revolution outside Russia, the Comintern became a department of the Soviet State. The various conferences held after Stalin's death, from the 1957 Moscow conference to the 1969 Moscow conference, had a different purpose. They were periodic and irregular meetings of sovereign parties. Their aim was to agree on a broad and very vague basis of action. Those that disagreed either did not turn up or left in the middle. In any case it was doubtful whether any communist party would really be bound by these decisions. The main result of the more recent conferences was to show the lack of unity.

As the conflict between Moscow and Peking became deeper the Soviets maintained that Mao Tse-tung and his group were in fact liquidating communism in China. Their racialist view of the world, their talk about the clash between world countryside and the world cities was an indication of this. For their part the Chinese accused the Russians of reverting to bourgeois capitalism. In a press conference in their embassy in Moscow they even accused the Russians of being fascists. They also charged the Soviet leaders with the territorial imperialist ambitions of the Tsars.

It was not only the clash with the Chinese and the Yugoslavs that weakened the unity of the Soviet bloc. In 1956 there were fears in Moscow that the Poles were pursuing the same path. From 1960 the Rumanians were doing the same. The case of Rumania is particularly interesting because unlike the Chinese there was no quarrel as to the way in which communism should be built. The disagreement was purely on foreign policy. Equally important was the case of Albania. Again the condemnation was not on ideology, it was on external factors. The Albanians feared that a reconciliation between Tito and Moscow would result in an extinction of their independence.

The schism among ruling communists had its effect, of course, on the non-ruling communist parties. Neither the Soviets nor the Chinese possessed the means of imposing control on them. In other words, neither the Red Army nor

the Chinese army could be used to impose ideological uni-
formity. Yet in the days of Stalin, even without such pressure,
unity was maintained. In 1936 the Comintern proclaimed the
policy of the popular front and socialists, liberals, Catholics
and all those prepared to oppose fascism were suddenly trans-
formed from enemies into allies of the communists. In 1939 an
even more remarkable change took place. Nazi Germany, the
arch-enemy of communist Russia, became its ally. Again this
necessitated a change in the orientation of communist parties.
Since 1956 such slavish following is no longer accepted. Even
such minuscule parties as the Communist Party of Great Britain
(membership 32,562) can flout Moscow's command. Another
communist party, that of Sweden, has since 1964 abandoned
the centralism which is a characteristic of all communist parties
and has become reformist rather than revolutionary. Some
parties were pro-Chinese, like that of Indonesia. The Japanese
Communist Party, 250,000 strong, had been pro-Chinese till
1966. Since then it has held an independent position though
its relations with the Soviet Communist Party have improved.
Many communist parties, like that of Belgium, have split into
a pro-Soviet and pro-Chinese party. India has also two communist parties, but in 1967 the pro-Peking communist party
split with China over the question of armed struggle. The
Israeli Communist Party split in 1956 into a Jewish communist
party and a mixed Jewish and Arab communist party, mirror-
ing the political struggles of the Middle East. Clearly there
can be little unity and no identity of views between the world's
ninety-three communist parties (excluding from this figure
those parties which have split on ideological or national lines).
A reformist party, like that of Italy, can find little in common
with a revolutionary one like that of China.

In some parts of the world the communist party is no longer
at the extreme left of the political spectrum, especially in its
refusal to use violence. Thus in Chile the communist party
co-operates with the Christian Democrats and is outshouted in
violence and extremism by the socialist party. And they all
together supported a Marxist, but non-communist, as president.

The conciliar stage of world communism does imply an
influence by non-Soviet communist parties, ruling and non-
ruling, on the decision-making process of the Soviet Union

itself. It is impossible to be very definite about this. Thus the Italian leader Togliatti clearly had much influence in the Kremlin. The very frequent consultations that are carried on between Soviet and other communist leaders would seem to indicate a desire on the part of Soviet leaders to explain their action to their foreign communist colleagues in order to elicit their support. Some agreement on informing each other on leadership changes has been made. But the Soviets violated even this undertaking. The communist leaders of eastern Europe were very angry indeed when they were informed of the overthrow of Khrushchev only after the news had been given to the press.

In the period under discussion the Soviet Union and the world communist movement have had two great successes. The building of socialism in Cuba has been an undeniable ideological success, although economically it has been an expensive one. It was hoped, of course, certainly by Fidel Castro, that Cuba would revolutionize the rest of Latin America. However, since the Cuban crisis and the failure of communist insurgency in other parts of America Cuba has remained ideologically, politically and economically isolated. She is still an off-shore island.

The other success has been in Vietnam. The never-ending war there, its off-shoot in Laos and its extension in Cambodia, have not brought communist victory. But it has shown the utter weakness of the South Vietnamese regime and has kept the strongest military power in the world involved there for years, unable to achieve either victory or a negotiated peace. As the Soviet Union, and not China, is now the chief supporter of North Vietnam, it must share some of the honour for this most tragic success.

The conclusion therefore must be drawn that from the point of view of ideology the directors of Soviet foreign policy have little cause to congratulate themselves. This is even more so if one considers the fact that the country which should have been the Soviet Union's chief ally, that is China, is now its worst enemy. China has challenged the Soviet leadership of the communist movement. She has been a rival in Asia, in Africa and in Latin America. She has intervened in the internal affairs of the Soviet Union and she has sought to prescribe to Soviet leaders the kind of policy that they should pursue both internally and externally. She has laid claim to vast areas of Soviet territory and she has challenged the Soviet Union in military combat. Soviet soldiers have died fighting the Chinese but no Soviets have shot or been shot at by Americans. The Chinese have attacked Soviet leaders in language which no responsible American statesman has ever used. Yet, in spite of all this, China is portrayed as a friend 'gone wrong' and the wish is piously repeated that when the present madness gripping the Chinese people and its Communist Party eventually passes China will once more take her place in the family of communist nations.

The United States and the other capitalist states are regarded, on the other hand, as deadly enemies whose only desire is to destroy the Soviet Union and wipe out communism. The aim of the Soviet Union must therefore be to defend itself against these imperialist aggressors. It is not, in the official propaganda view, the aim of the Soviet Union to impose a system of government on the United States and the other capitalist countries contrary to their wishes. Marxism teaches that capitalism will certainly collapse, but that it will collapse by its own contradictions and not by external military pressure.

It is clear from the kind of relations that the Soviets have had with the Americans since the death of Stalin that they do not really believe in the supposed aggressiveness of the United States. The present state of Soviet-American relations is good. Yet the Soviet leaders cannot escape from their ideological heritage, on the foundations of which Soviet society exists. The United States must be the foe because it is the major capitalist power in the world. China, in spite of bloodshed, will again become a friend because she is a communist state.

There are other ways in which one may measure the success or lack of it achieved by Soviet foreign policy. One can treat the question from a different perspective, from the point of view of Soviet 'power' competing with other powers. One can, so to speak, disregard ideology. Militarily the Soviet Union has become stronger and the defence of the country now depends on weapons as sophisticated as those possessed by the Americans. It is true that nuclear parity, not to speak of superiority, over the United States has not been achieved. This is no great loss because few Soviet leaders really believe in the likelihood of an American attack on the Soviet Union. In any case the success, limited though it is, of the Partial Test Ban Treaty, the Nuclear Non-proliferation Treaty, and the hot line, is to the advantage of the Soviet Union as much as to the United States.

In the European theatre the attempts to break up the satellite empire have failed—on three occasions. Clearly as long as the Red Army continues to exist and as long as the directors of Soviet policy have the will to do so, the communist regimes in eastern Europe will also continue to exist. It is true that the plan to neutralize central Europe has failed and the plan to conclude a European security pact still eludes the Soviets. Yet the signing in 1970 of a non-aggression pact with the Federal Republic of Germany is an important stage in the normalization of relations with Bonn, second only to the establishment of diplomatic relations between the two countries.

The Mediterranean and the Middle East have been an area of spectacular success. Soviet naval forces are present in the Mediterranean and although much inferior to the NATO forces they clearly influence the course of events there. The Soviet influence in Egypt is considerable although it has been challenged by Nasser's successor Sadat. The Soviet Union is now the main champion of the Arab states and the exponent of Arab nationalism.

Even though the first flush of friendship between the Soviet Union and various African states is now a thing of the past, the influence of the Soviet Union in some states of Africa should also not be minimized. The Congo episode was no success, in spite of the continuing Soviet exploitation of the name of Patrice Lumumba. In Guinea the close ties between Sekou Touré and the Soviet bloc countries were quickly ruptured. Everywhere the Russians have had to contend with Chinese agitators and with local nationalists only a little less suspicious of them than they are of the west.

In Asia too there has been success. Moscow can claim to have cordial relations with virtually all states in the area with the exception of those that one may regard as American puppets and of course the People's Republic of China. Even Indonesia still receives Soviet favours although it is only five years since the government there liquidated the communists. The relations with India are excellent and with India's rival Pakistan they have continued to improve. In January 1956 the world was treated to the amazing spectacle of a meeting in the Soviet Asian city of Tashkent of the Indian and Pakistani prime ministers presided over by Kosygin. At this meeting Kosygin managed to mediate between the two sides, then at war, and they concluded a cease-fire. Indeed, in Tashkent the Soviet Union was acting the role traditionally reserved for great powers—that of a guardian of peace.

The preservation of peace has surely been the most splendid Soviet achievement since the end of the war. No doubt the policy of peaceful co-existence is regarded as a temporary stage before the walls of capitalism crumble under the trumpet blasts of the working class. But, in politics, the temporary so often becomes the permanent. Certainly this is what the average Soviet citizen would wish.

Select Bibliography

ASPATURIAN, Vernon, *The Soviet Union in the World Communist System*, Stanford University Press, 1966.

BRZEZINSKI, Zbigniew (ed.), *Africa and the Communist World*, Stanford University Press, 1963.

BRZEZINSKI, Zbigniew, *The Soviet Bloc: Unity and Conflict*, Cambridge, Mass.: Harvard University Press, 1967.

CRANKSHAW, Edward, *The New Cold War: Moscow vs. Pekin*, Penguin, 1963.

DALLIN, Alexander, *The Soviet Union and the United Nations: An Inquiry into Soviet Motives and Objectives*, New York: Praeger, 1962.

DINERSTEIN, H. S., *War and the Soviet Union: Nuclear Weapons and the Revolution in Soviet Military and Political Thinking*, New York: Praeger, 1962.

GEHLEN, Michael, *The Politics of Coexistence*, Bloomington: Indiana University Press, 1967.

GOLDMAN, Marshall, *Soviet Foreign Aid*, London: Praeger, 1967.

HORELICK, Arnold and RUSH, Myron, *Strategic Power and Soviet Foreign Policy*, University of Chicago Press, 1966.

KASER, Michael, *Comecon: Integration Problems of the Planned Economies*, Oxford University Press, 1967.

LAQUEUR, Walter Z. (ed.), *The Middle East in Transition*, New York: Praeger, 1958.

LINDEN, Carl, *Khrushchev and the Soviet Leadership*, Baltimore: Johns Hopkins Press, 1966.

LOWENTHAL, Richard, *World Communism: The Disintegration of a Secular Faith*, New York: Oxford University Press, 1966.

MACKINTOSH, J. M., *Strategy and Tactics of Soviet Foreign Policy*, Oxford University Press, 1962.

MORRISON, David, *The USSR and Africa*, Oxford University Press, 1964.

RA'ANAN, Uri, *U.S.S.R. arms the Third World*, Cambridge, Mass.: M.I.T. Press, 1970.

STEIN, A., *India and the Soviet Union: The Nehru Era*, University of Chicago Press, 1969.

TRISKA, Jan and FINLEY, David, *Soviet Foreign Policy*, New York: Macmillan, 1968.

ULAN, Adam, *Expansion and Coexistence, The History of Soviet Foreign Policy, 1917-1967*, New York: Praeger, 1968.

WOLFE, Thomas W., *Soviet and Europe, 1945–1970*, Baltimore: Johns Hopkins Press, 1970.

ZAGORIA, Donald S., *The Sino-Soviet Conflict, 1965–1971*, Princeton University Press, 1962.

Index

337